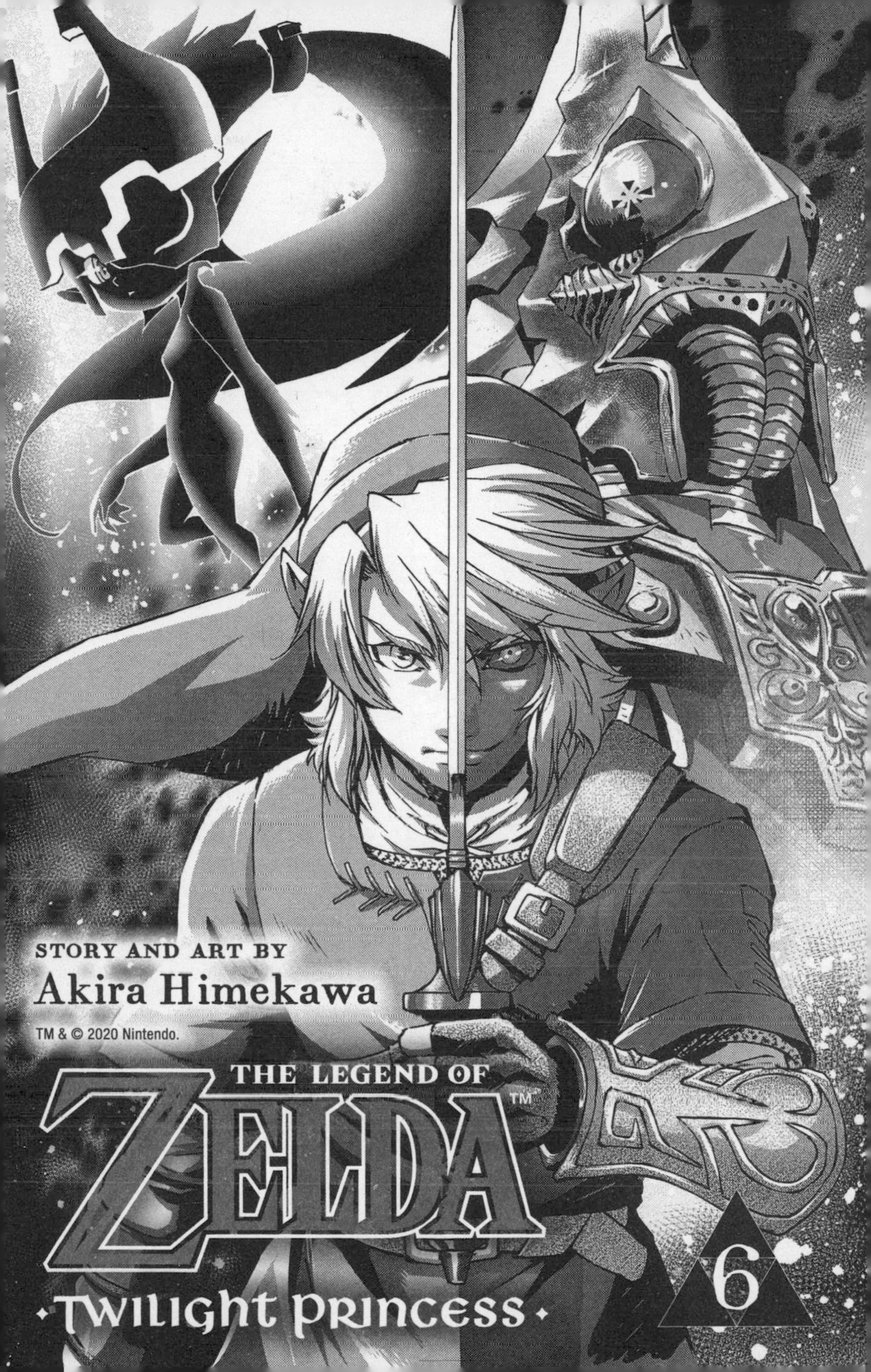
STORY AND ART BY
Akira Himekawa
TM & © 2020 Nintendo.
THE LEGEND OF
ZELDA™
·TWILIGHT PRINCESS·
6

THE LEGEND OF ZELDA™

·TWILIGHT PRINCESS·

6

CONTENTS

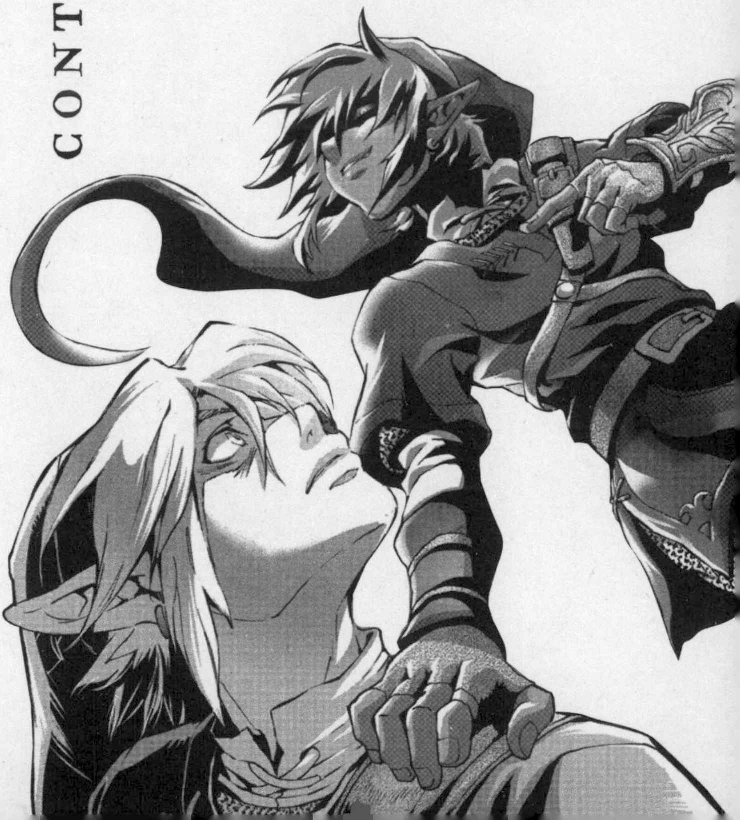

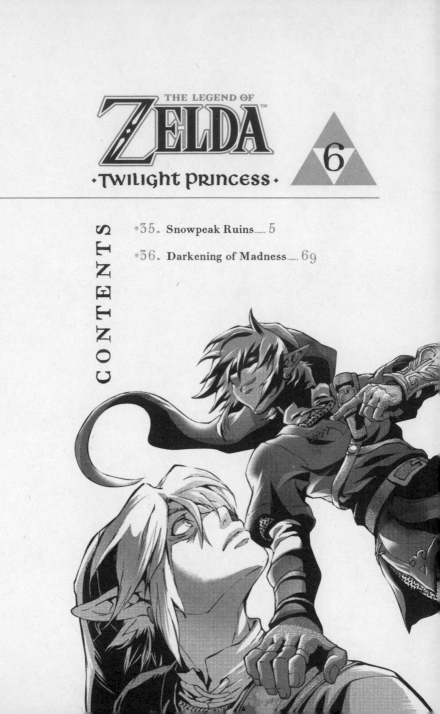

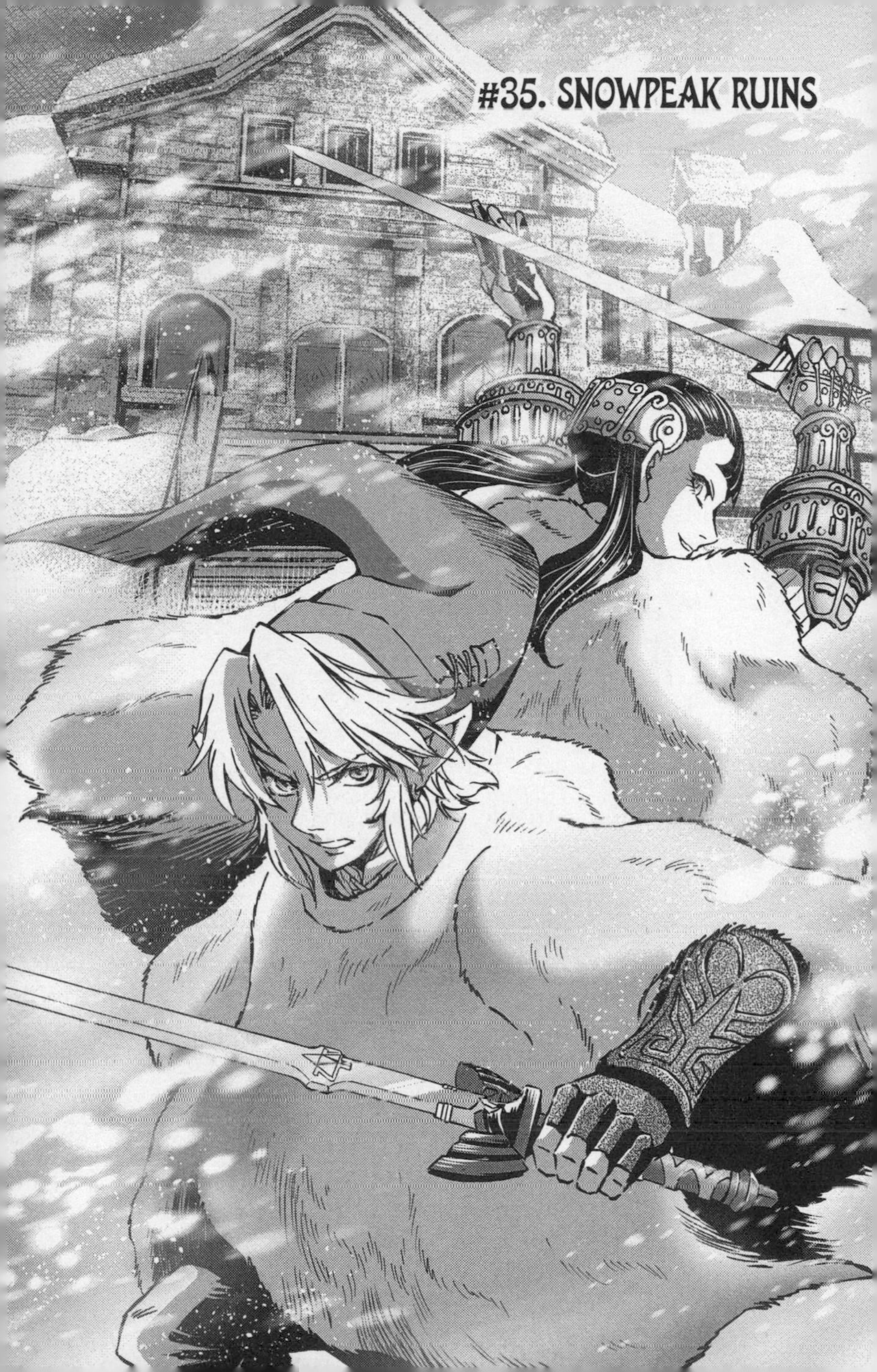
#35. SNOWPEAK RUINS

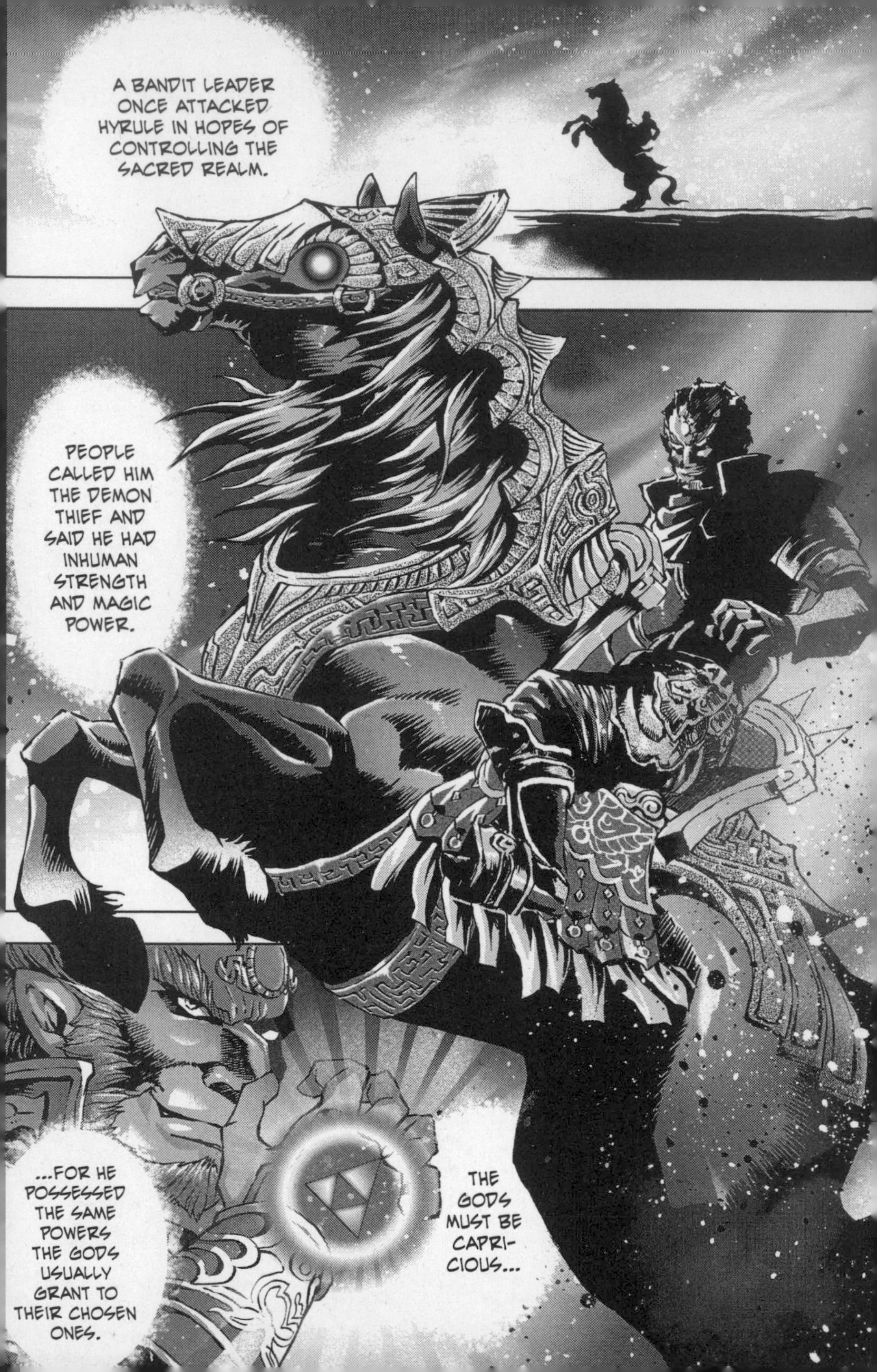
A BANDIT LEADER ONCE ATTACKED HYRULE IN HOPES OF CONTROLLING THE SACRED REALM.
PEOPLE CALLED HIM THE DEMON THIEF AND SAID HE HAD INHUMAN STRENGTH AND MAGIC POWER.
THE GODS MUST BE CAPRI-CIOUS...
...FOR HE POSSESSED THE SAME POWERS THE GODS USUALLY GRANT TO THEIR CHOSEN ONES.

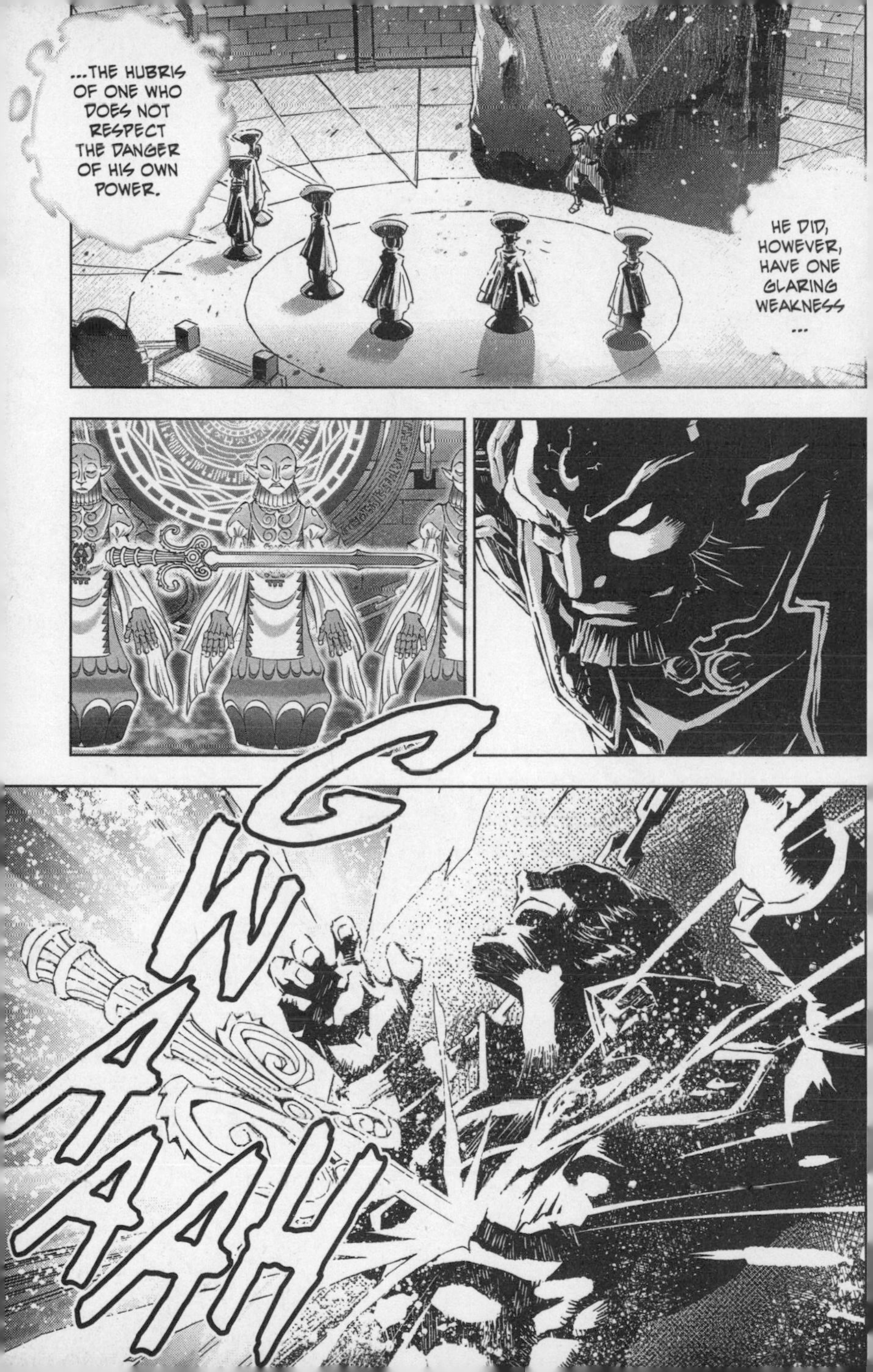
...THE HUBRIS OF ONE WHO DOES NOT RESPECT THE DANGER OF HIS OWN POWER.
HE DID, HOWEVER, HAVE ONE GLARING WEAKNESS ...
GWAAAAH

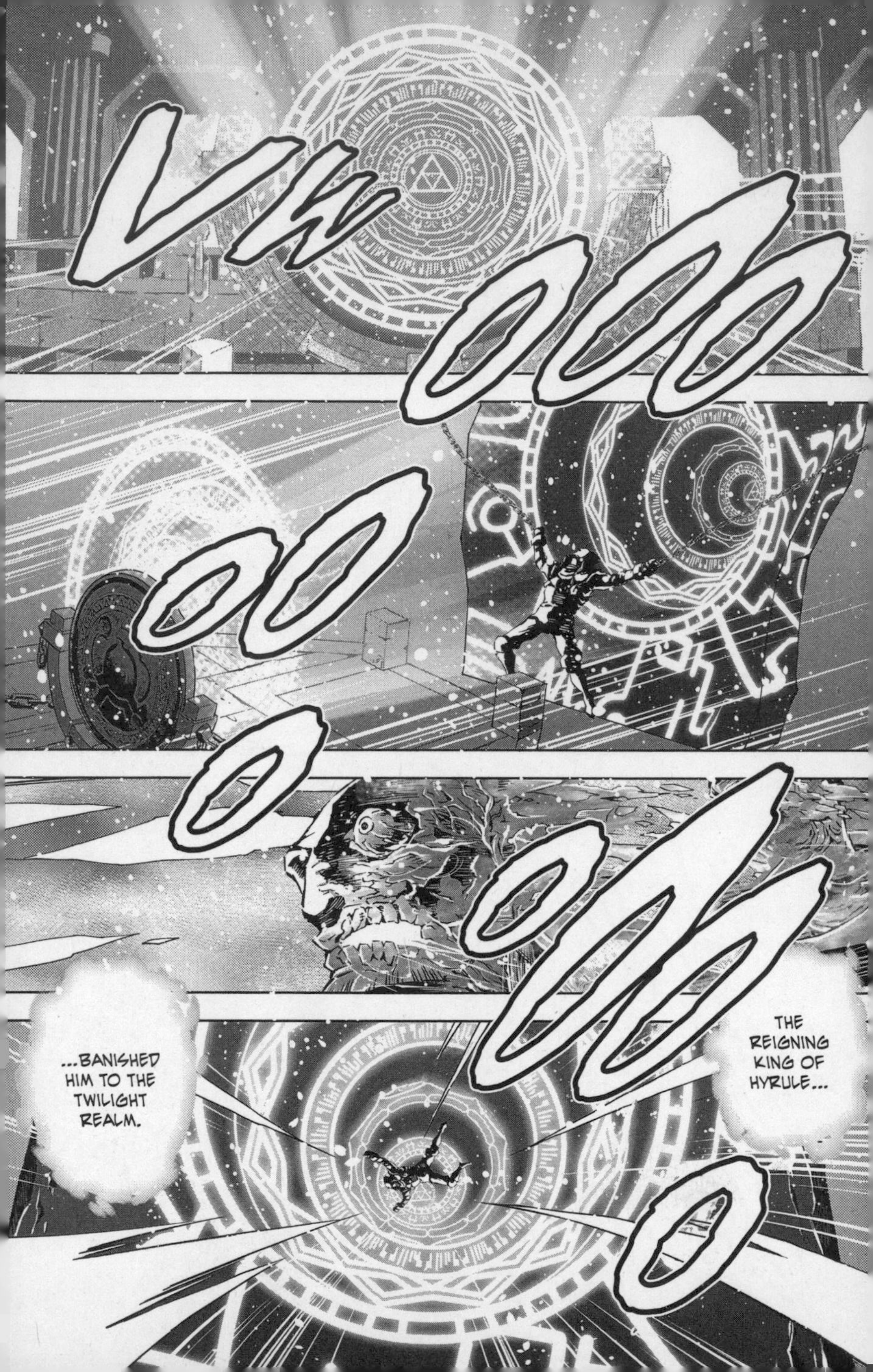
THE REIGNING KING OF HYRULE...
...BANISHED HIM TO THE TWILIGHT REALM.

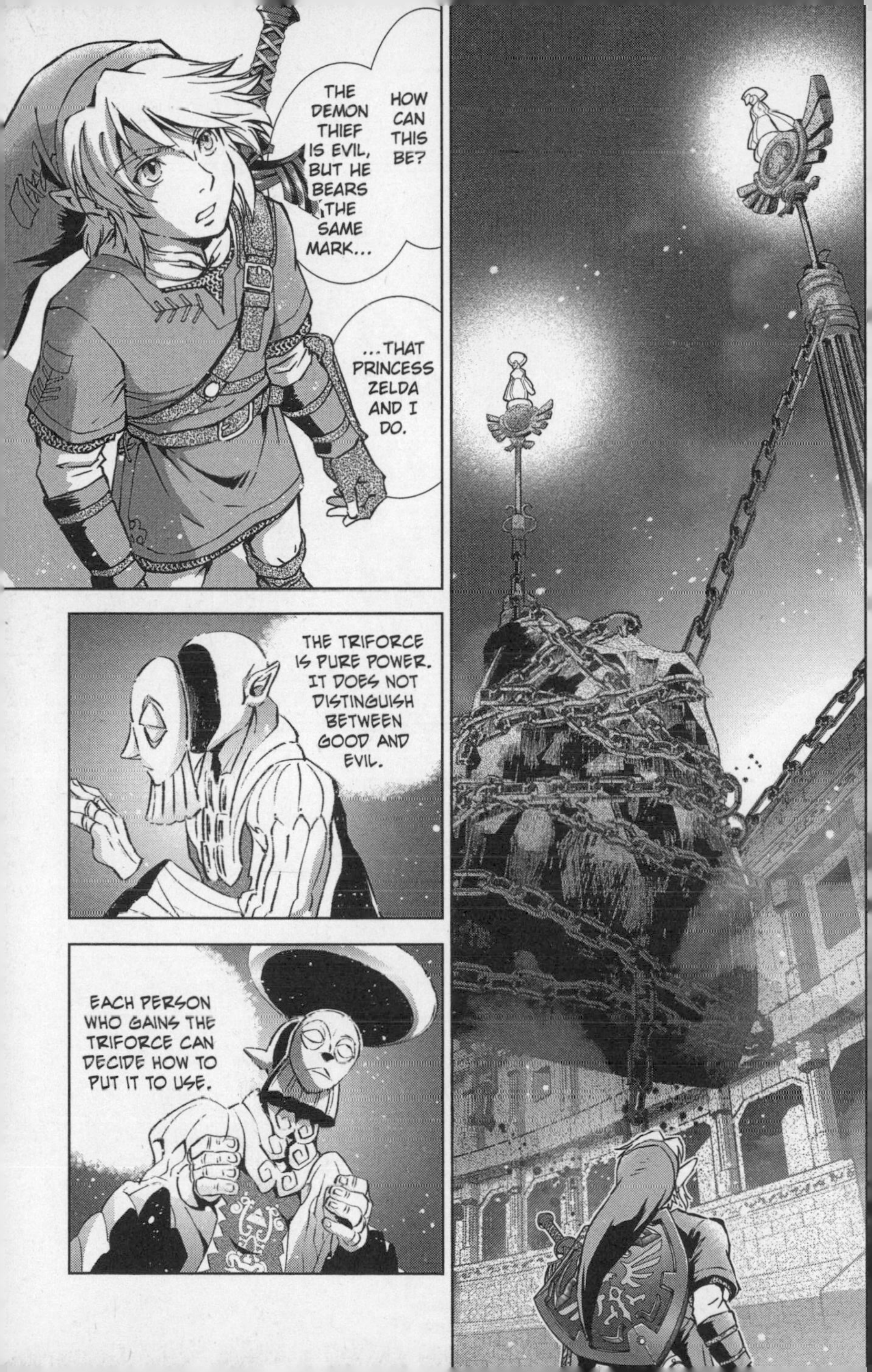
HOW CAN THIS BE?
THE DEMON THIEF IS EVIL, BUT HE BEARS THE SAME MARK...
...THAT PRINCESS ZELDA AND I DO.
THE TRIFORCE IS PURE POWER. IT DOES NOT DISTINGUISH BETWEEN GOOD AND EVIL.
EACH PERSON WHO GAINS THE TRIFORCE CAN DECIDE HOW TO PUT IT TO USE.

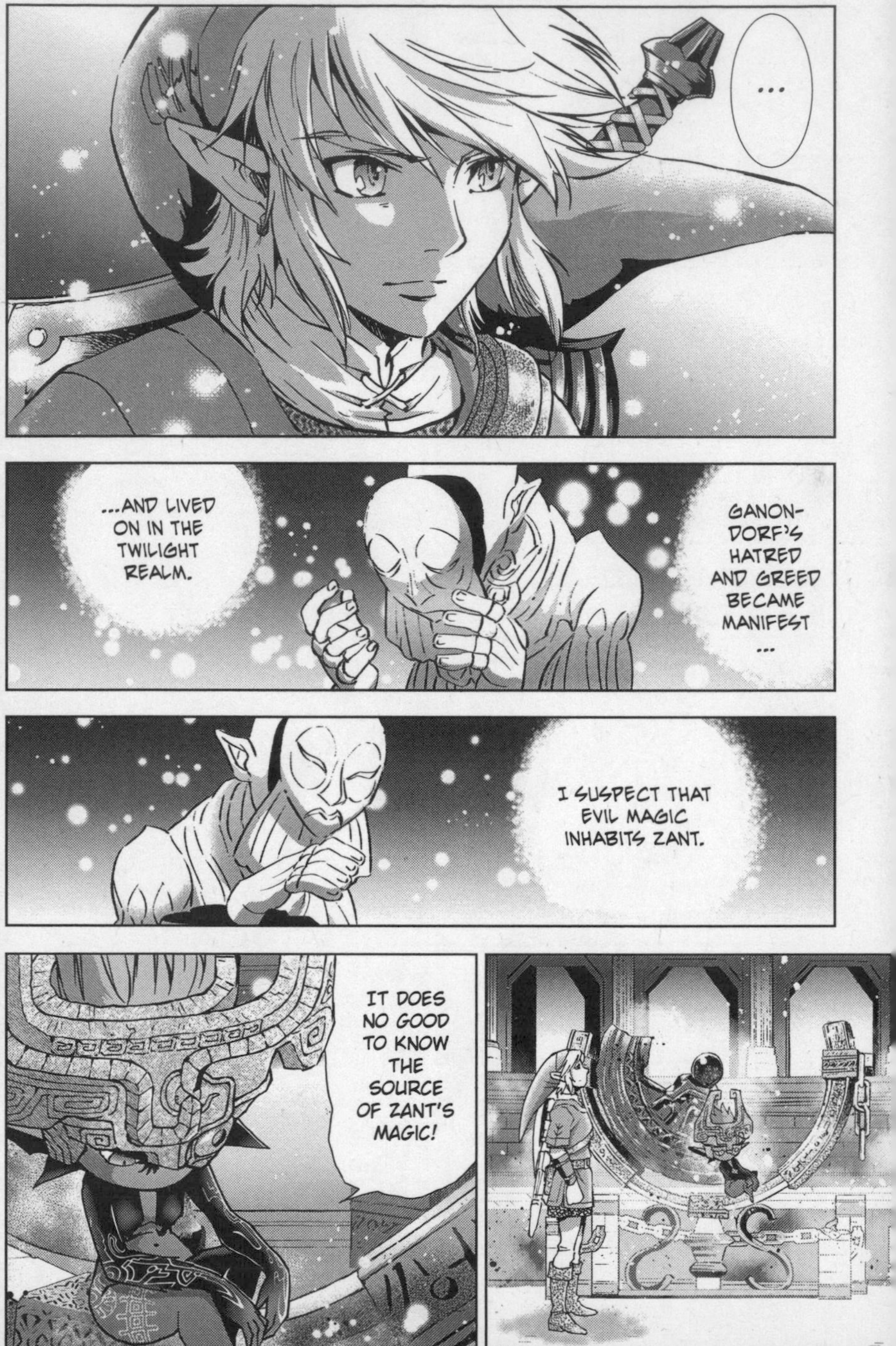
...
GANON-DORF'S HATRED AND GREED BECAME MANIFEST...
...AND LIVED ON IN THE TWILIGHT REALM.
I SUSPECT THAT EVIL MAGIC INHABITS ZANT.
IT DOES NO GOOD TO KNOW THE SOURCE OF ZANT'S MAGIC!

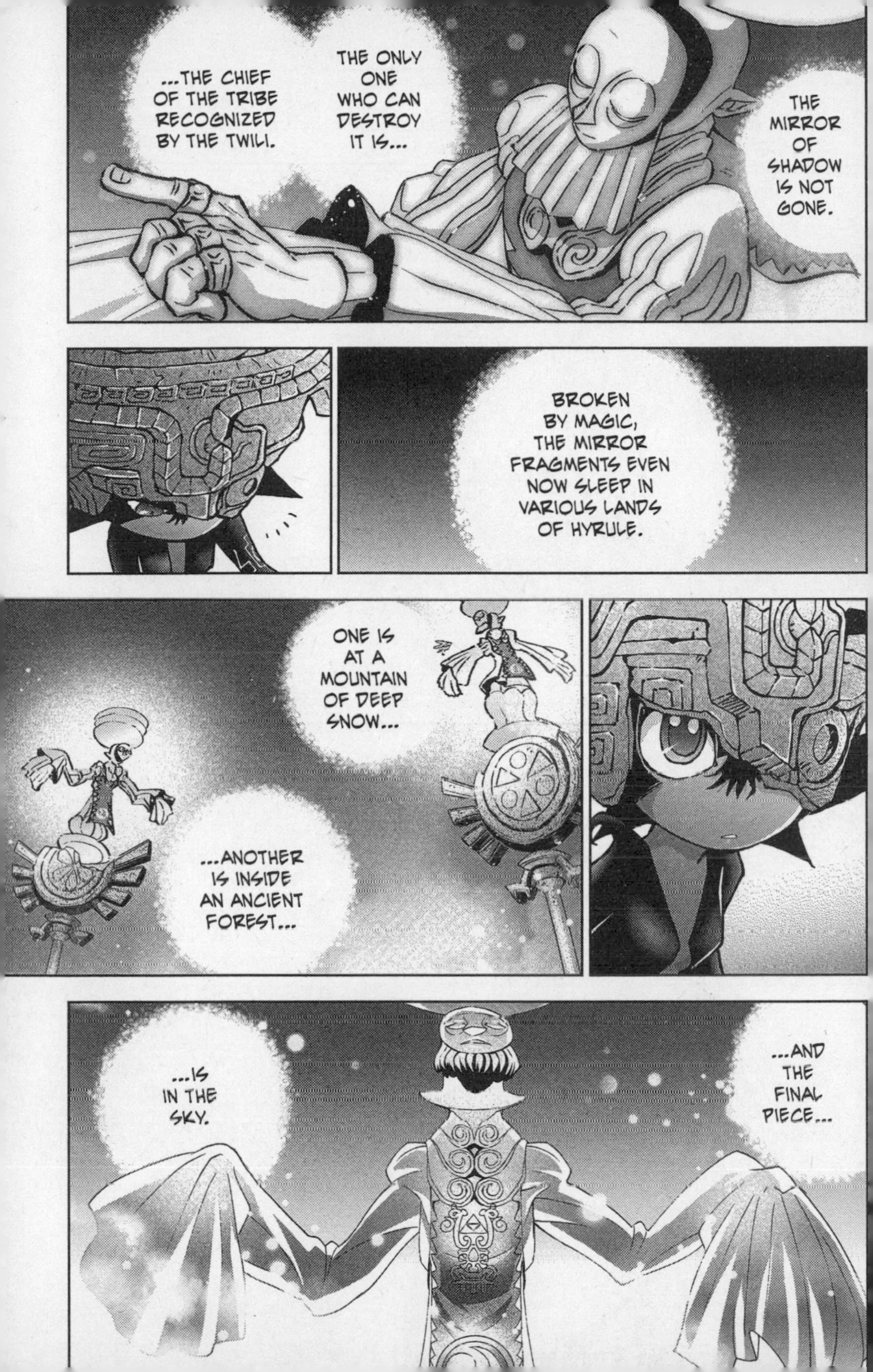
THE MIRROR OF SHADOW IS NOT GONE.
THE ONLY ONE WHO CAN DESTROY IT IS...
...THE CHIEF OF THE TRIBE RECOGNIZED BY THE TWILI.
BROKEN BY MAGIC, THE MIRROR FRAGMENTS EVEN NOW SLEEP IN VARIOUS LANDS OF HYRULE.
...
ONE IS AT A MOUNTAIN OF DEEP SNOW...
...ANOTHER IS INSIDE AN ANCIENT FOREST...
...AND THE FINAL PIECE...
...IS IN THE SKY.

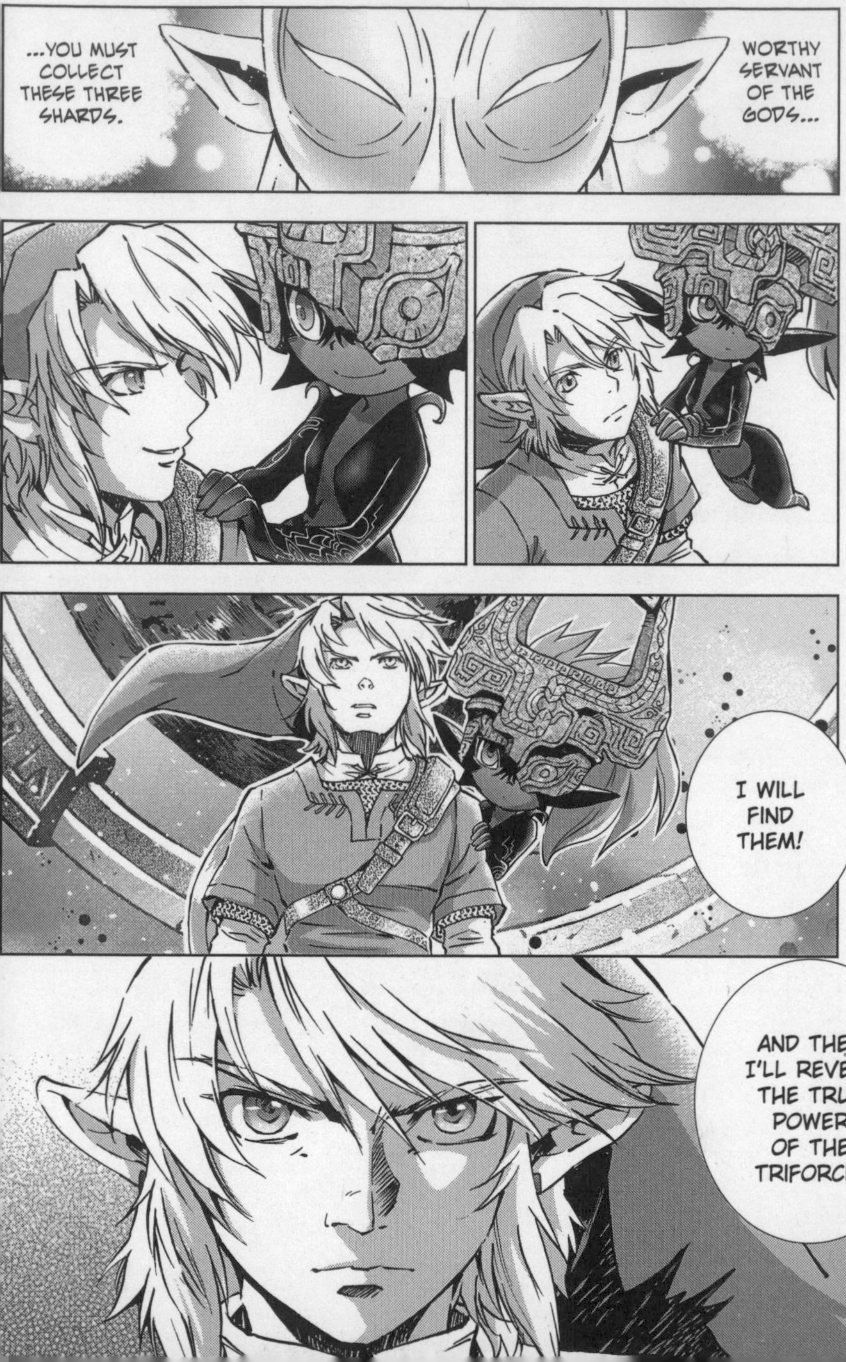
WORTHY SERVANT OF THE GODS...
...YOU MUST COLLECT THESE THREE SHARDS.
I WILL FIND THEM!
AND THEN I'LL REVEAL THE TRUE POWER OF THE TRIFORCE!

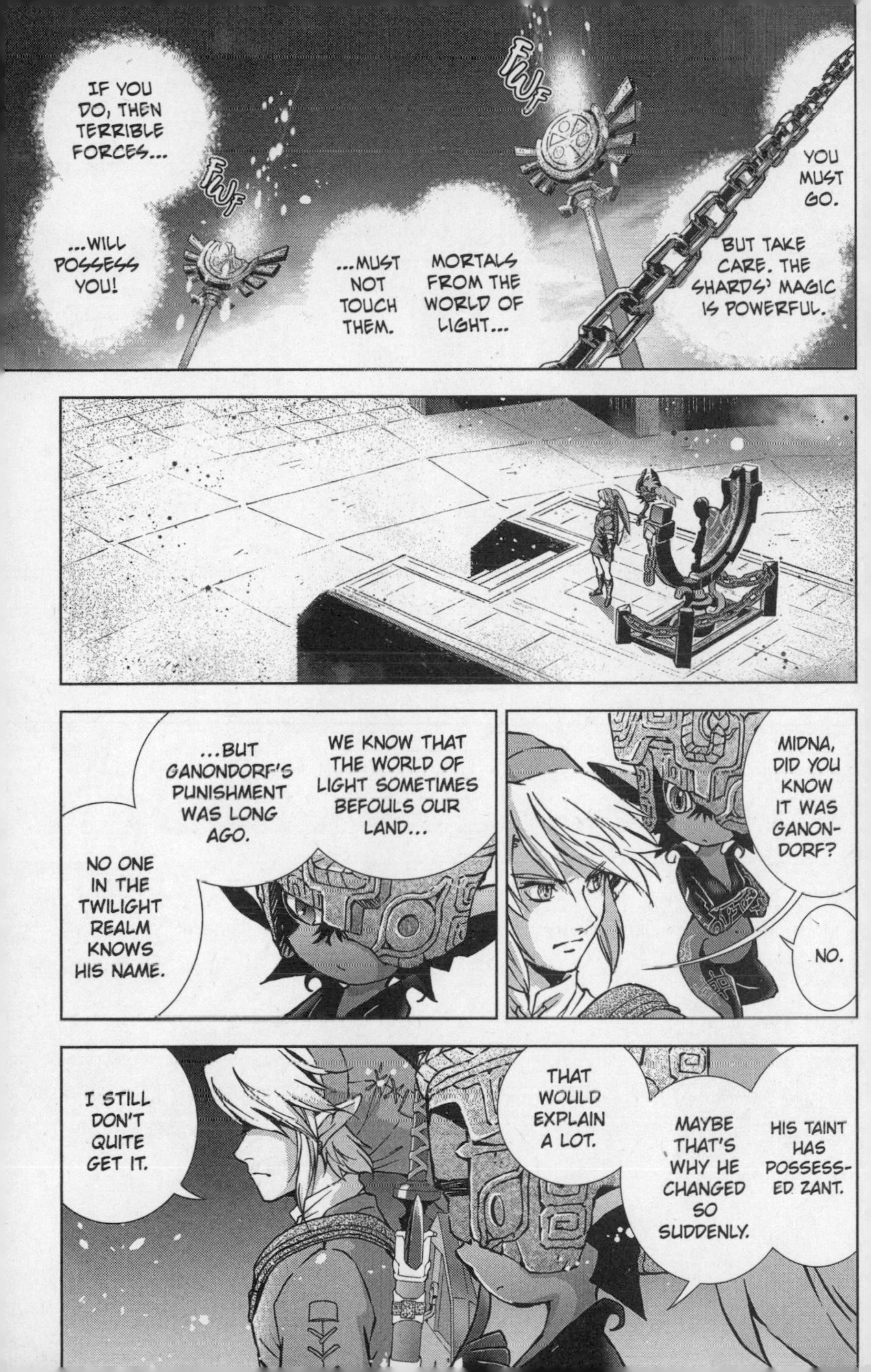
YOU MUST GO.
BUT TAKE CARE. THE SHARDS' MAGIC IS POWERFUL.
FWF
MORTALS FROM THE WORLD OF LIGHT...
...MUST NOT TOUCH THEM.
FWF
IF YOU DO, THEN TERRIBLE FORCES...
...WILL POSSESS YOU!
MIDNA, DID YOU KNOW IT WAS GANON-DORF?
NO.
WE KNOW THAT THE WORLD OF LIGHT SOMETIMES BEFOULS OUR LAND...
...BUT GANONDORF'S PUNISHMENT WAS LONG AGO.
NO ONE IN THE TWILIGHT REALM KNOWS HIS NAME.
HIS TAINT HAS POSSESS-ED ZANT.
MAYBE THAT'S WHY HE CHANGED SO SUDDENLY.
THAT WOULD EXPLAIN A LOT.
I STILL DON'T QUITE GET IT.

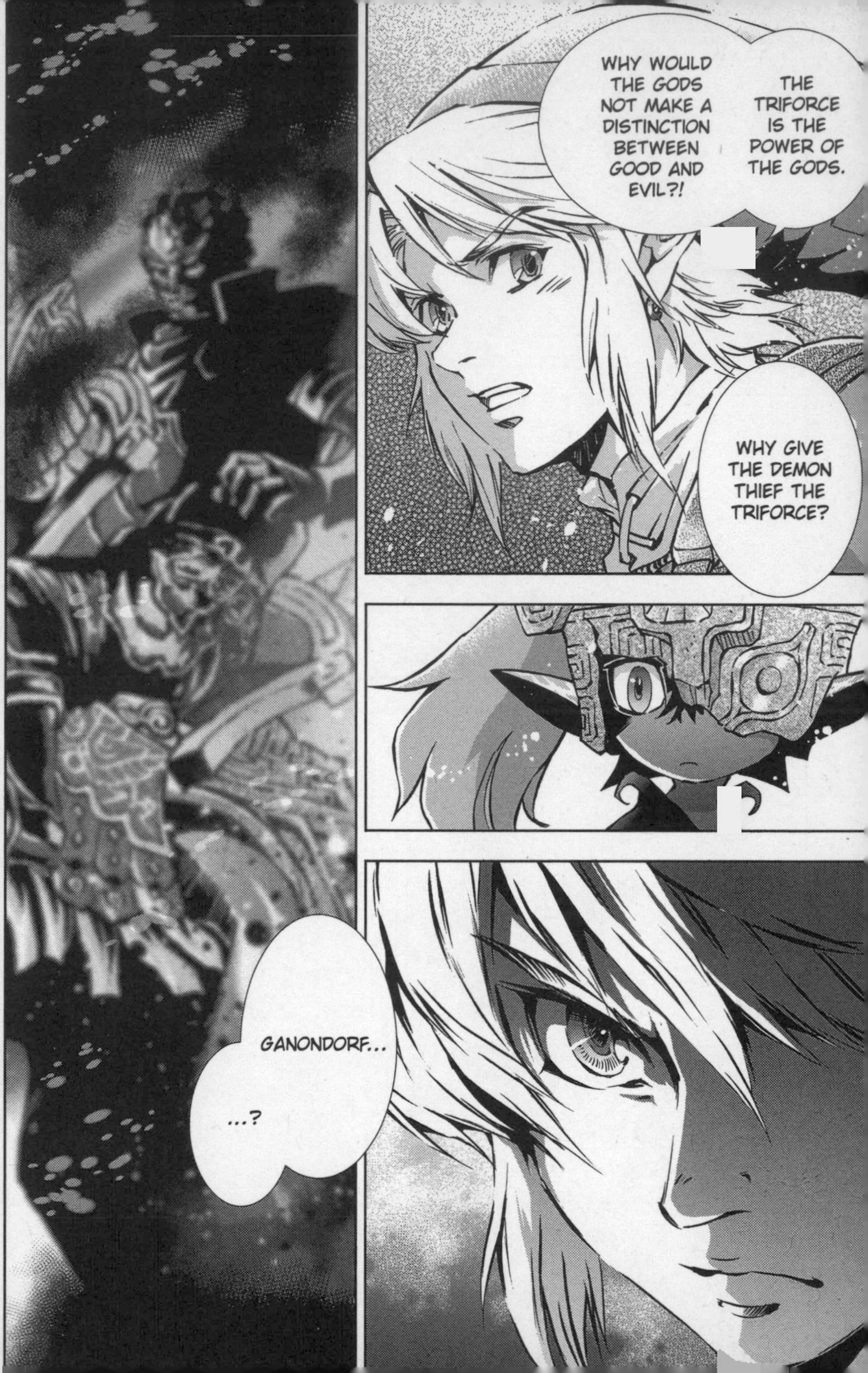
THE TRIFORCE IS THE POWER OF THE GODS.
WHY WOULD THE GODS NOT MAKE A DISTINCTION BETWEEN GOOD AND EVIL?!
WHY GIVE THE DEMON THIEF THE TRIFORCE?
GANONDORF...
...?

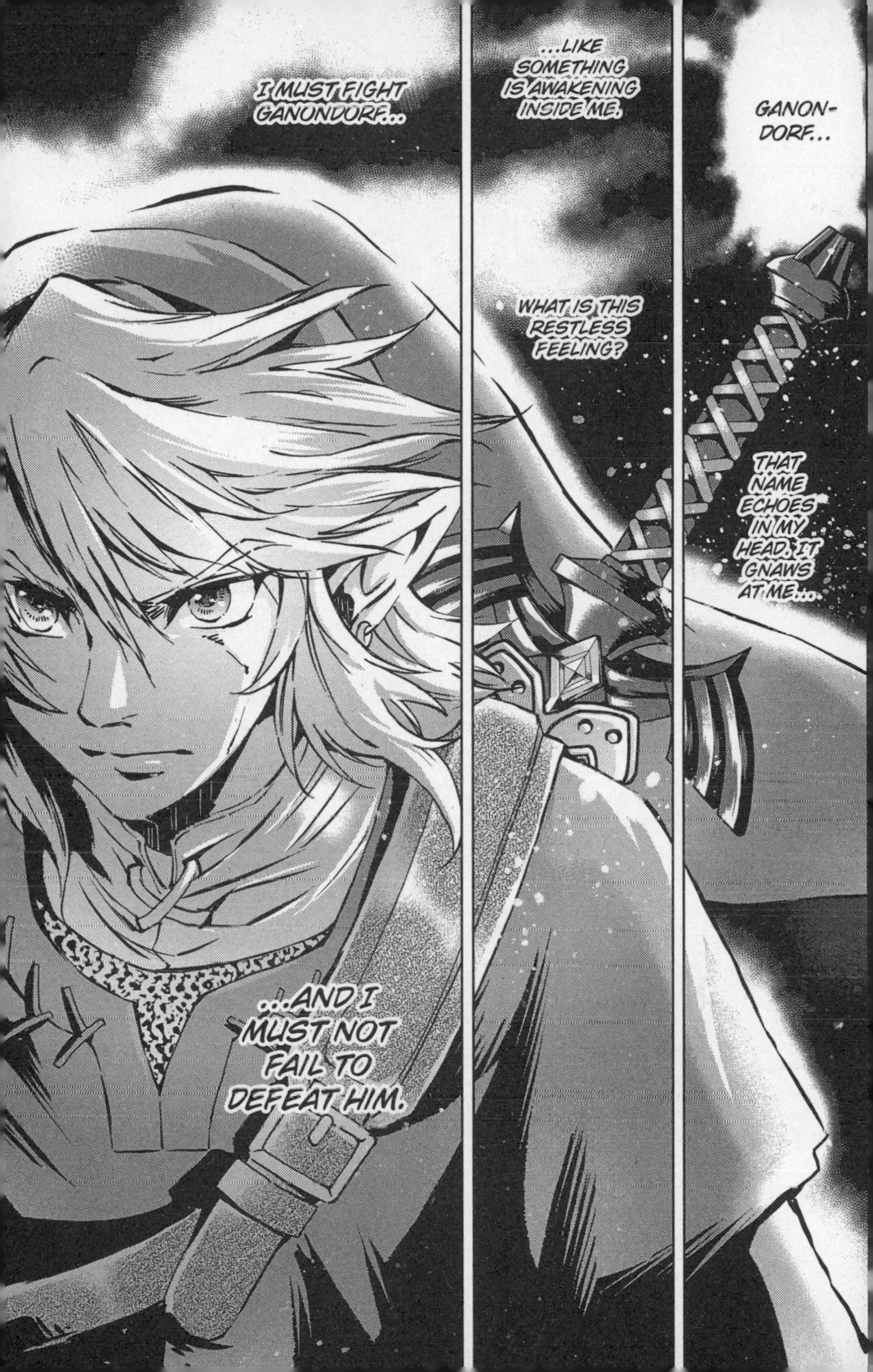
GANON-DORF...
THAT NAME ECHOES IN MY HEAD. IT GNAWS AT ME...
...LIKE SOMETHING IS AWAKENING INSIDE ME.
WHAT IS THIS RESTLESS FEELING?
I MUST FIGHT GANONDORF...
...AND I MUST NOT FAIL TO DEFEAT HIM.

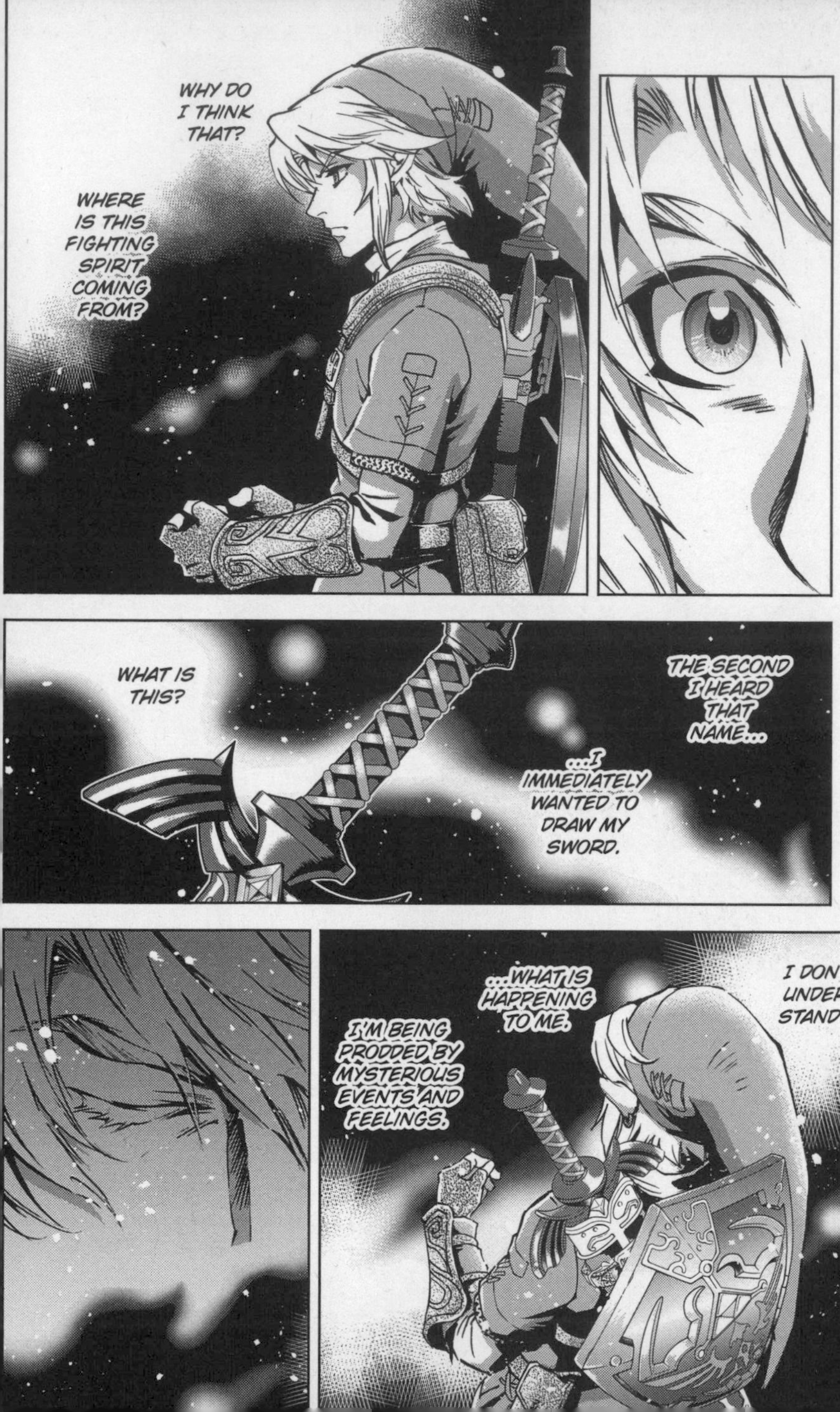
WHY DO I THINK THAT?
WHERE IS THIS FIGHTING SPIRIT COMING FROM?
THE SECOND I HEARD THAT NAME...
...I IMMEDIATELY WANTED TO DRAW MY SWORD.
WHAT IS THIS?
I DON'T UNDER-STAND...
...WHAT IS HAPPENING TO ME.
I'M BEING PRODDED BY MYSTERIOUS EVENTS AND FEELINGS.

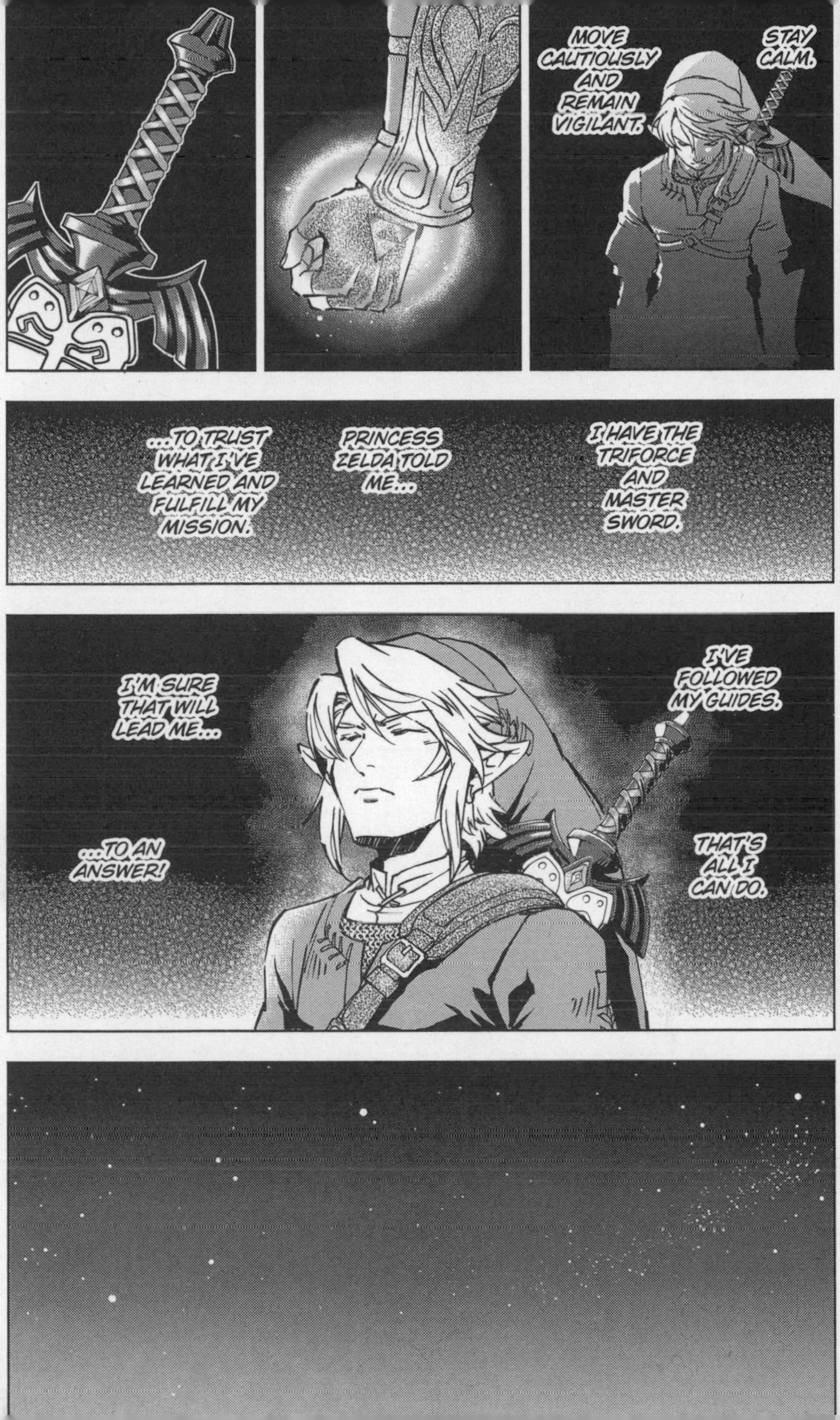
STAY CALM.
MOVE CAUTIOUSLY AND REMAIN VIGILANT.
I HAVE THE TRIFORCE AND MASTER SWORD.
PRINCESS ZELDA TOLD ME...
...TO TRUST WHAT I'VE LEARNED AND FULFILL MY MISSION.
I'VE FOLLOWED MY GUIDES.
THAT'S ALL I CAN DO.
I'M SURE THAT WILL LEAD ME...
...TO AN ANSWER!

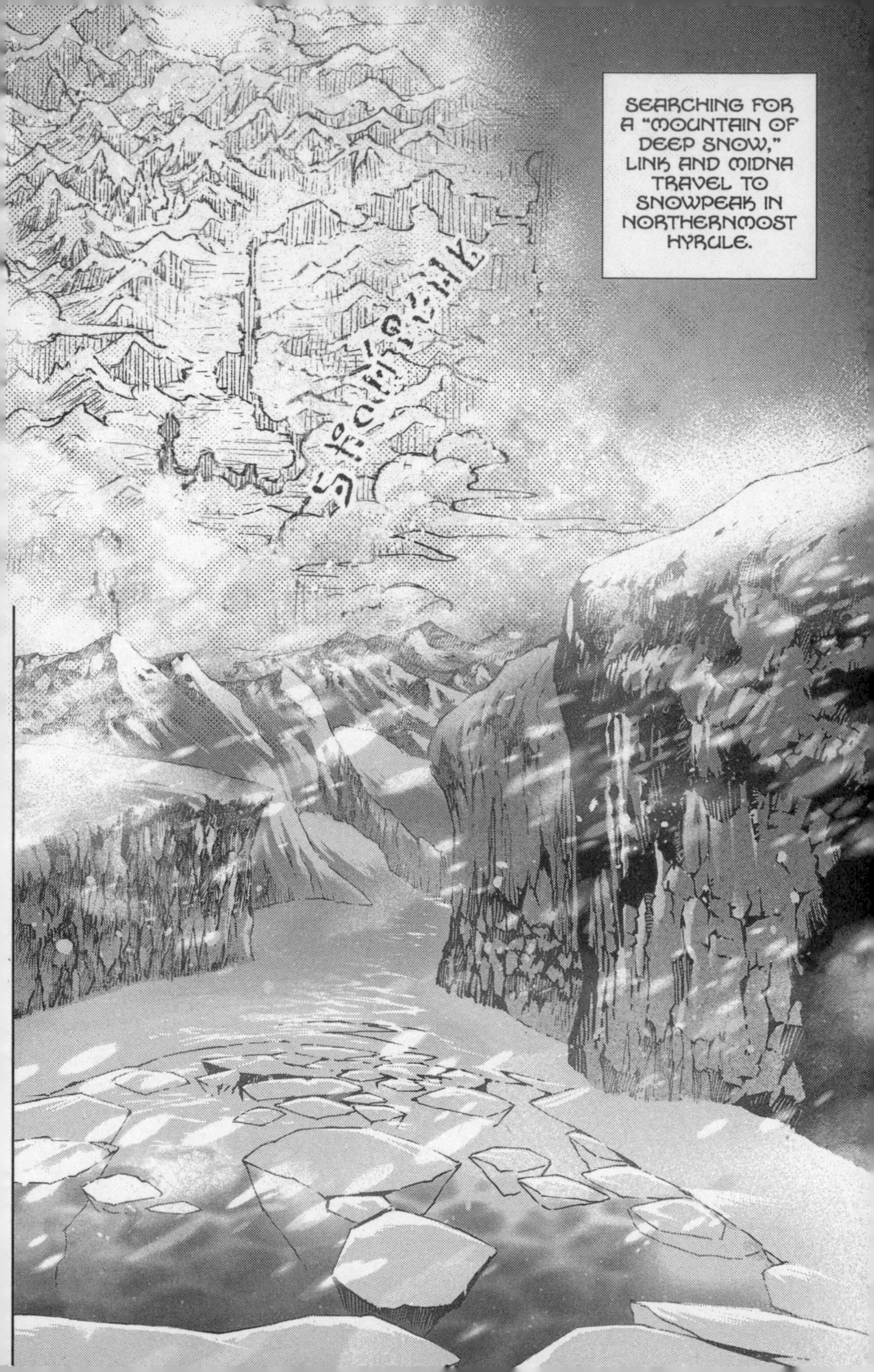
SEARCHING FOR A "MOUNTAIN OF DEEP SNOW," LINK AND MIDNA TRAVEL TO SNOWPEAK IN NORTHERNMOST HYRULE.

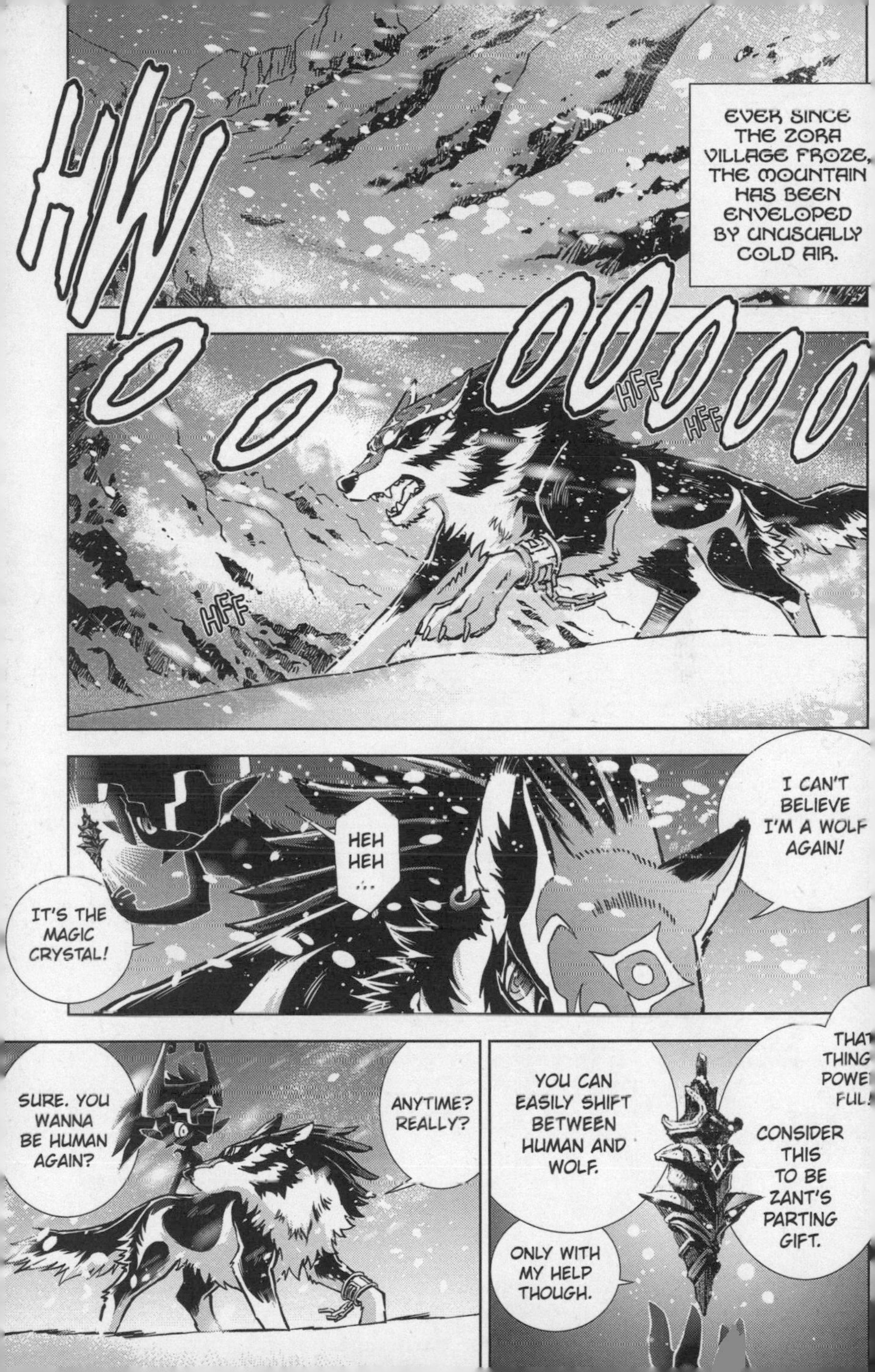
EVER SINCE THE ZORA VILLAGE FROZE, THE MOUNTAIN HAS BEEN ENVELOPED BY UNUSUALLY COLD AIR.
HWOOOOOOOO
HFF
HFF
HFF
I CAN'T BELIEVE I'M A WOLF AGAIN!
HEH HEH ...
IT'S THE MAGIC CRYSTAL!
THAT THING POWE FUL!
CONSIDER THIS TO BE ZANT'S PARTING GIFT.
YOU CAN EASILY SHIFT BETWEEN HUMAN AND WOLF.
ONLY WITH MY HELP THOUGH.
ANYTIME? REALLY?
SURE. YOU WANNA BE HUMAN AGAIN?

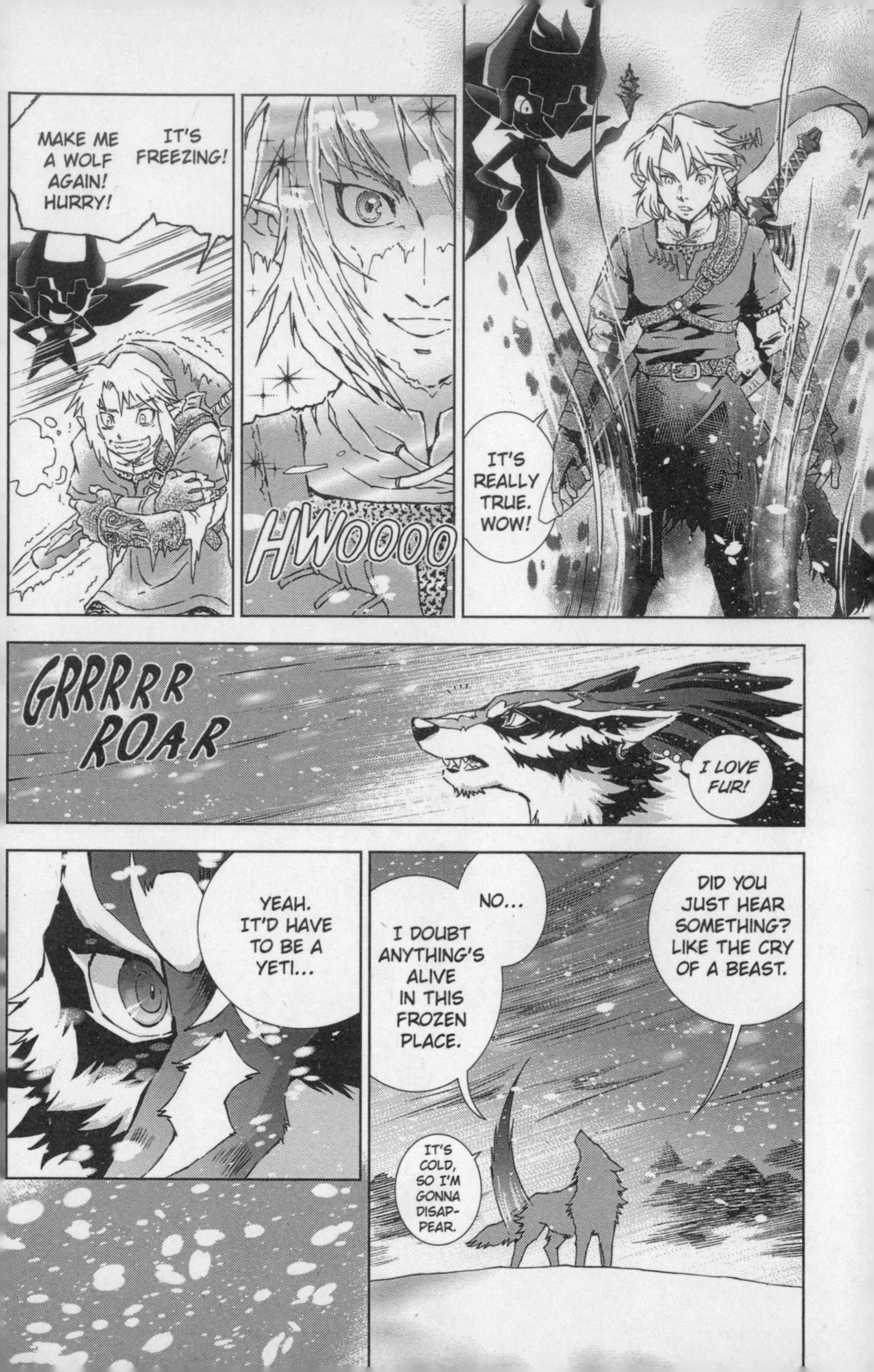
IT'S REALLY TRUE. WOW!
HWOOOO
IT'S FREEZING!
MAKE ME A WOLF AGAIN! HURRY!
GRRRRR ROAR
I LOVE FUR!
DID YOU JUST HEAR SOMETHING? LIKE THE CRY OF A BEAST.
NO...
I DOUBT ANYTHING'S ALIVE IN THIS FROZEN PLACE.
IT'S COLD, SO I'M GONNA DISAP-PEAR.
YEAH. IT'D HAVE TO BE A YETI...

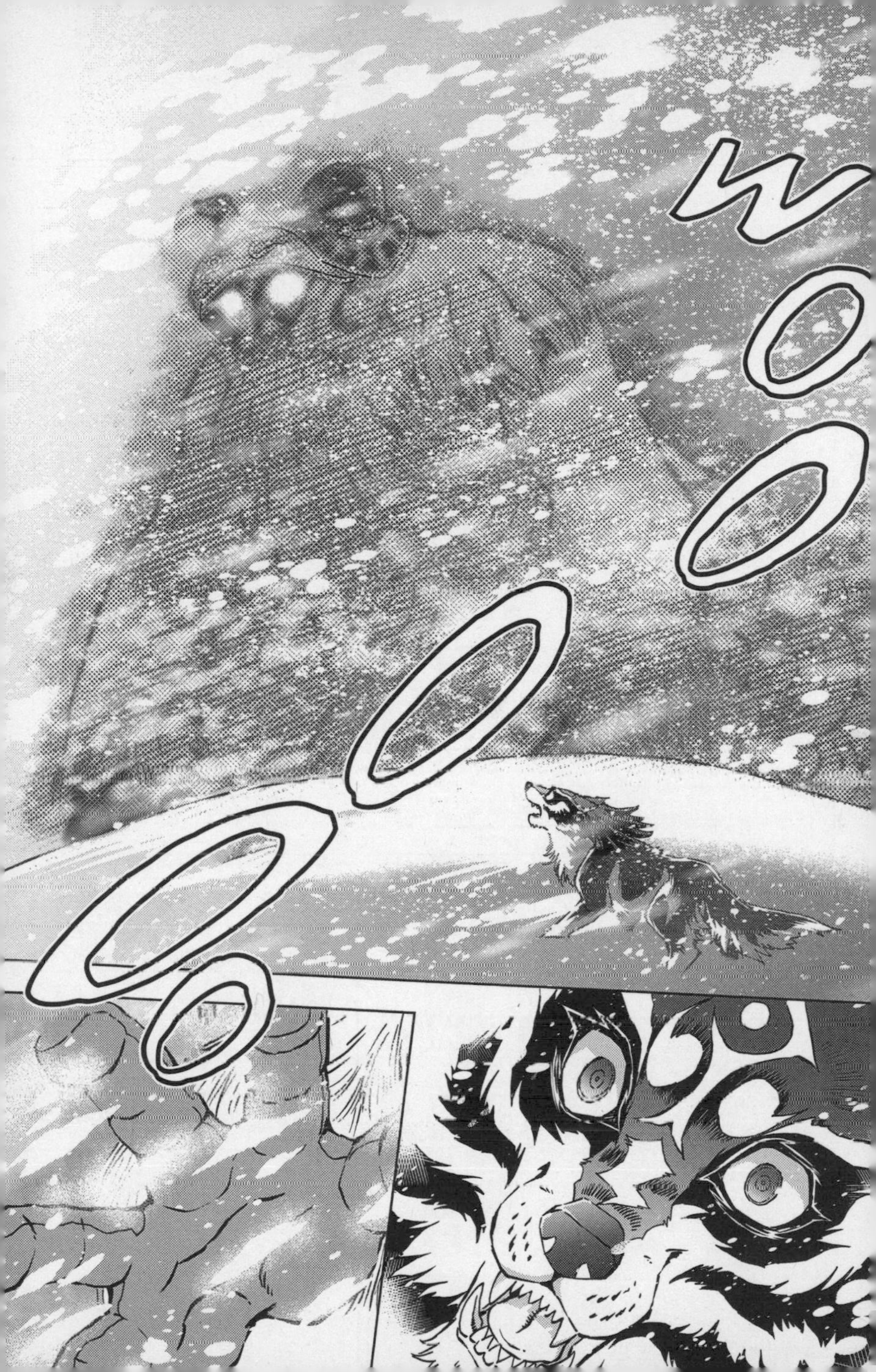
WOOOOO

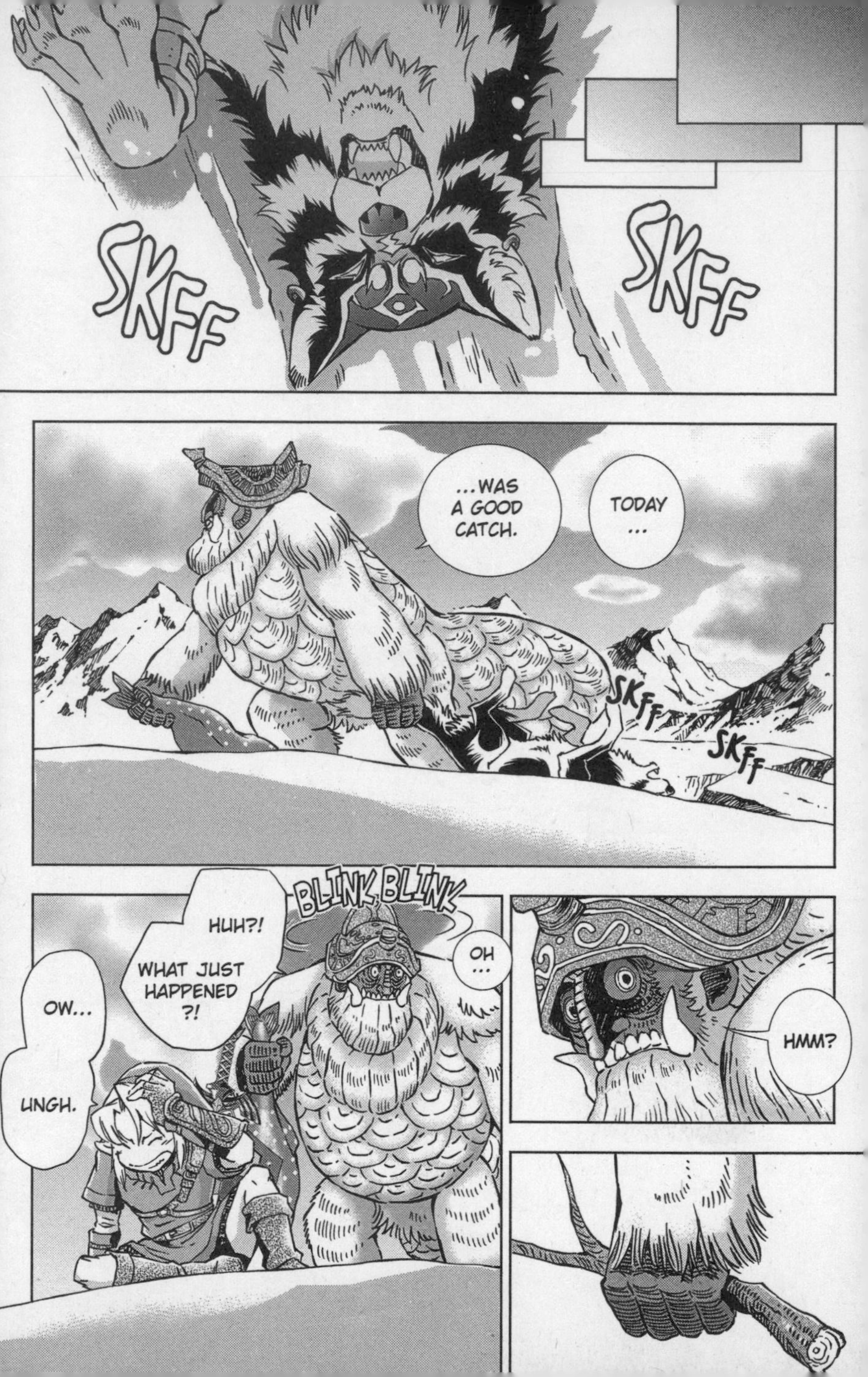
SKFF
SKFF
TODAY ...
...WAS A GOOD CATCH.
SKFF
SKFF
HMM?
BLINK, BLINK
OH ...
HUH?! WHAT JUST HAPPENED ?!
OW...
UNGH.

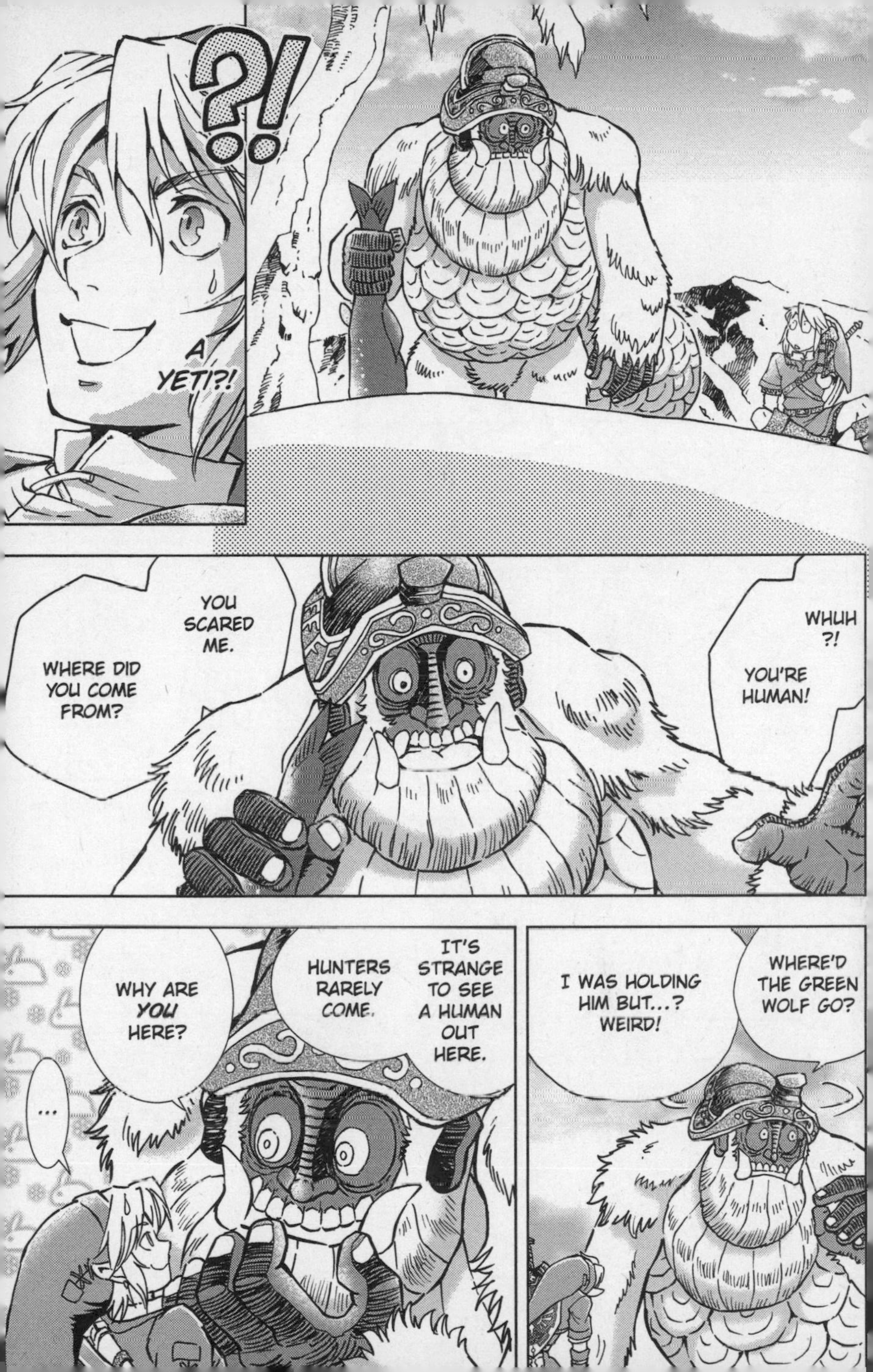
?!
A YETI?!
WHUH ?!
YOU'RE HUMAN!
YOU SCARED ME.
WHERE DID YOU COME FROM?
WHERE'D THE GREEN WOLF GO?
I WAS HOLDING HIM BUT...? WEIRD!
IT'S STRANGE TO SEE A HUMAN OUT HERE.
HUNTERS RARELY COME.
WHY ARE *YOU* HERE?
...

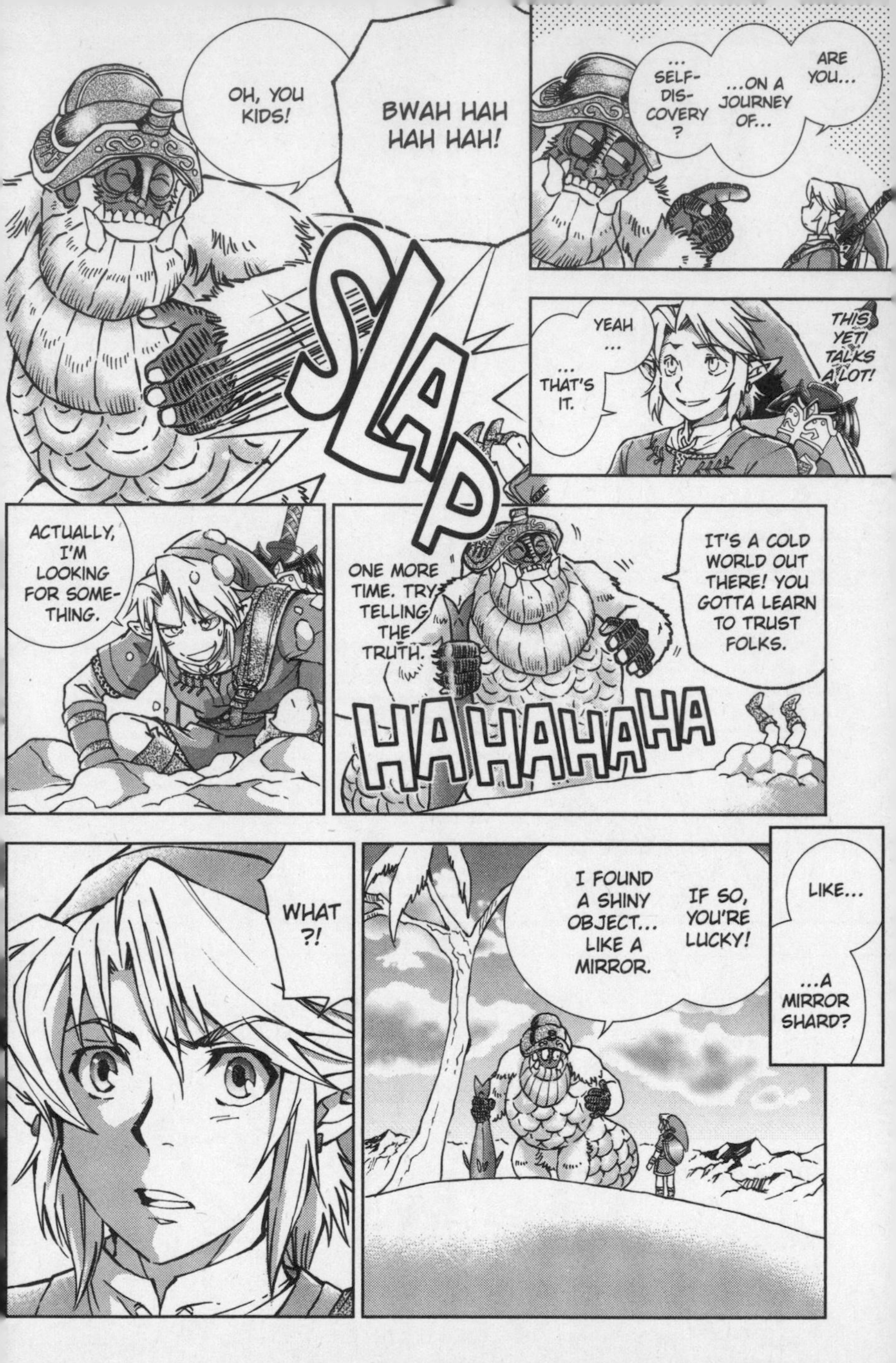
ARE YOU... ...ON A JOURNEY OF... ...SELF-DISCOVERY?
YEAH... ...THAT'S IT.
THIS YETI TALKS A LOT!
OH, YOU KIDS!
BWAH HAH HAH HAH!
SLAP
IT'S A COLD WORLD OUT THERE! YOU GOTTA LEARN TO TRUST FOLKS.
ONE MORE TIME. TRY TELLING THE TRUTH.
HAHAHAHAHA
ACTUALLY, I'M LOOKING FOR SOME-THING.
LIKE... ...A MIRROR SHARD?
IF SO, YOU'RE LUCKY!
I FOUND A SHINY OBJECT... LIKE A MIRROR.
WHAT?!

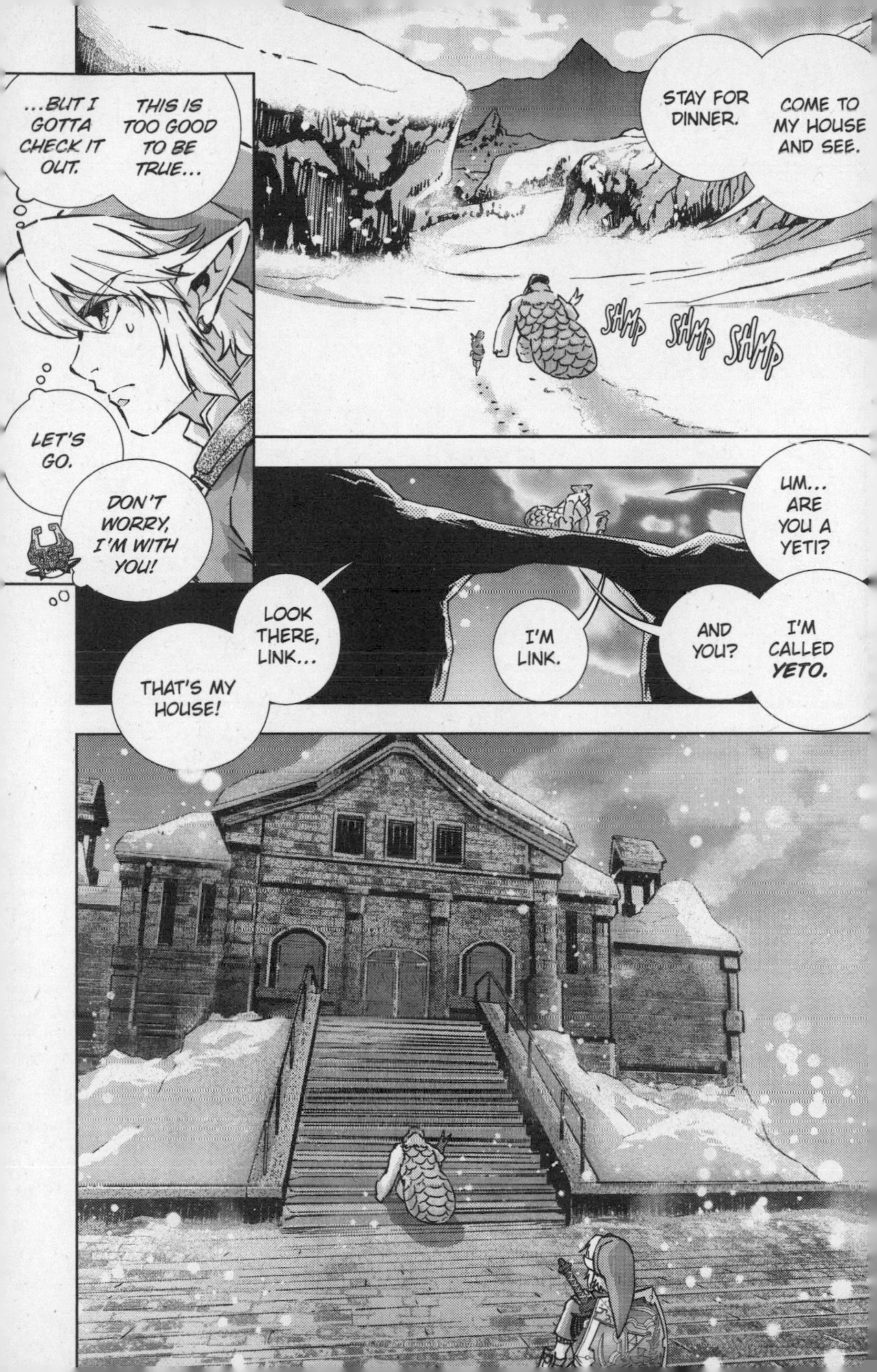
COME TO MY HOUSE AND SEE.
STAY FOR DINNER.
SHMP SHMP SHMP
UM... ARE YOU A YETI?
THIS IS TOO GOOD TO BE TRUE...
...BUT I GOTTA CHECK IT OUT.
LET'S GO.
DON'T WORRY, I'M WITH YOU!
I'M CALLED YETO.
AND YOU?
I'M LINK.
LOOK THERE, LINK...
THAT'S MY HOUSE!

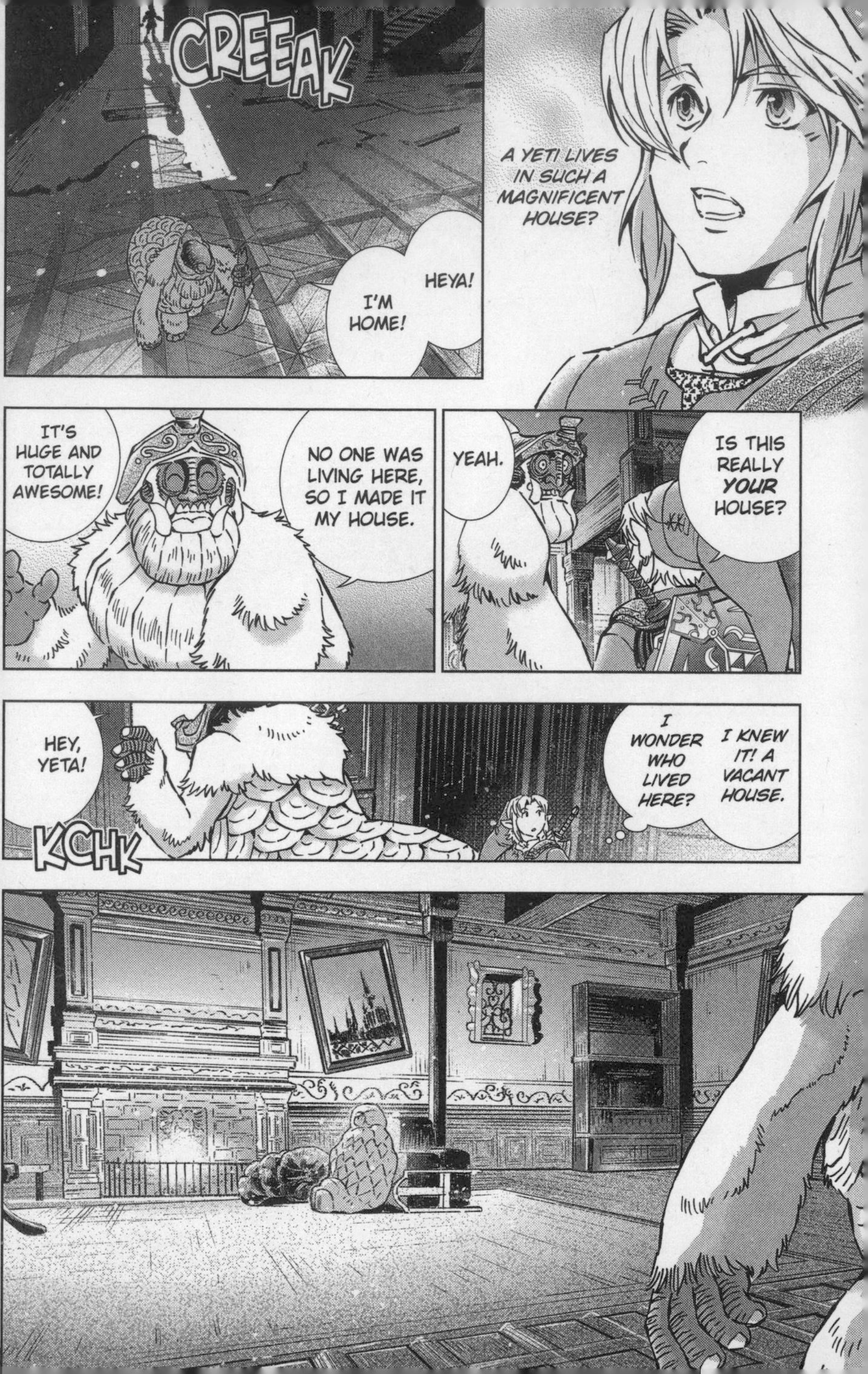
A YETI LIVES IN SUCH A MAGNIFICENT HOUSE?
CREEAK
HEYA!
I'M HOME!
IS THIS REALLY *YOUR* HOUSE?
YEAH.
NO ONE WAS LIVING HERE, SO I MADE IT MY HOUSE.
IT'S HUGE AND TOTALLY AWESOME!
I KNEW IT! A VACANT HOUSE.
I WONDER WHO LIVED HERE?
HEY, YETA!
KCHK

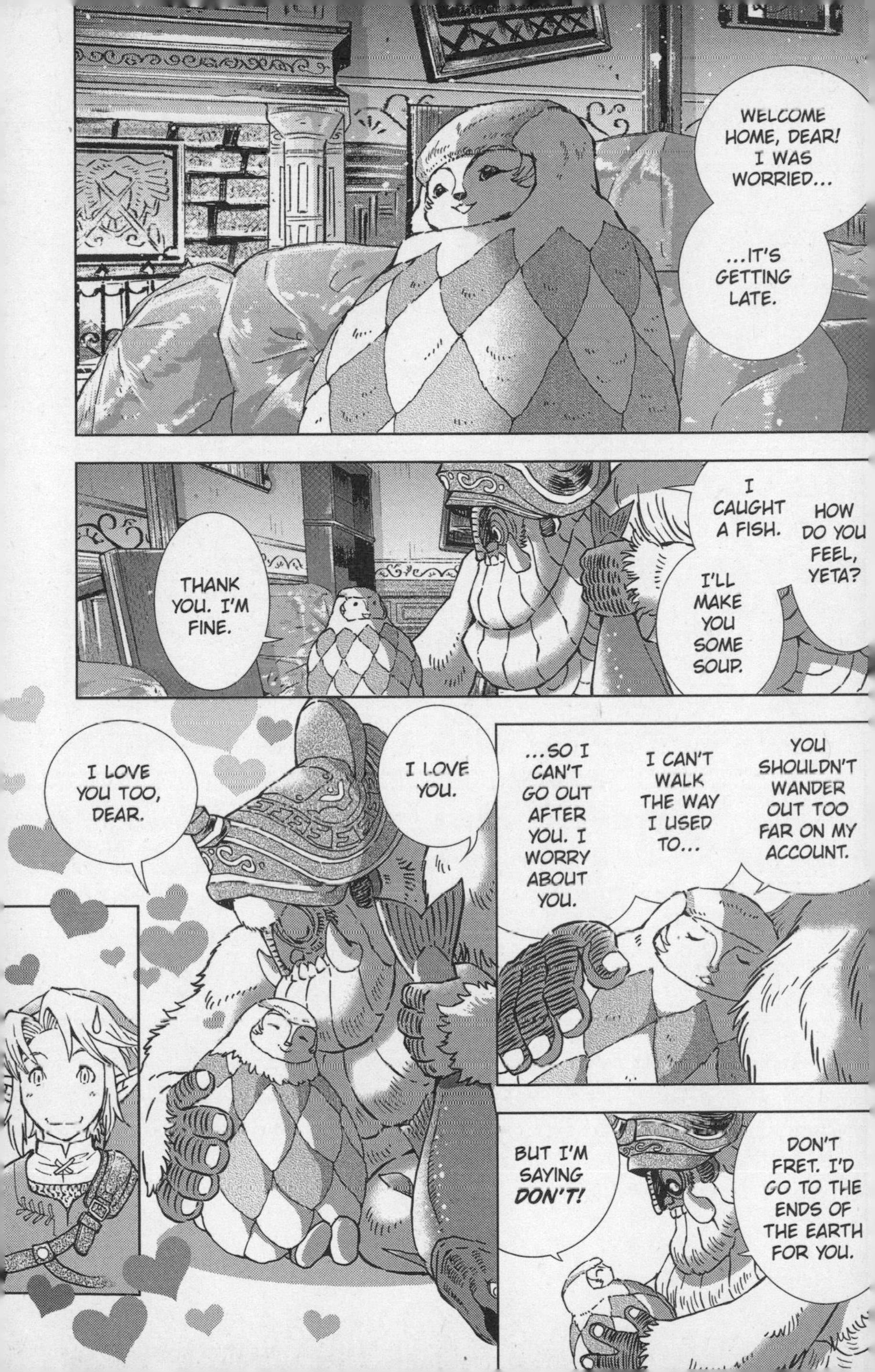
WELCOME HOME, DEAR! I WAS WORRIED...
...IT'S GETTING LATE.
HOW DO YOU FEEL, YETA?
I CAUGHT A FISH.
I'LL MAKE YOU SOME SOUP.
THANK YOU. I'M FINE.
YOU SHOULDN'T WANDER OUT TOO FAR ON MY ACCOUNT.
I CAN'T WALK THE WAY I USED TO...
...SO I CAN'T GO OUT AFTER YOU. I WORRY ABOUT YOU.
DON'T FRET. I'D GO TO THE ENDS OF THE EARTH FOR YOU.
BUT I'M SAYING ***DON'T!***
I LOVE YOU.
I LOVE YOU TOO, DEAR.

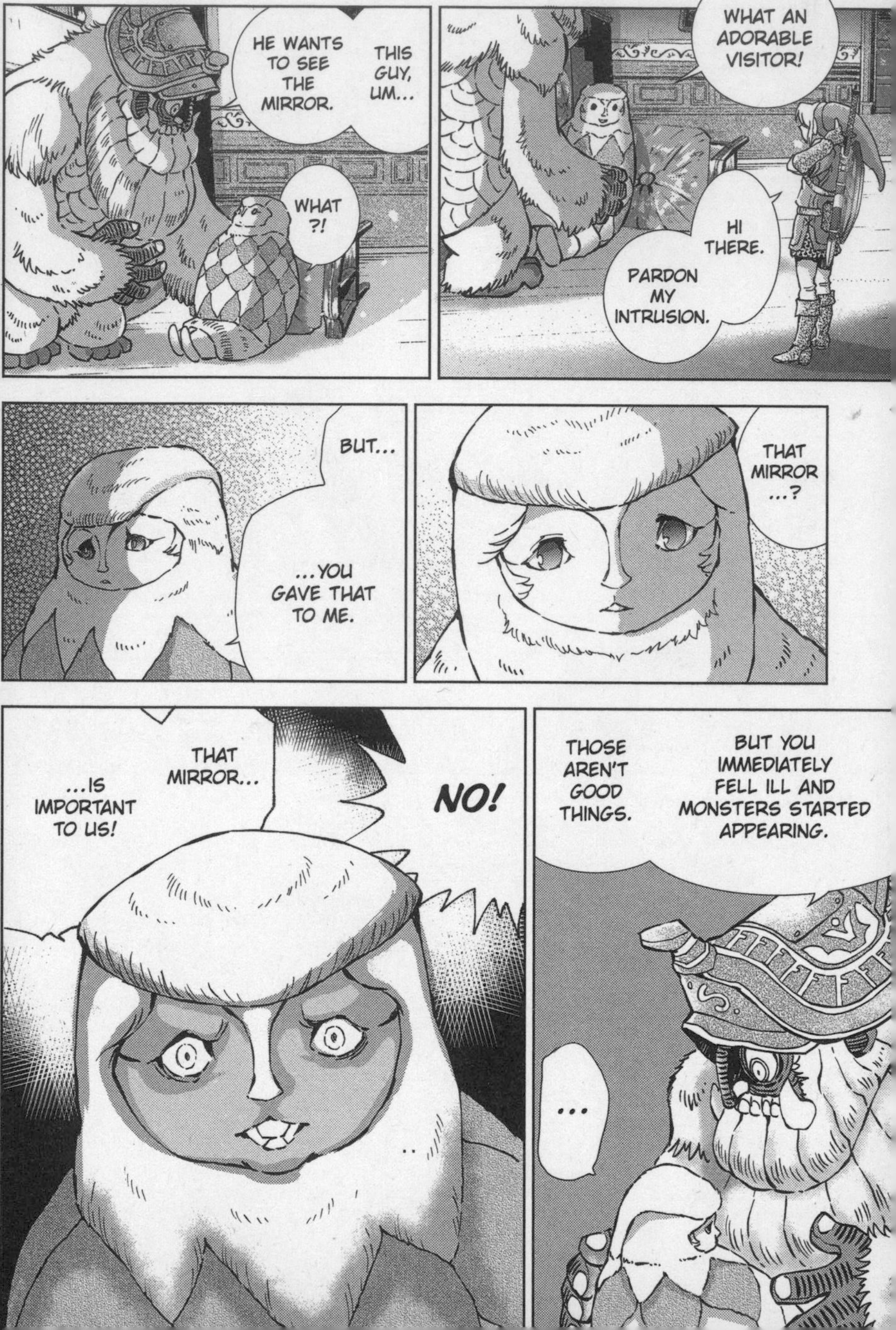
WHAT AN ADORABLE VISITOR!
HI THERE.
PARDON MY INTRUSION.
THIS GUY, UM...
HE WANTS TO SEE THE MIRROR.
WHAT ?!
THAT MIRROR ...?
BUT...
...YOU GAVE THAT TO ME.
BUT YOU IMMEDIATELY FELL ILL AND MONSTERS STARTED APPEARING.
THOSE AREN'T GOOD THINGS.
...
NO!
THAT MIRROR...
...IS IMPORTANT TO US!

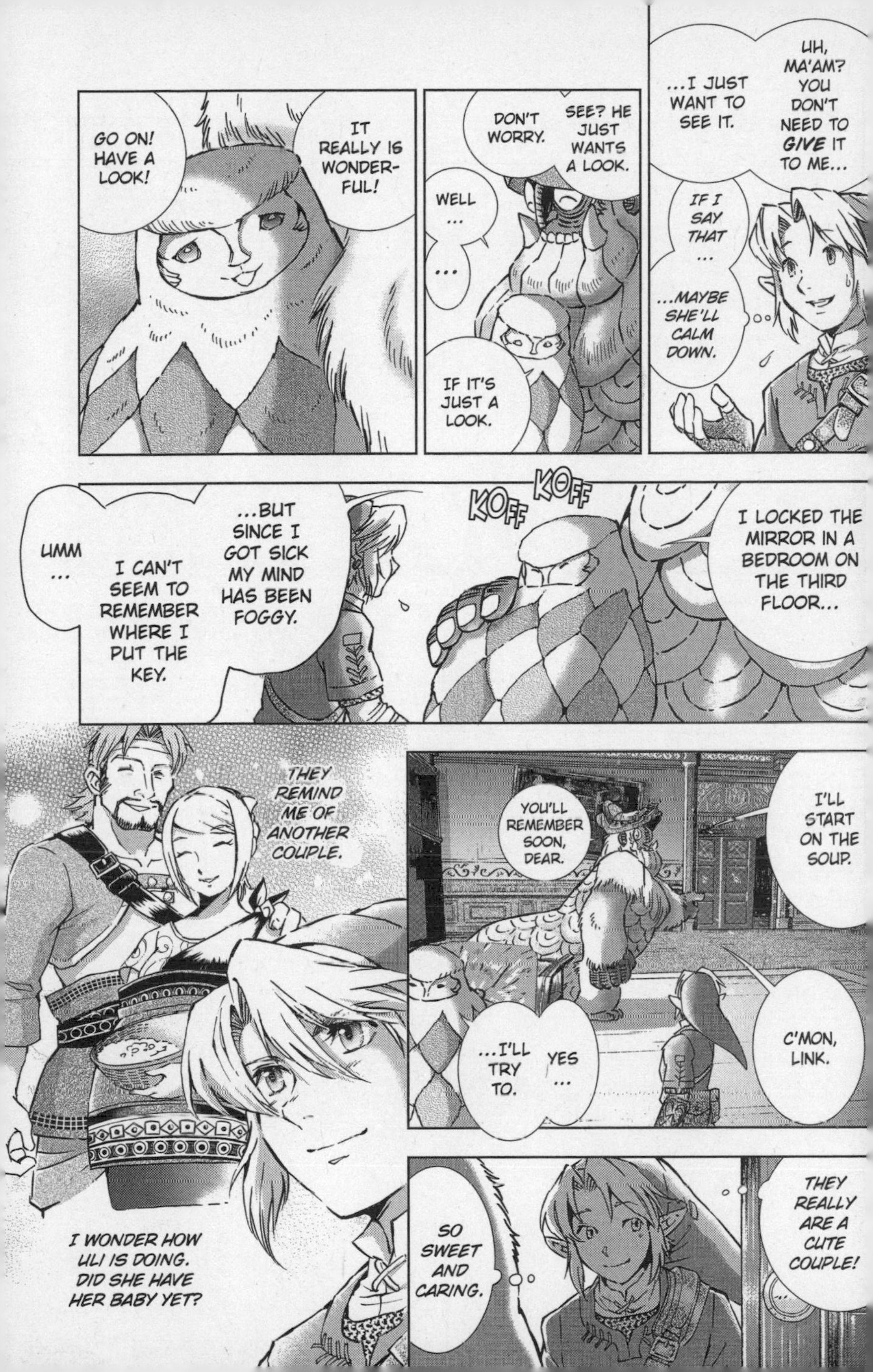
UH, MA'AM? YOU DON'T NEED TO GIVE IT TO ME...
...I JUST WANT TO SEE IT.
IF I SAY THAT...
...MAYBE SHE'LL CALM DOWN.
SEE? HE JUST WANTS A LOOK.
DON'T WORRY.
WELL...
...
IF IT'S JUST A LOOK.
IT REALLY IS WONDERFUL!
GO ON! HAVE A LOOK!
KOFF
KOFF
I LOCKED THE MIRROR IN A BEDROOM ON THE THIRD FLOOR...
...BUT SINCE I GOT SICK MY MIND HAS BEEN FOGGY.
I CAN'T SEEM TO REMEMBER WHERE I PUT THE KEY.
UMM...
I'LL START ON THE SOUP.
YOU'LL REMEMBER SOON, DEAR.
C'MON, LINK.
YES...
...I'LL TRY TO.
THEY REALLY ARE A CUTE COUPLE!
SO SWEET AND CARING.
THEY REMIND ME OF ANOTHER COUPLE.
I WONDER HOW ULI IS DOING. DID SHE HAVE HER BABY YET?

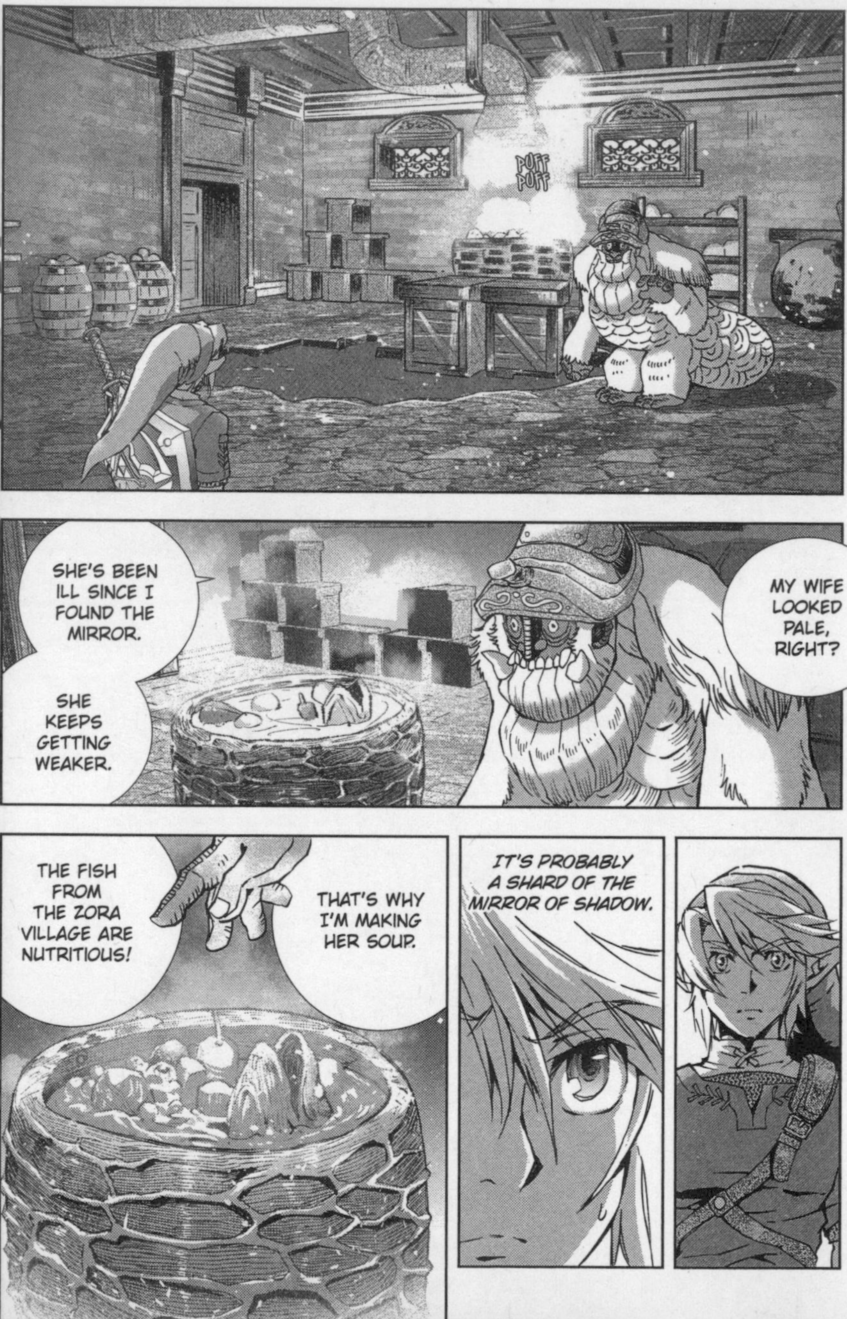
PUFF PUFF
MY WIFE LOOKED PALE, RIGHT?
SHE'S BEEN ILL SINCE I FOUND THE MIRROR.
SHE KEEPS GETTING WEAKER.
IT'S PROBABLY A SHARD OF THE MIRROR OF SHADOW.
THAT'S WHY I'M MAKING HER SOUP.
THE FISH FROM THE ZORA VILLAGE ARE NUTRITIOUS!

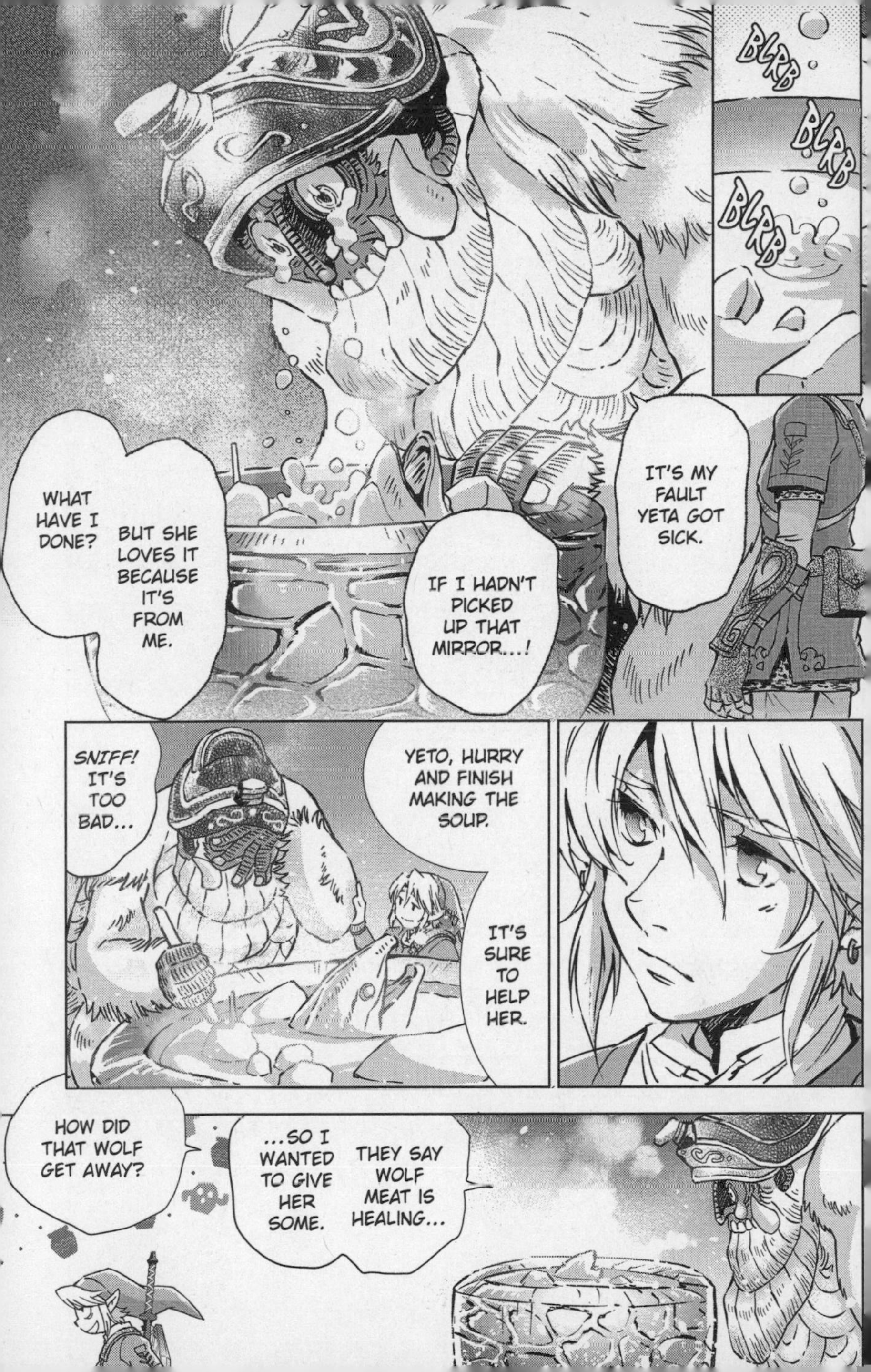
BLRB
BLRB
BLRB
IT'S MY FAULT YETA GOT SICK.
IF I HADN'T PICKED UP THAT MIRROR...!
BUT SHE LOVES IT BECAUSE IT'S FROM ME.
WHAT HAVE I DONE?
YETO, HURRY AND FINISH MAKING THE SOUP.
IT'S SURE TO HELP HER.
SNIFF! IT'S TOO BAD...
THEY SAY WOLF MEAT IS HEALING...
...SO I WANTED TO GIVE HER SOME.
HOW DID THAT WOLF GET AWAY?

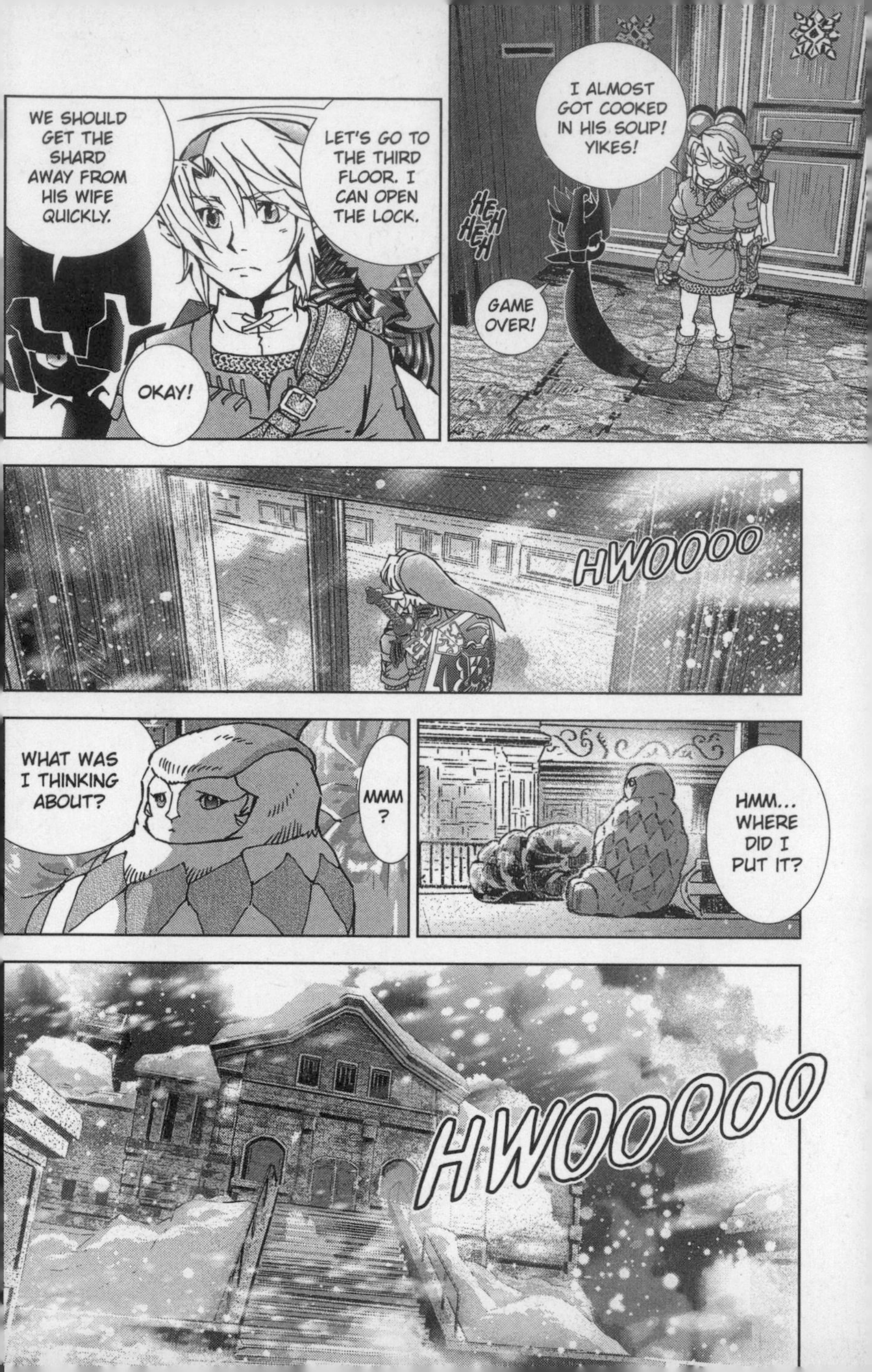
I ALMOST GOT COOKED IN HIS SOUP! YIKES!
HEH HEH HEH
GAME OVER!
LET'S GO TO THE THIRD FLOOR. I CAN OPEN THE LOCK.
WE SHOULD GET THE SHARD AWAY FROM HIS WIFE QUICKLY.
OKAY!
HWOOOO
HMM... WHERE DID I PUT IT?
MMM ?
WHAT WAS I THINKING ABOUT?
HWOOOOO

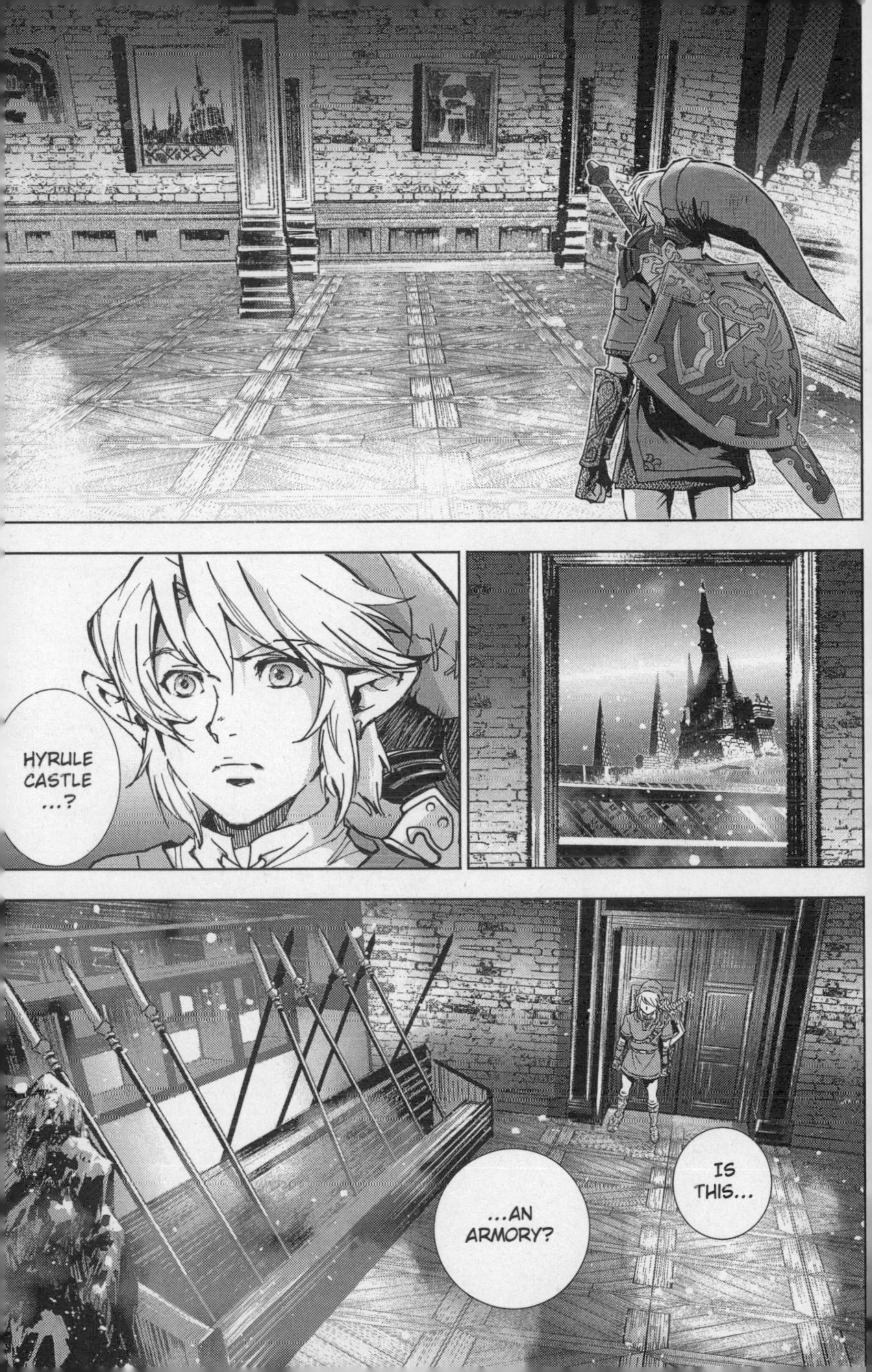
HYRULE CASTLE ...?
IS THIS...
...AN ARMORY?

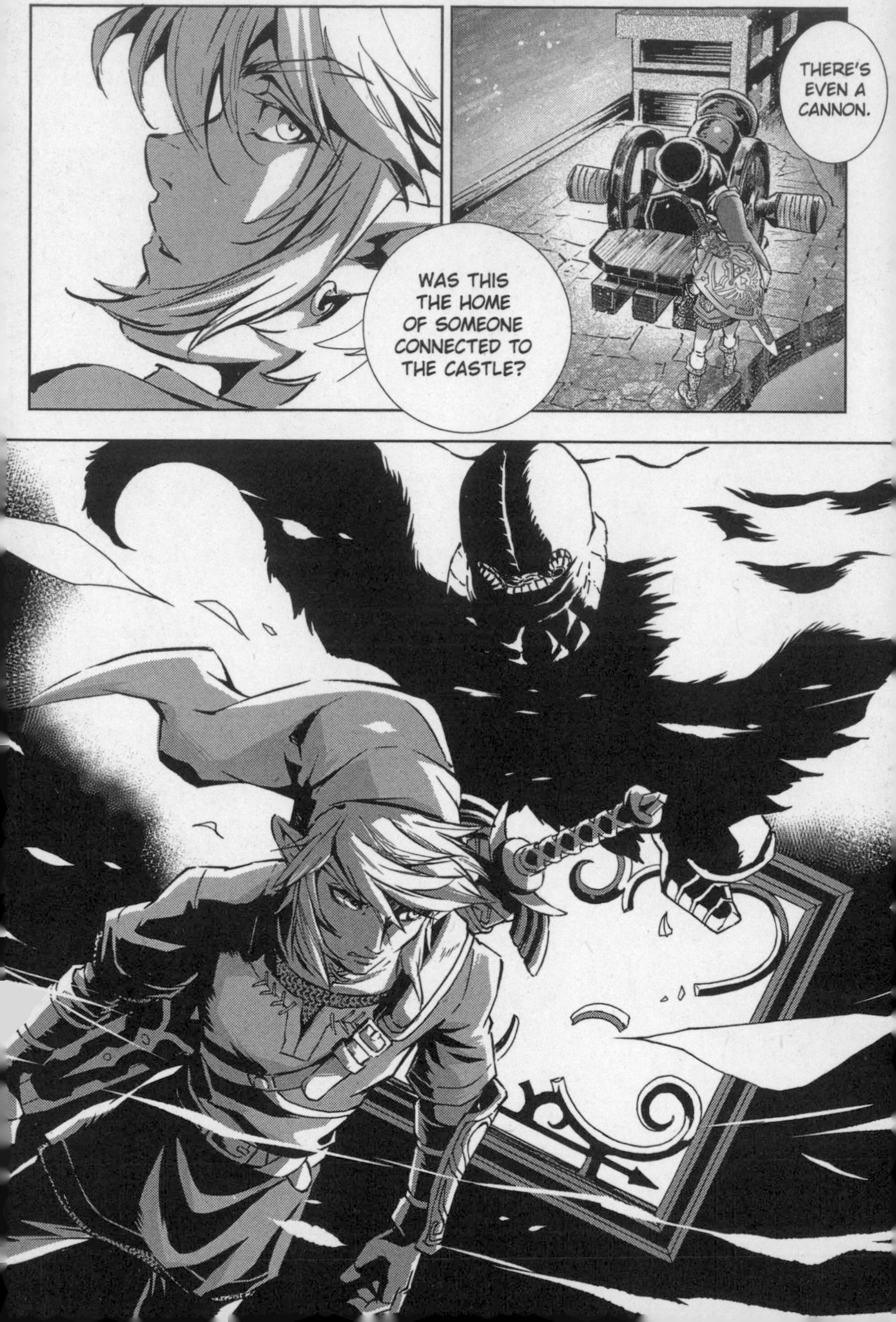
THERE'S EVEN A CANNON.
WAS THIS THE HOME OF SOMEONE CONNECTED TO THE CASTLE?

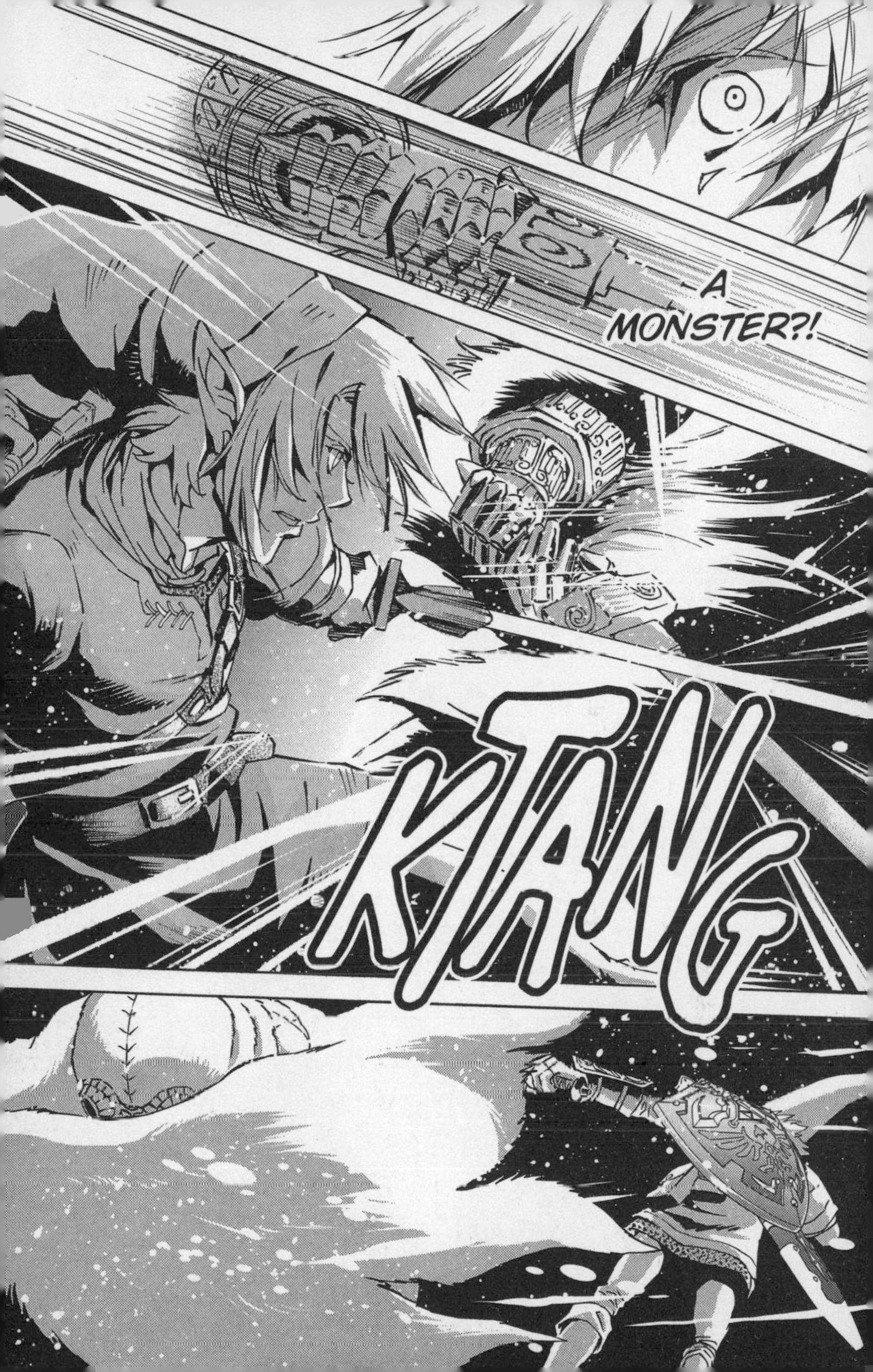
A MONSTER?!
KTANG

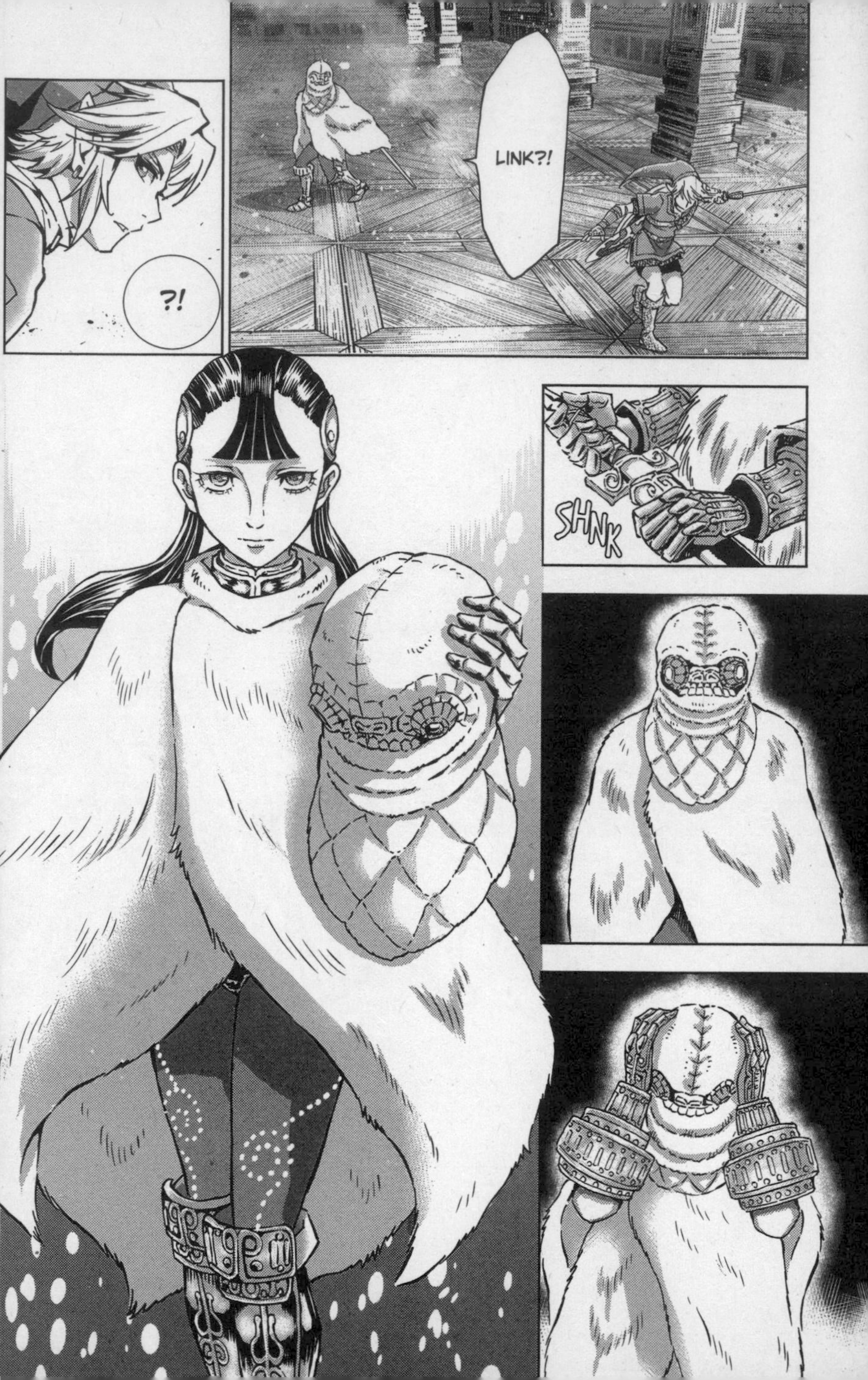
LINK?!
?!
SHNK

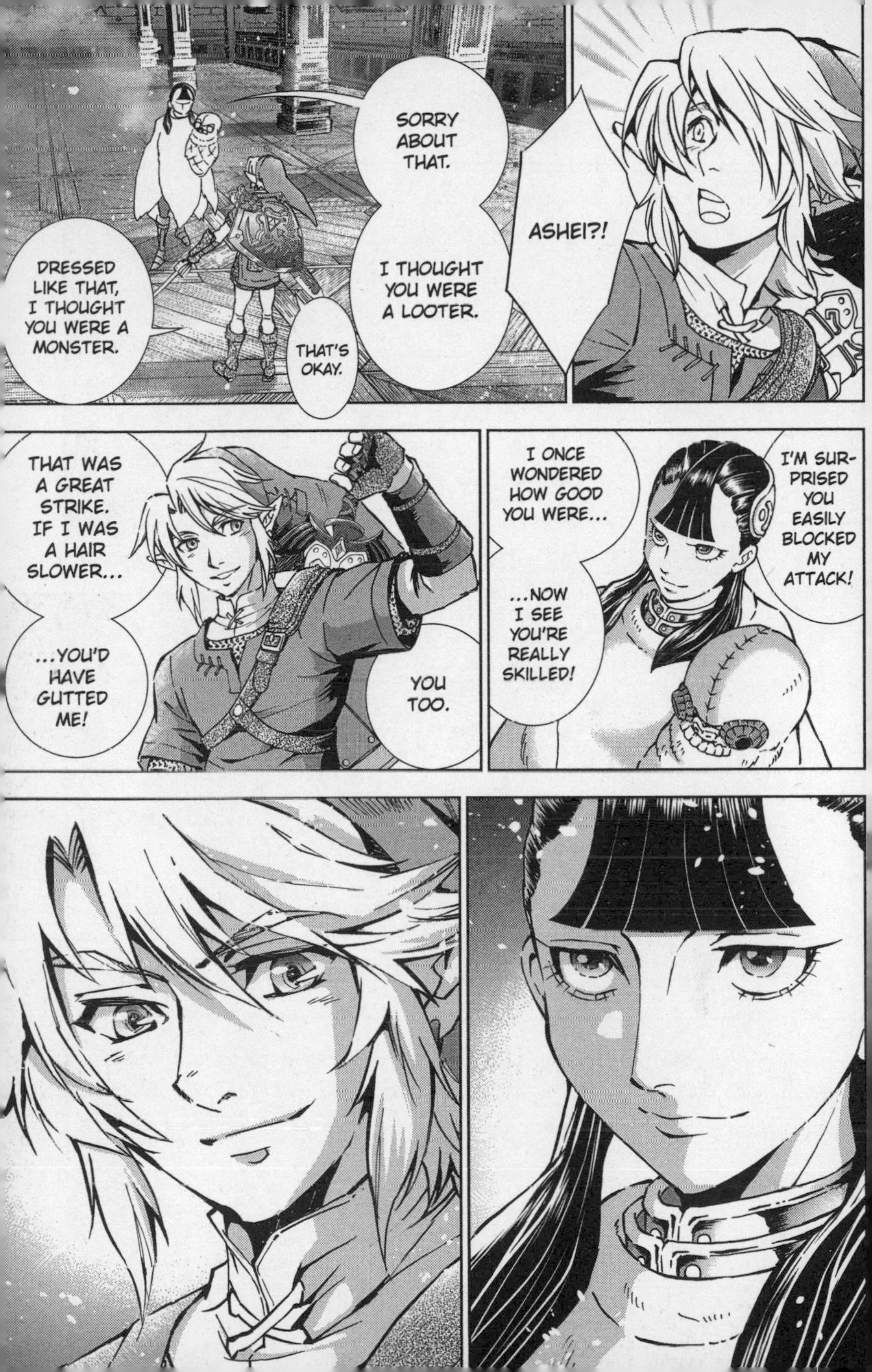
ASHEI?!
SORRY ABOUT THAT.
I THOUGHT YOU WERE A LOOTER.
THAT'S OKAY.
DRESSED LIKE THAT, I THOUGHT YOU WERE A MONSTER.
I'M SUR-PRISED YOU EASILY BLOCKED MY ATTACK!
I ONCE WONDERED HOW GOOD YOU WERE...
...NOW I SEE YOU'RE REALLY SKILLED!
YOU TOO.
THAT WAS A GREAT STRIKE. IF I WAS A HAIR SLOWER...
...YOU'D HAVE GUTTED ME!

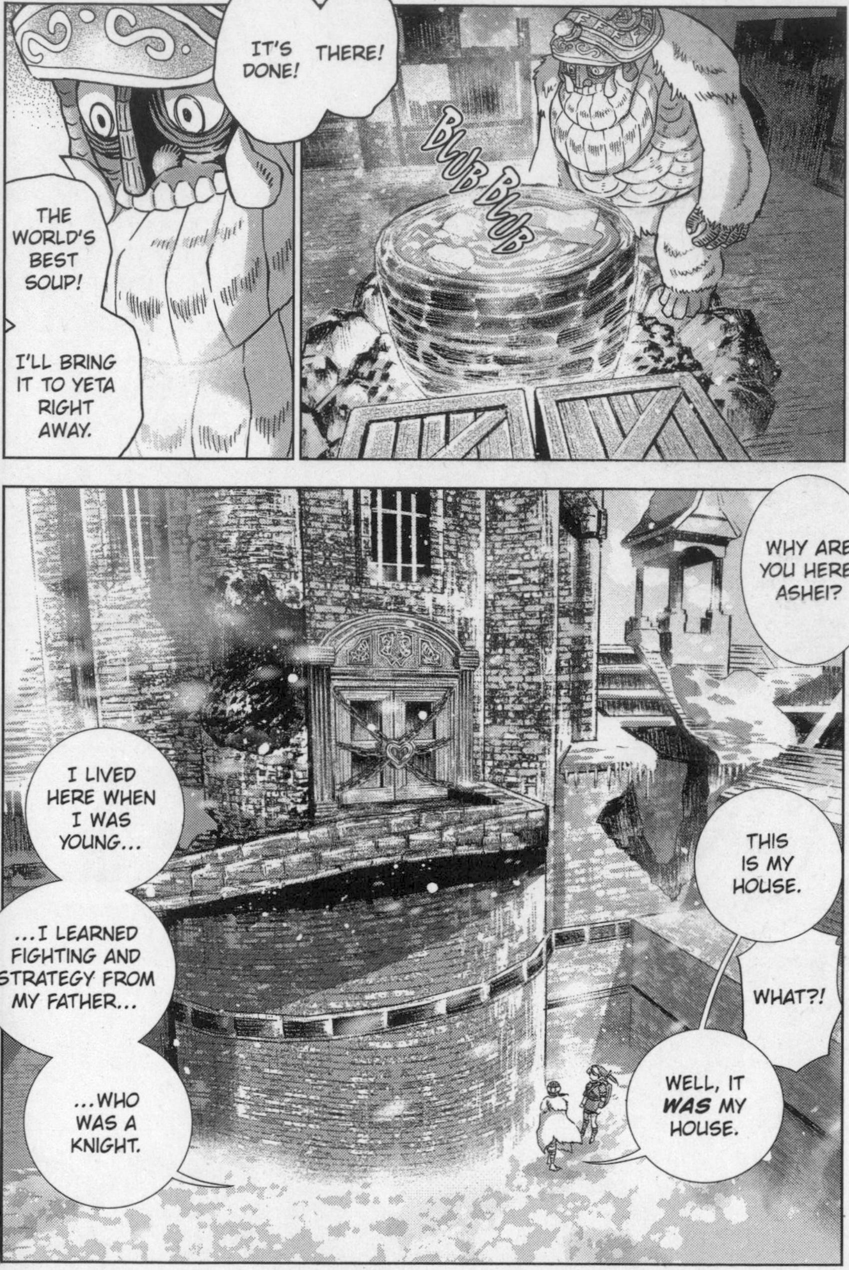
THERE!
IT'S DONE!
BLUB BLUB
THE WORLD'S BEST SOUP!
I'LL BRING IT TO YETA RIGHT AWAY.
WHY ARE YOU HERE, ASHEI?
THIS IS MY HOUSE.
WHAT?!
WELL, IT *WAS* MY HOUSE.
I LIVED HERE WHEN I WAS YOUNG...
...I LEARNED FIGHTING AND STRATEGY FROM MY FATHER...
...WHO WAS A KNIGHT.

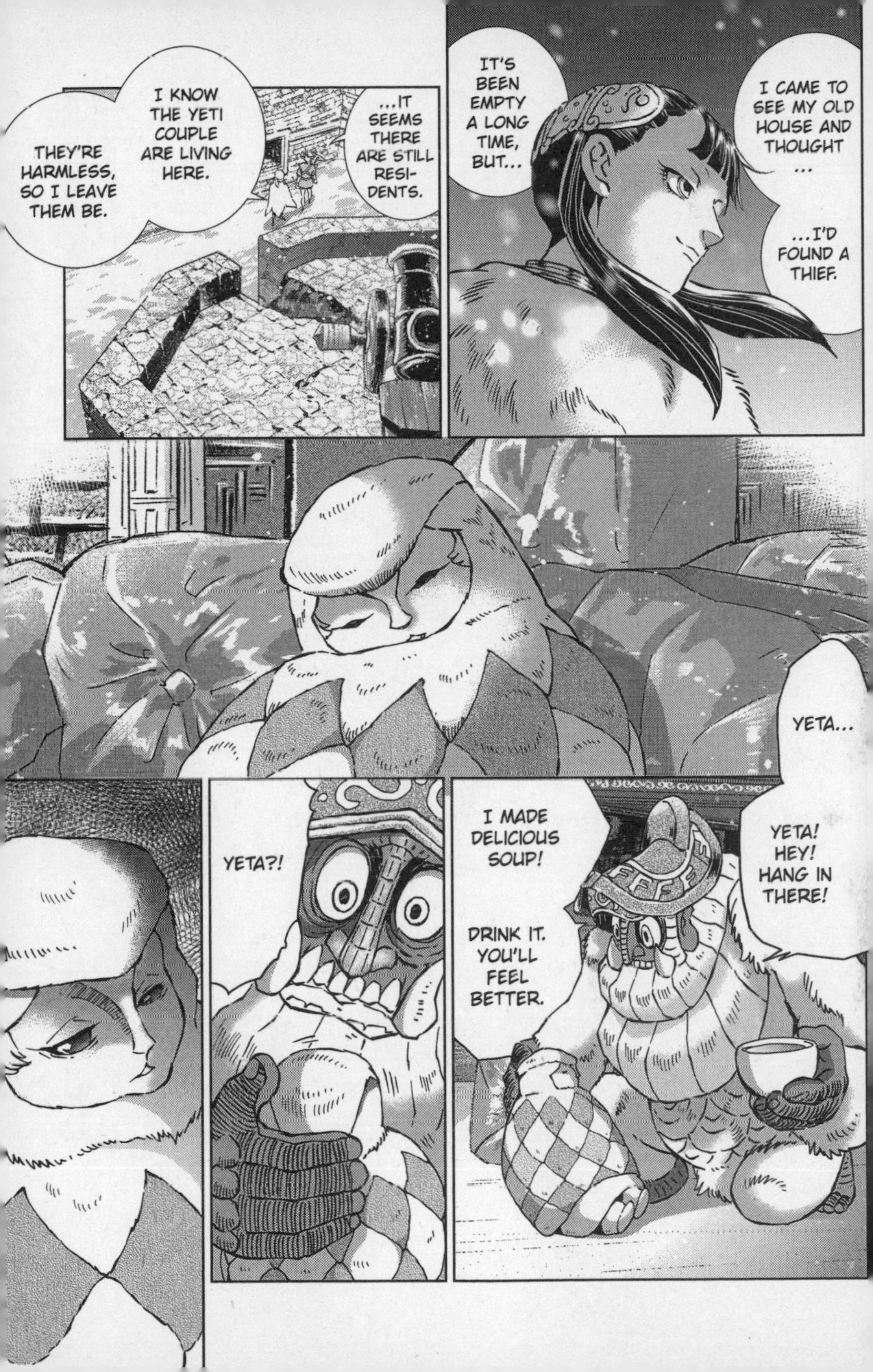
I CAME TO SEE MY OLD HOUSE AND THOUGHT ...
...I'D FOUND A THIEF.
IT'S BEEN EMPTY A LONG TIME, BUT...
...IT SEEMS THERE ARE STILL RESIDENTS.
I KNOW THE YETI COUPLE ARE LIVING HERE.
THEY'RE HARMLESS, SO I LEAVE THEM BE.
YETA...
YETA! HEY! HANG IN THERE!
I MADE DELICIOUS SOUP!
DRINK IT. YOU'LL FEEL BETTER.
YETA?!

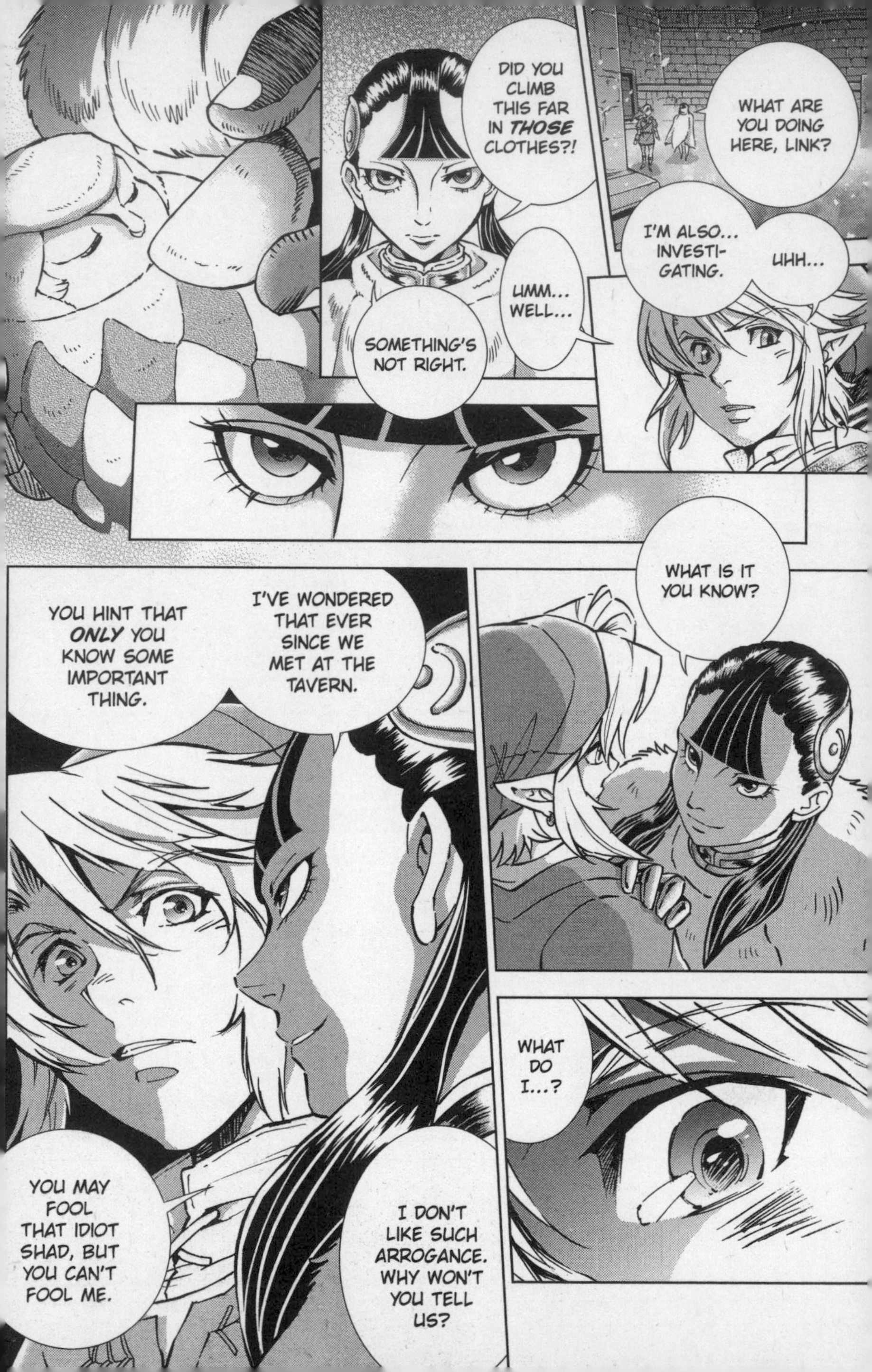
WHAT ARE YOU DOING HERE, LINK?
UHH...
I'M ALSO... INVESTIGATING.
DID YOU CLIMB THIS FAR IN THOSE CLOTHES?!
UMM... WELL...
SOMETHING'S NOT RIGHT.
WHAT IS IT YOU KNOW?
WHAT DO I...?
I'VE WONDERED THAT EVER SINCE WE MET AT THE TAVERN.
YOU HINT THAT ONLY YOU KNOW SOME IMPORTANT THING.
I DON'T LIKE SUCH ARROGANCE. WHY WON'T YOU TELL US?
YOU MAY FOOL THAT IDIOT SHAD, BUT YOU CAN'T FOOL ME.

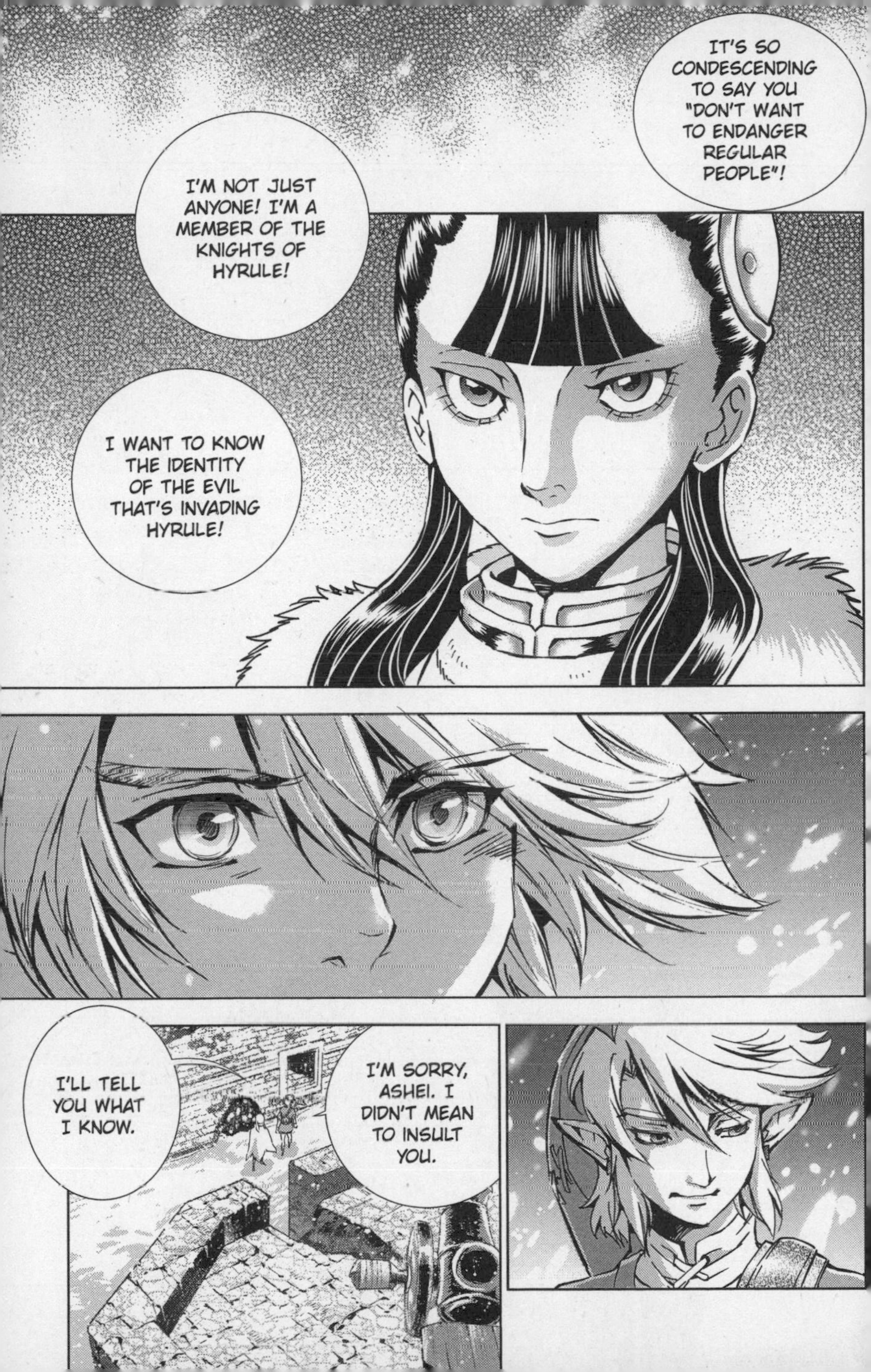
IT'S SO CONDESCENDING TO SAY YOU "DON'T WANT TO ENDANGER REGULAR PEOPLE"!
I'M NOT JUST ANYONE! I'M A MEMBER OF THE KNIGHTS OF HYRULE!
I WANT TO KNOW THE IDENTITY OF THE EVIL THAT'S INVADING HYRULE!
I'M SORRY, ASHEI. I DIDN'T MEAN TO INSULT YOU.
I'LL TELL YOU WHAT I KNOW.

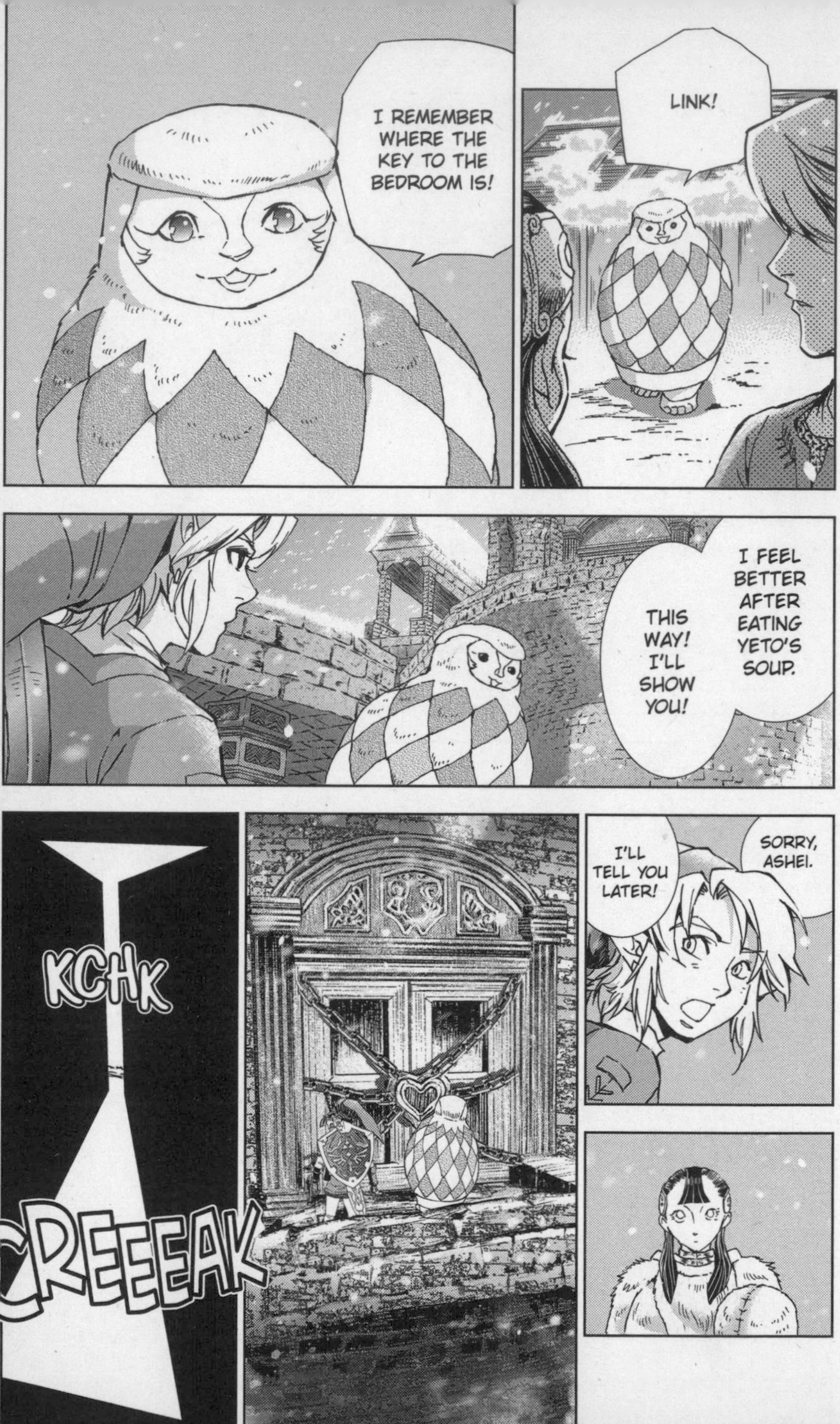
LINK!
I REMEMBER WHERE THE KEY TO THE BEDROOM IS!
I FEEL BETTER AFTER EATING YETO'S SOUP.
THIS WAY! I'LL SHOW YOU!
SORRY, ASHEI.
I'LL TELL YOU LATER!
KCHK
CREEEAK

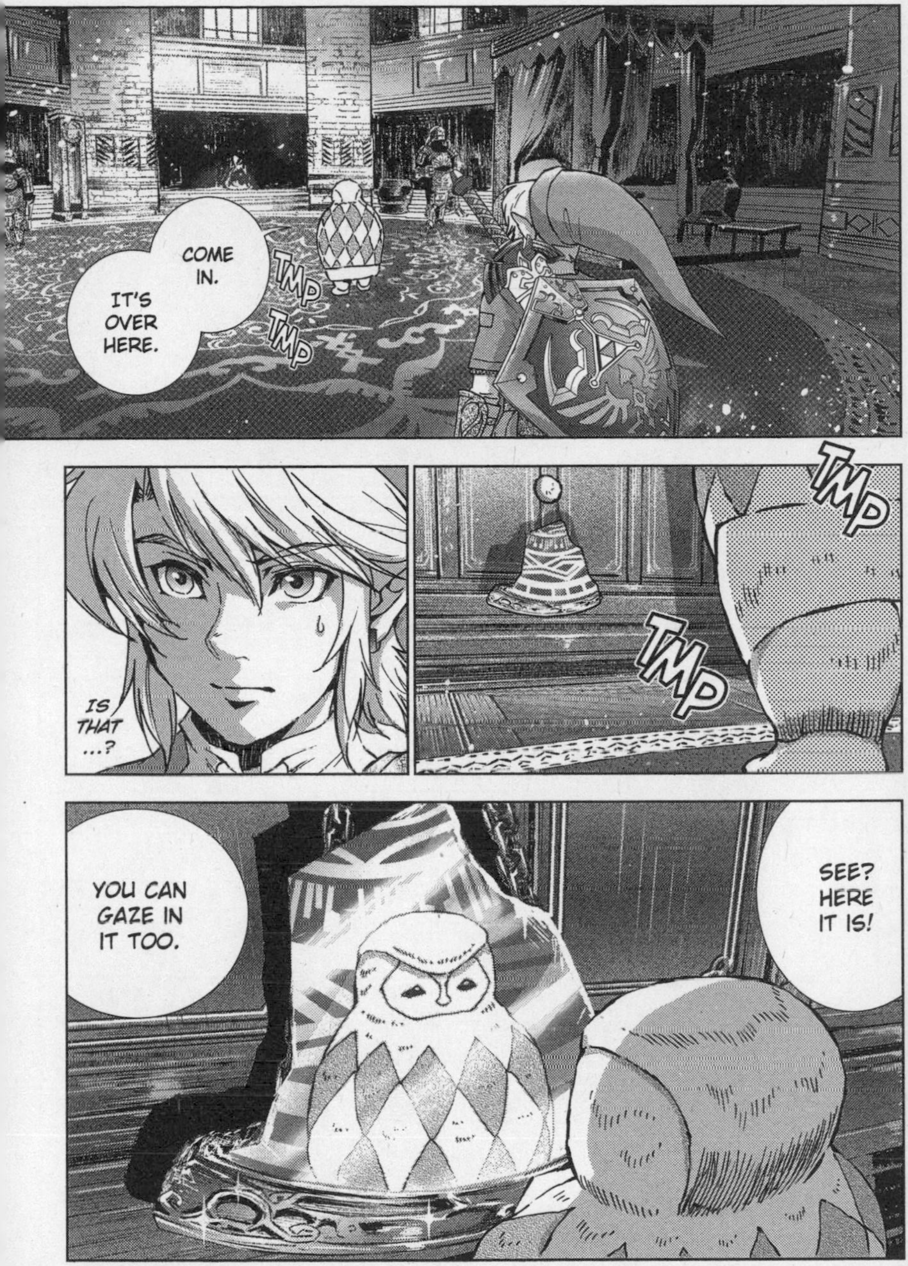
COME IN.
IT'S OVER HERE.
TMP
TMP
TMP
TMP
IS THAT ...?
SEE? HERE IT IS!
YOU CAN GAZE IN IT TOO.

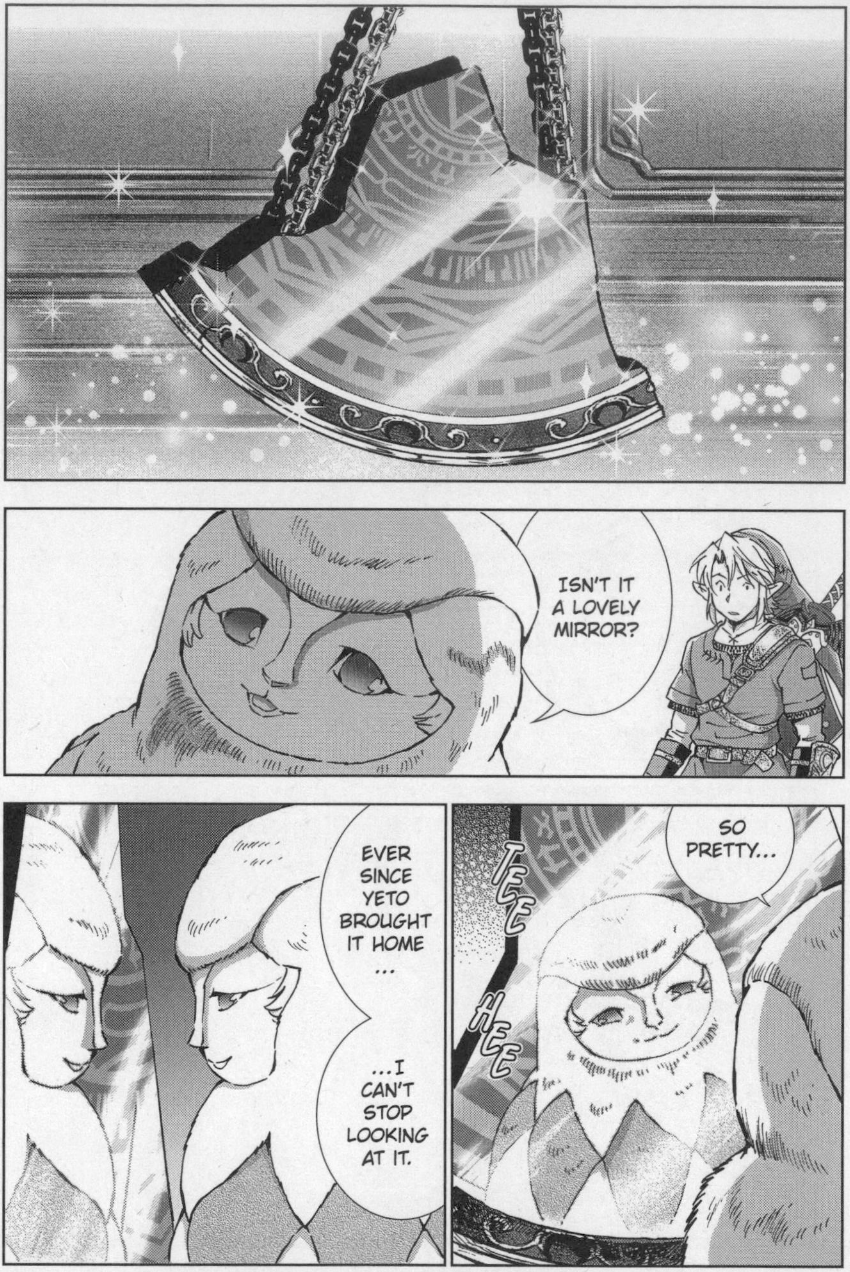

ISN'T IT A LOVELY MIRROR?
SO PRETTY...
TEE HEE
EVER SINCE YETO BROUGHT IT HOME ...
...I CAN'T STOP LOOKING AT IT.

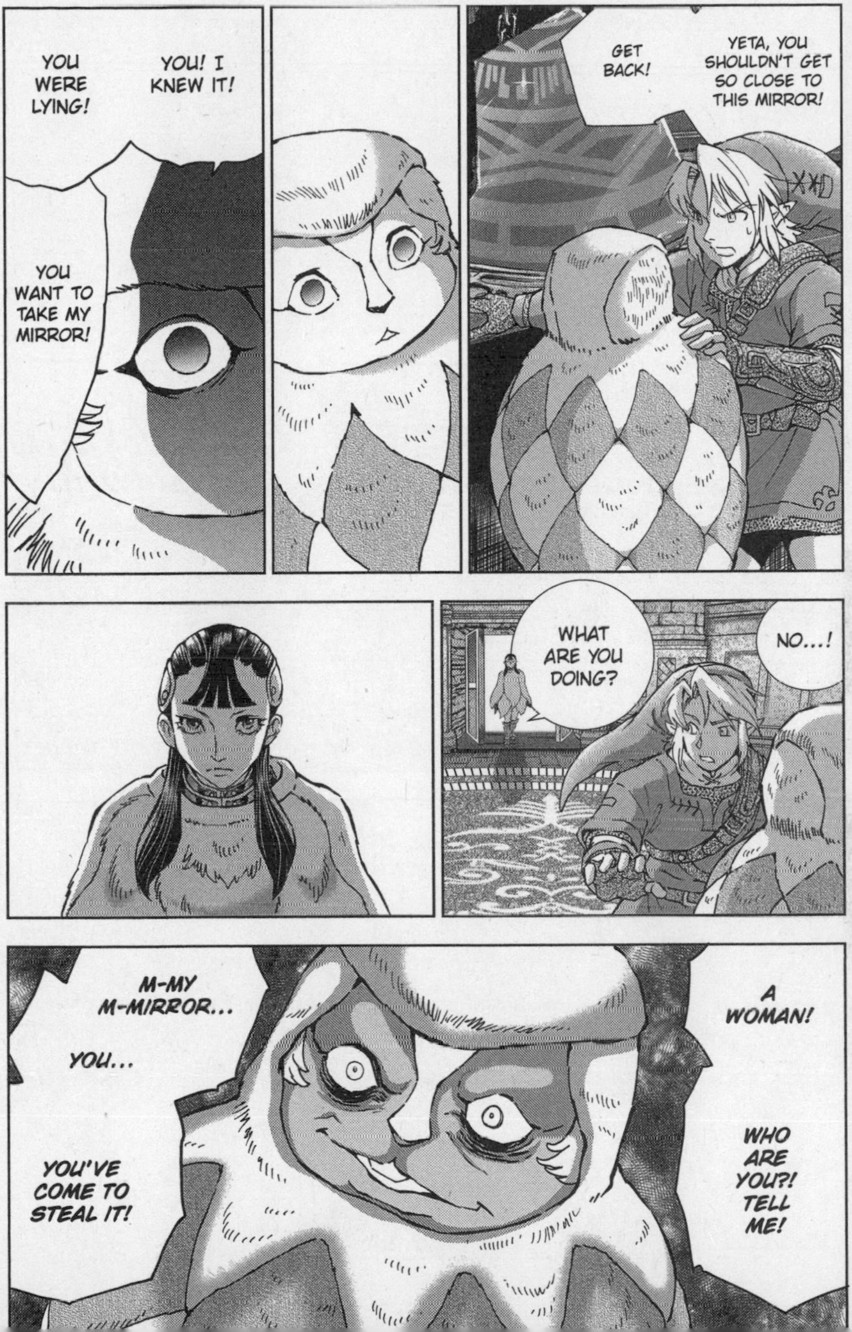
YETA, YOU SHOULDN'T GET SO CLOSE TO THIS MIRROR!
GET BACK!
YOU! I KNEW IT!
YOU WERE LYING!
YOU WANT TO TAKE MY MIRROR!
NO...!
WHAT ARE YOU DOING?
A WOMAN!
WHO ARE YOU?! TELL ME!
M-MY M-MIRROR...
YOU...
YOU'VE COME TO STEAL IT!

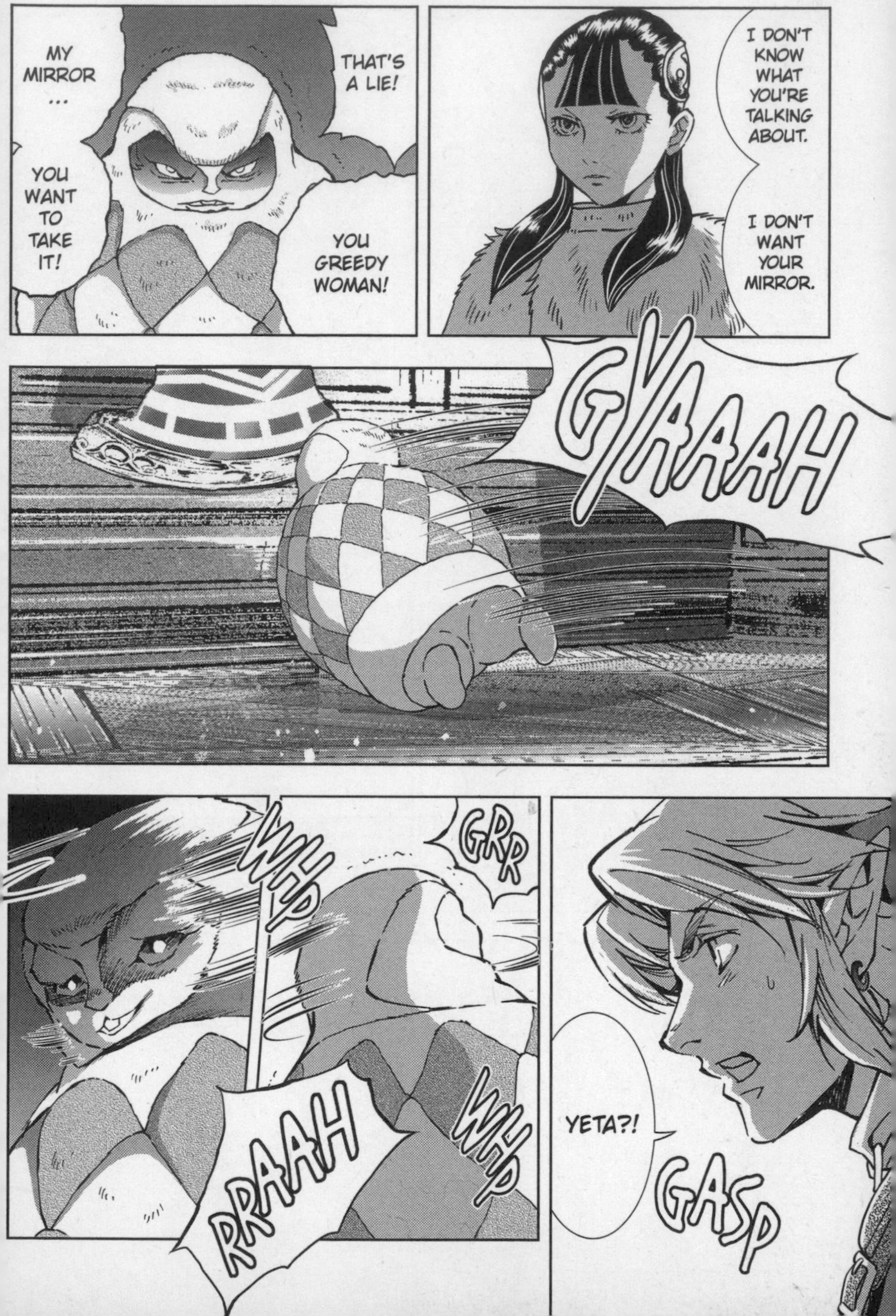
I DON'T KNOW WHAT YOU'RE TALKING ABOUT.
I DON'T WANT YOUR MIRROR.
THAT'S A LIE!
MY MIRROR ...
YOU GREEDY WOMAN!
YOU WANT TO TAKE IT!
GYAAAH
YETA?!
GASP
GRR
WHIP
WHIP
RRAAH

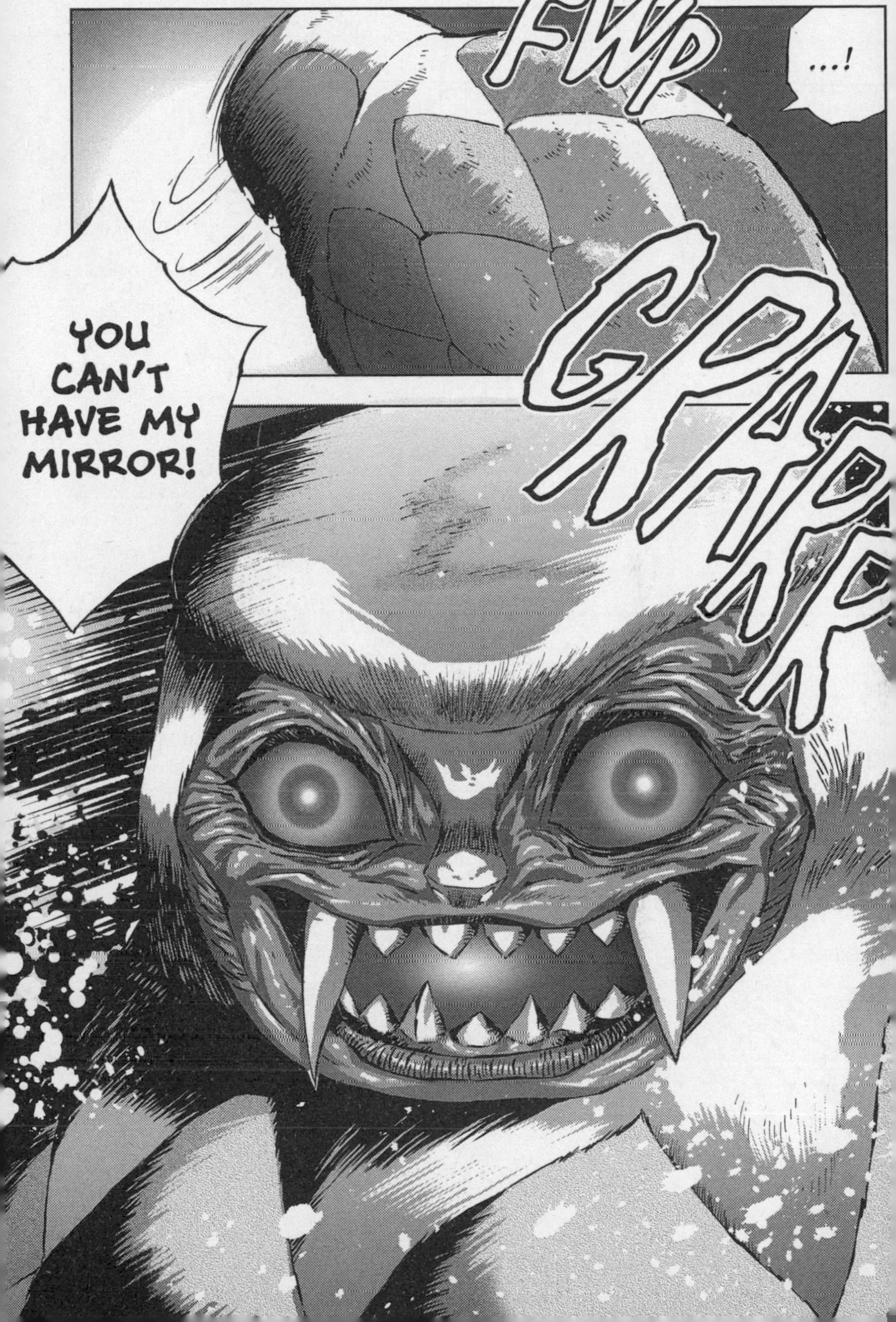
...!
FWP
YOU CAN'T HAVE MY MIRROR!
GARR

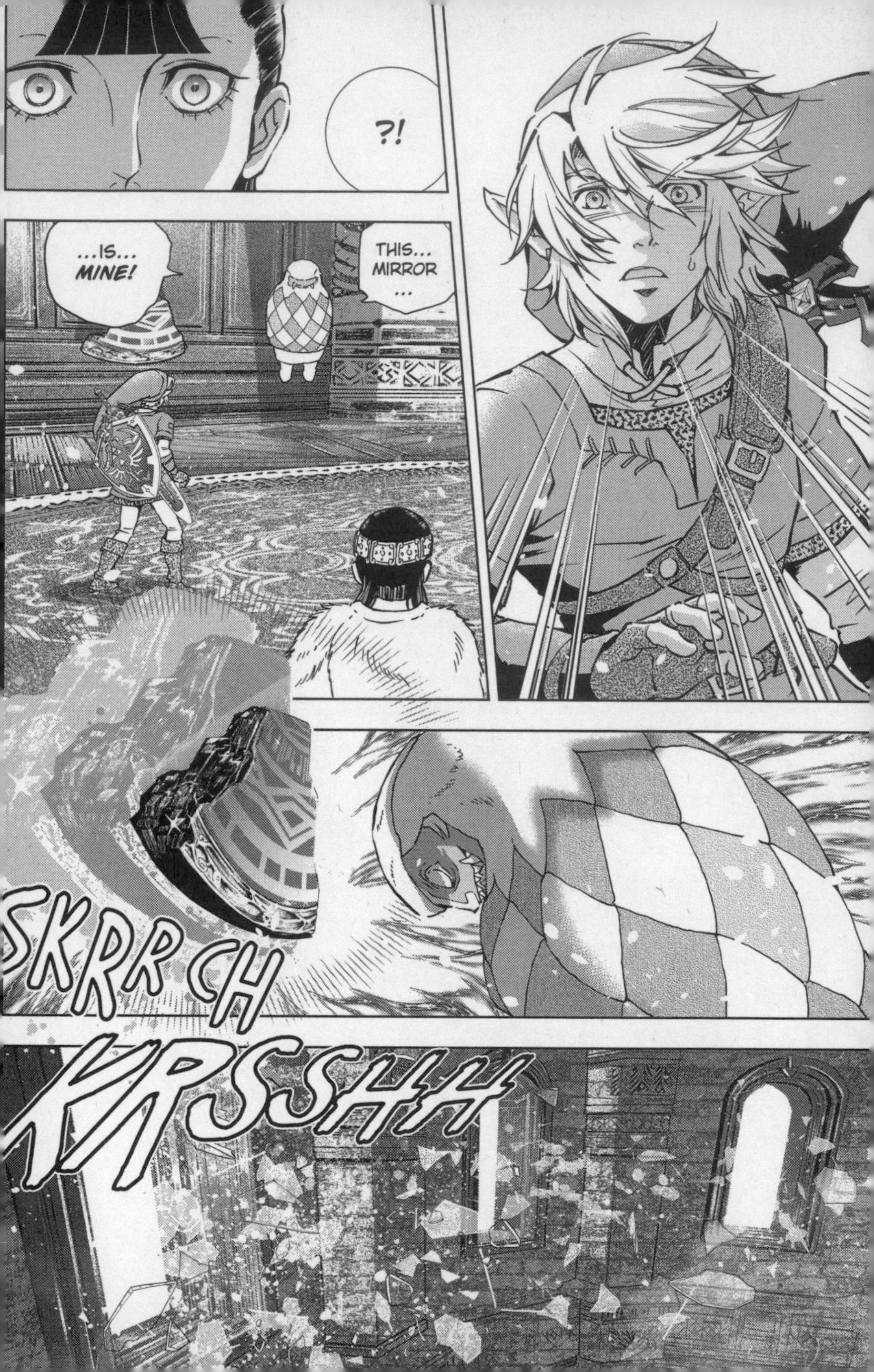
?!
THIS... MIRROR ...
...IS... MINE!
SKRRCH
KRSSHH

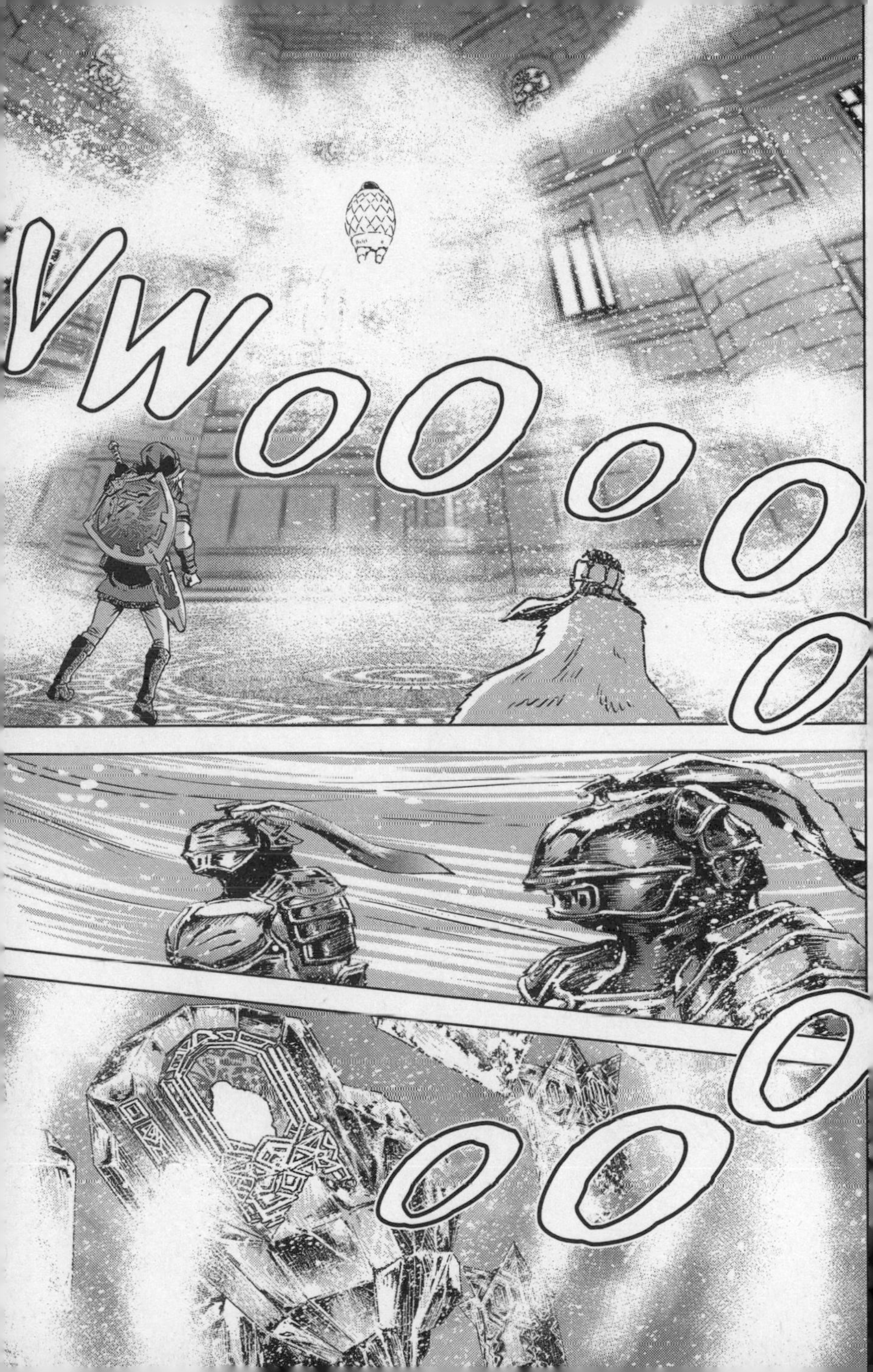
VWOOOOOOOO

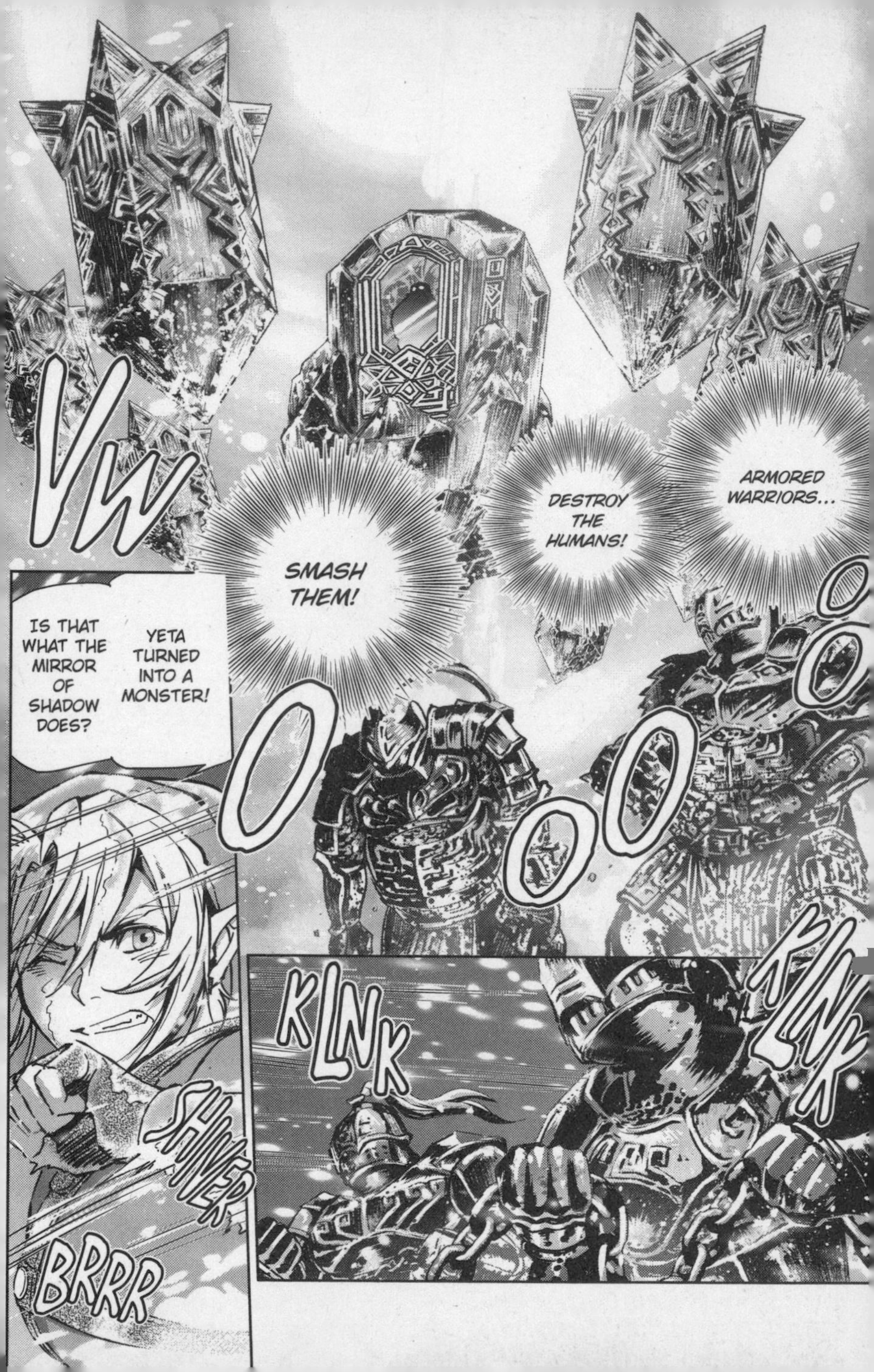
ARMORED WARRIORS...
DESTROY THE HUMANS!
SMASH THEM!
VW
OOOOOO
KLNK
KLNK
YETA TURNED INTO A MONSTER!
IS THAT WHAT THE MIRROR OF SHADOW DOES?
SHIVER
BRRR

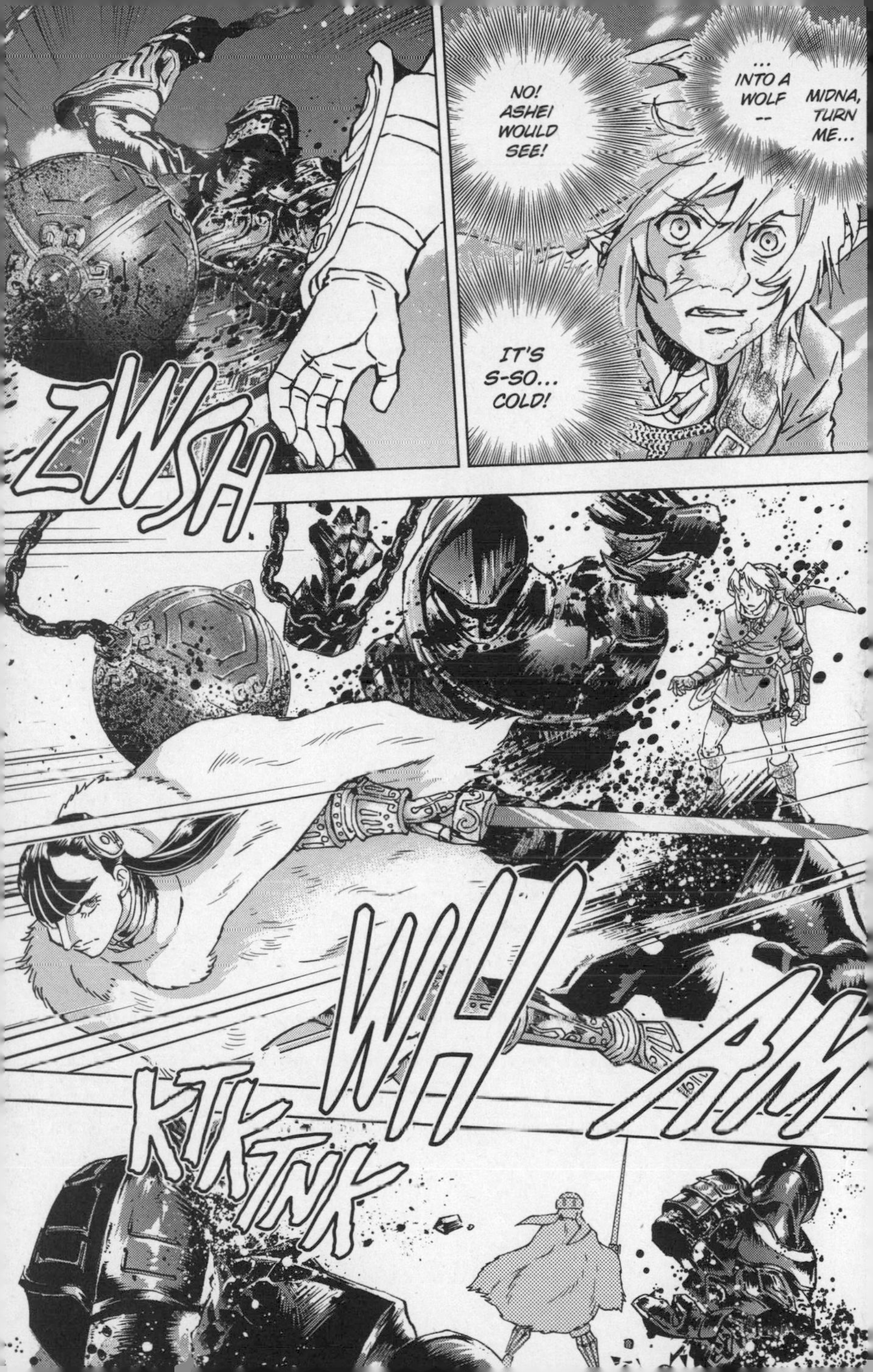
MIDNA, TURN ME...
... INTO A WOLF --
NO! ASHEI WOULD SEE!
IT'S S-SO... COLD!
ZWSH
WHAM
KTKTNK

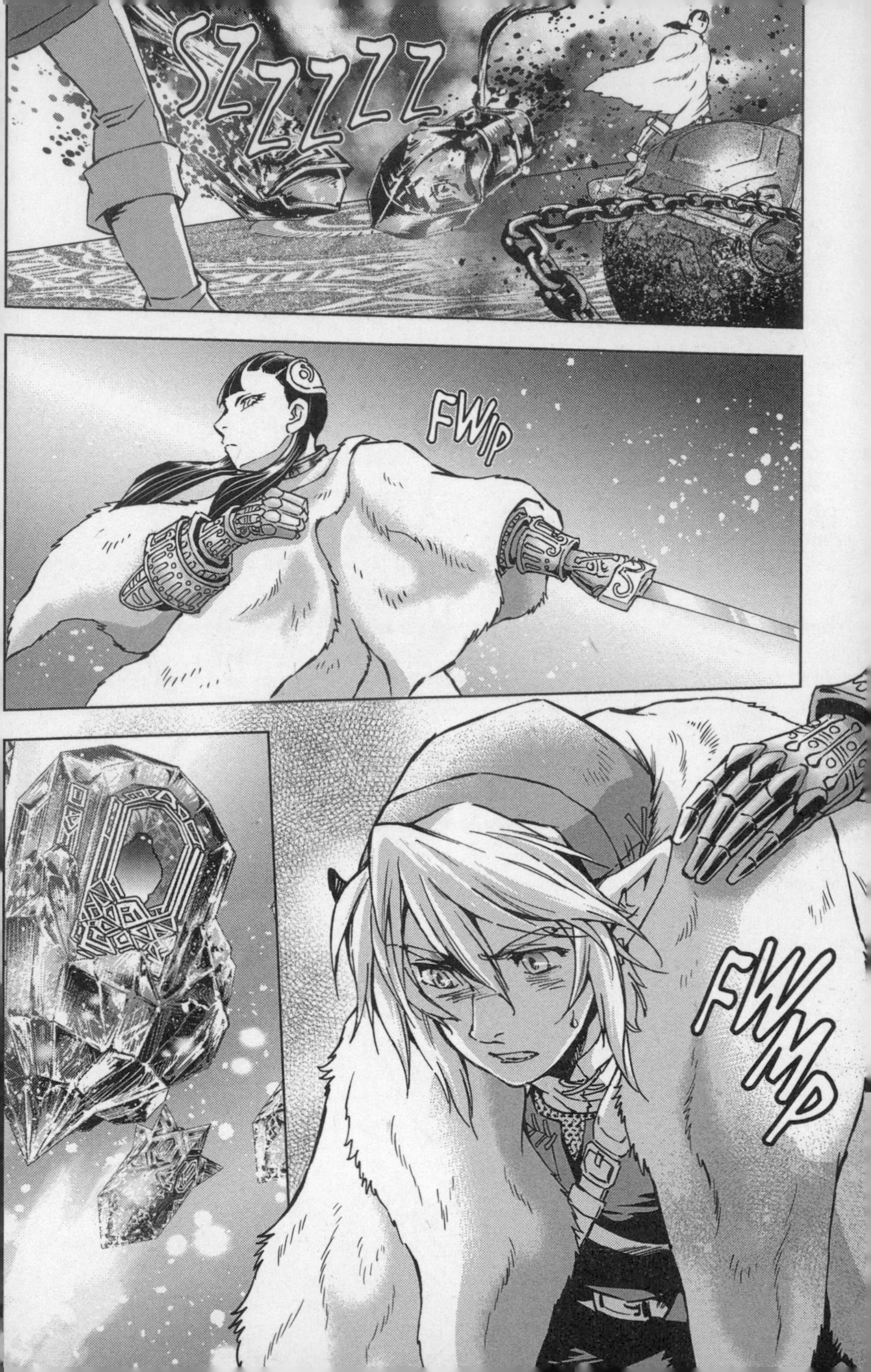
SZZZZZ
FWIP
FWUMP

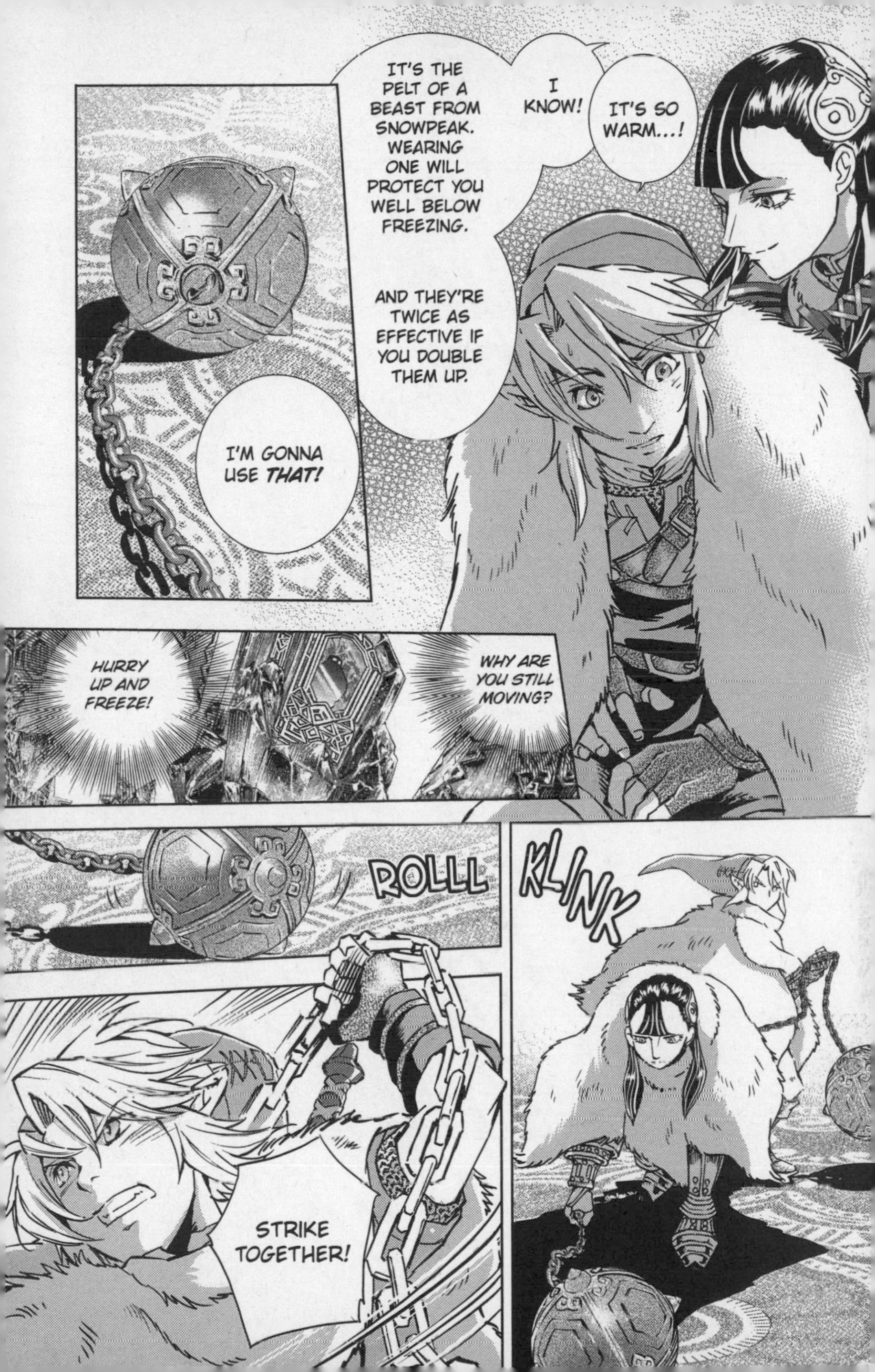
IT'S SO WARM...!
I KNOW!
IT'S THE PELT OF A BEAST FROM SNOWPEAK. WEARING ONE WILL PROTECT YOU WELL BELOW FREEZING.
AND THEY'RE TWICE AS EFFECTIVE IF YOU DOUBLE THEM UP.
I'M GONNA USE *THAT!*
WHY ARE YOU STILL MOVING?
HURRY UP AND FREEZE!
KLINK
ROLLL
STRIKE TOGETHER!

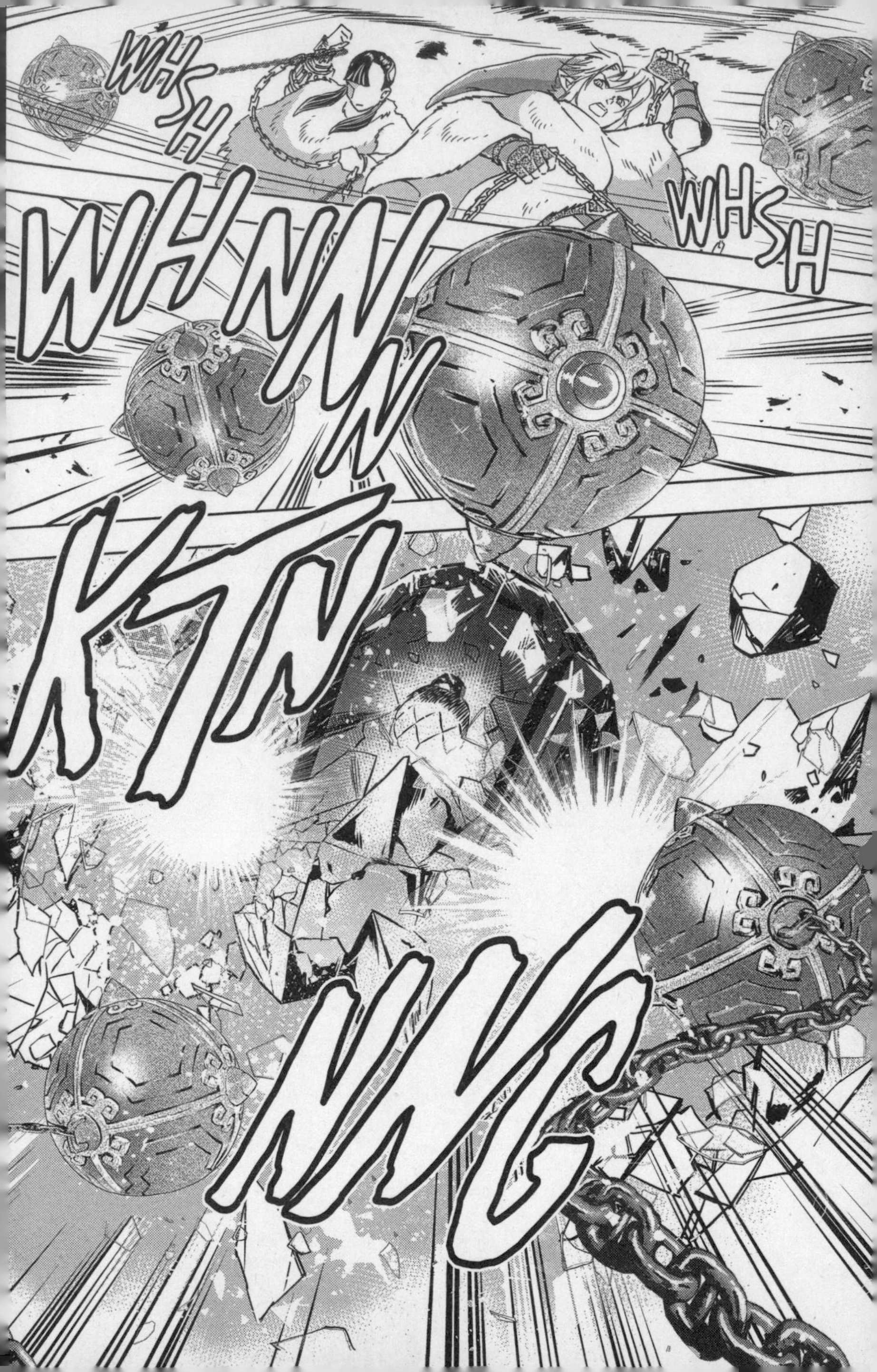
WHSH
WHSH
WHNNN
KTN
NNG

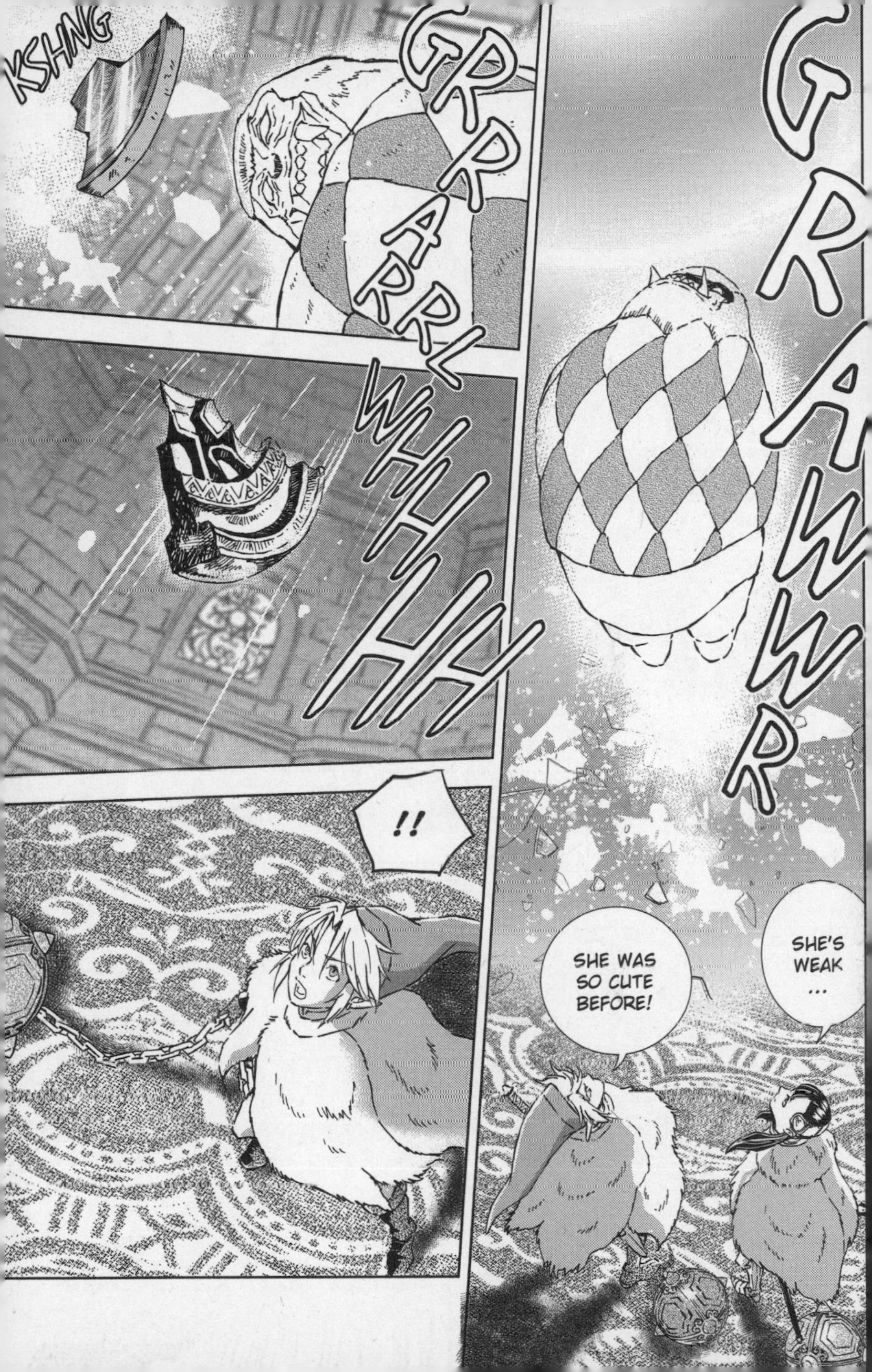
GRAWWR
SHE'S WEAK ...
SHE WAS SO CUTE BEFORE!
KSHNG
GRRARRL
WHHHHH
!!

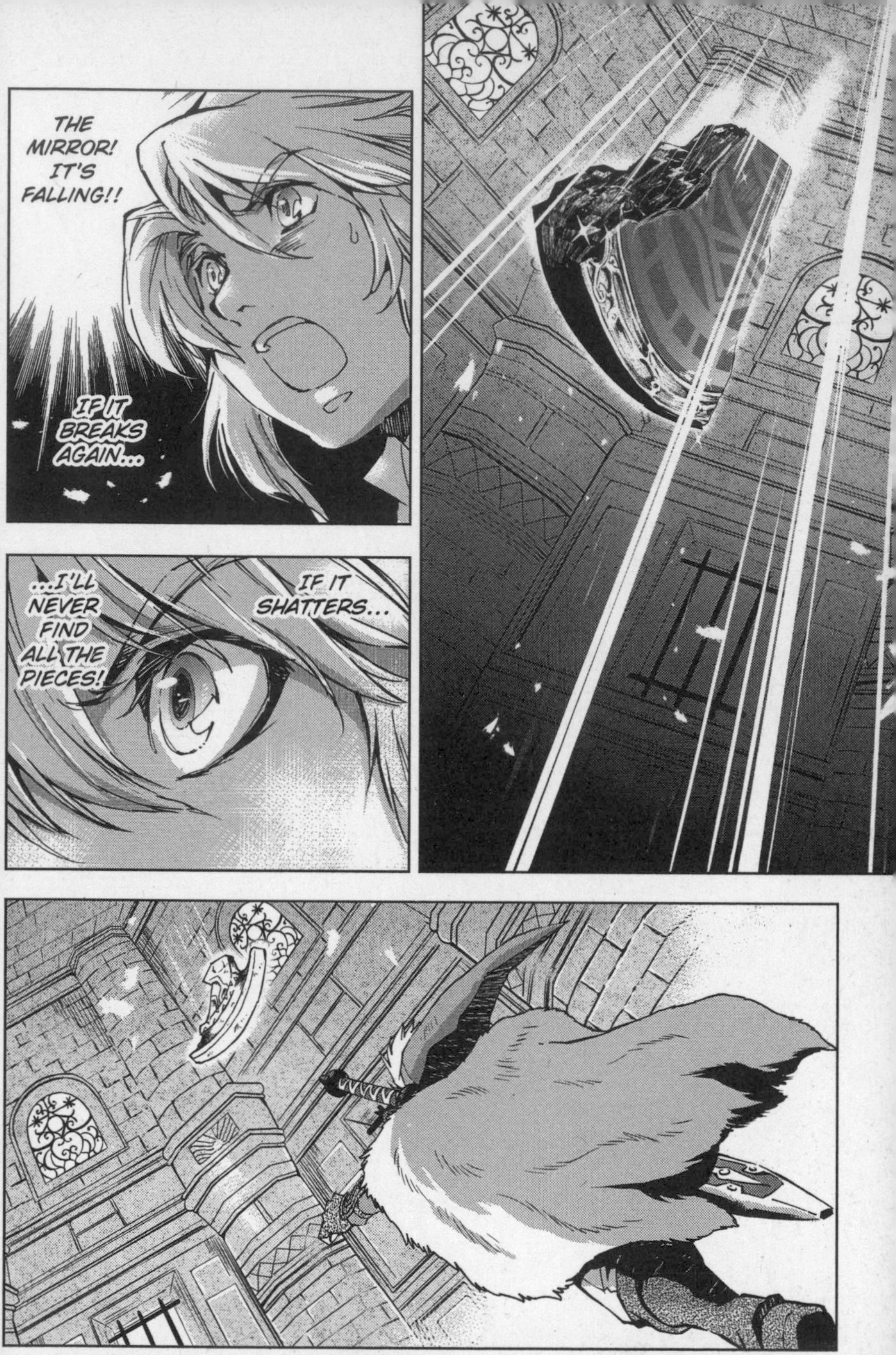
THE MIRROR! IT'S FALLING!!
IF IT BREAKS AGAIN...
IF IT SHATTERS...
...I'LL NEVER FIND ALL THE PIECES!

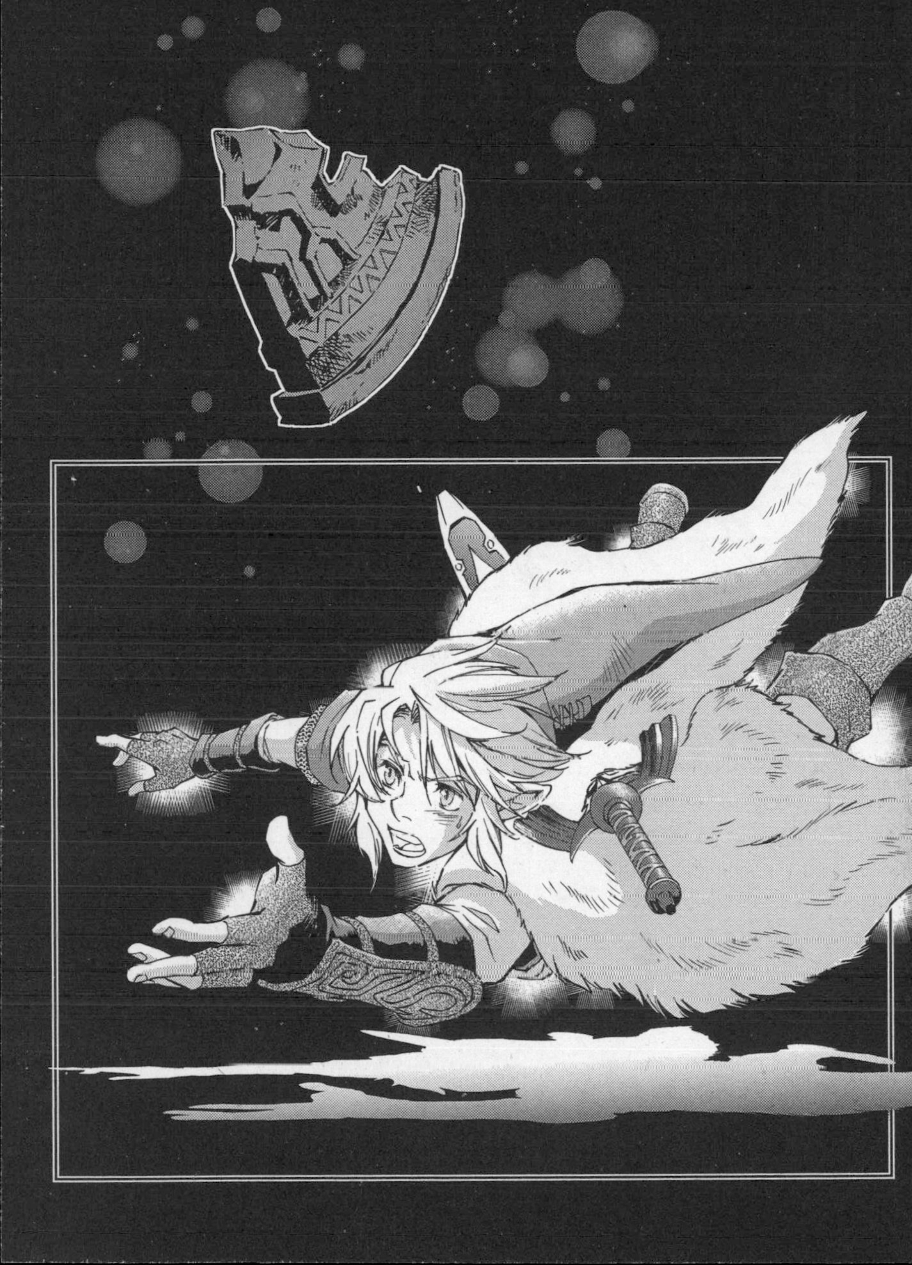

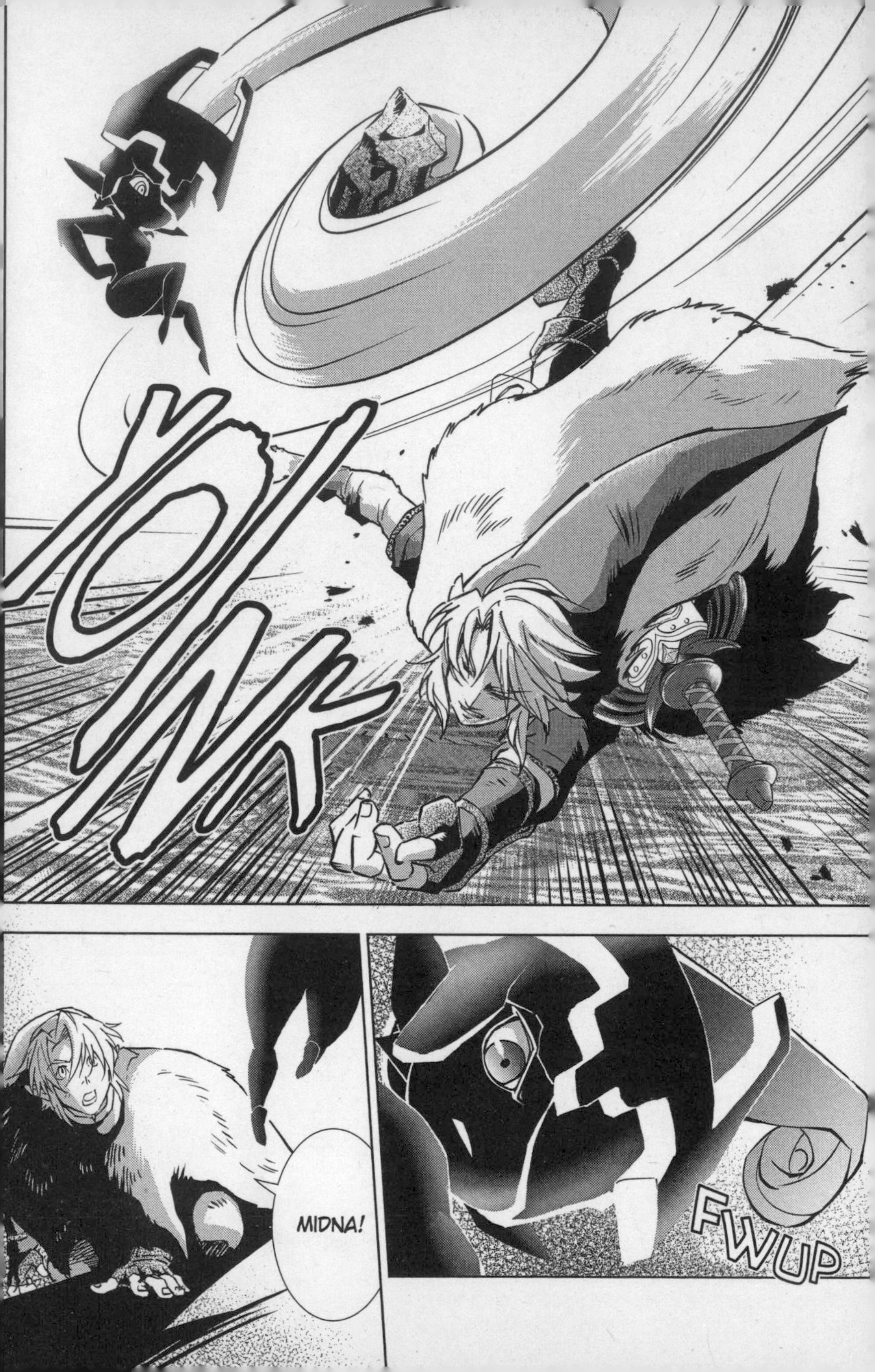
YOINK
FWUP
MIDNA!

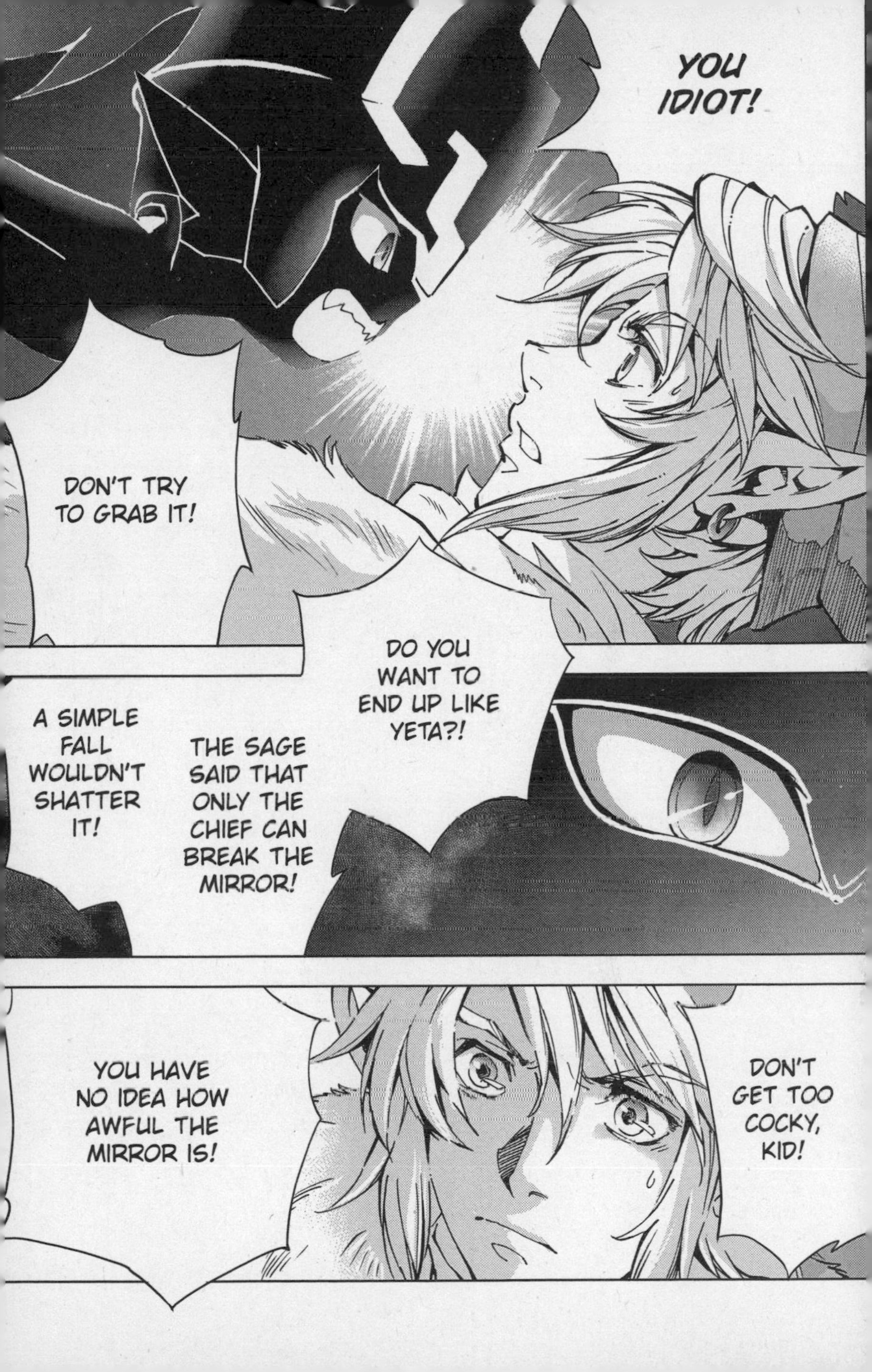
YOU IDIOT!
DON'T TRY TO GRAB IT!
DO YOU WANT TO END UP LIKE YETA?!
THE SAGE SAID THAT ONLY THE CHIEF CAN BREAK THE MIRROR!
A SIMPLE FALL WOULDN'T SHATTER IT!
DON'T GET TOO COCKY, KID!
YOU HAVE NO IDEA HOW AWFUL THE MIRROR IS!

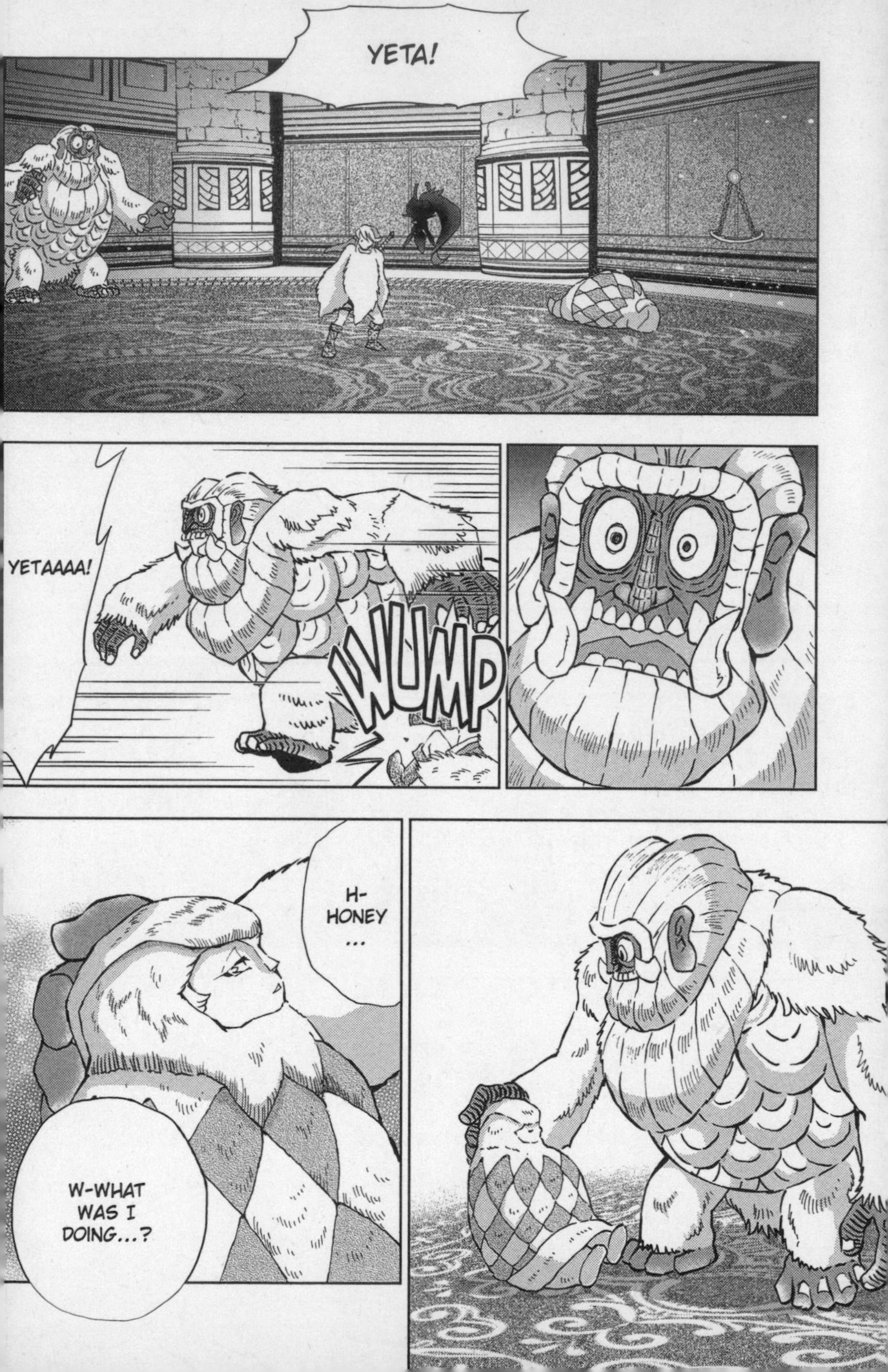
YETA!
YETAAAA!
WUMP
H-HONEY...
W-WHAT WAS I DOING...?

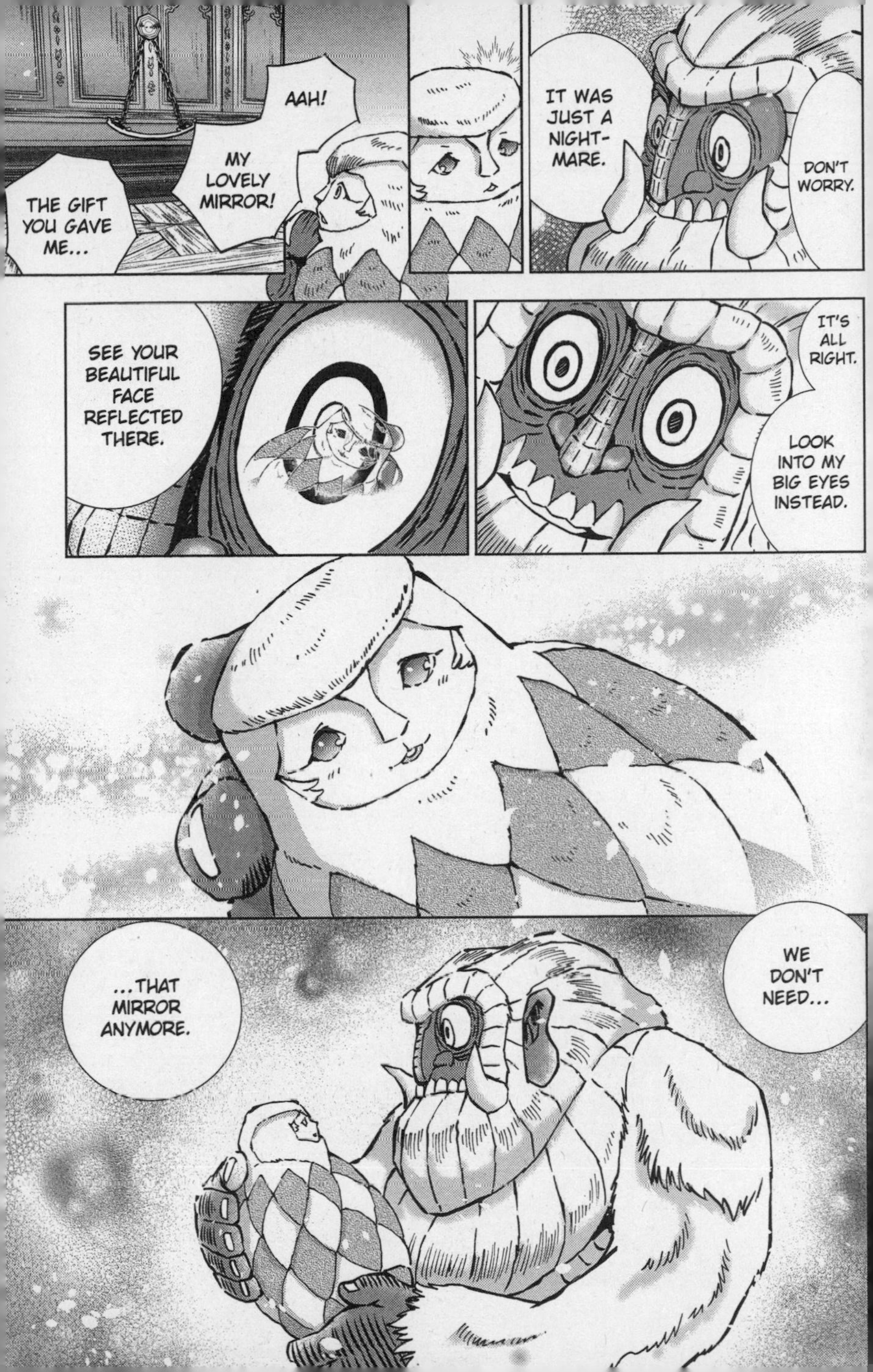
DON'T WORRY.
IT WAS JUST A NIGHT-MARE.
AAH!
MY LOVELY MIRROR!
THE GIFT YOU GAVE ME...
IT'S ALL RIGHT.
LOOK INTO MY BIG EYES INSTEAD.
SEE YOUR BEAUTIFUL FACE REFLECTED THERE.
WE DON'T NEED...
...THAT MIRROR ANYMORE.

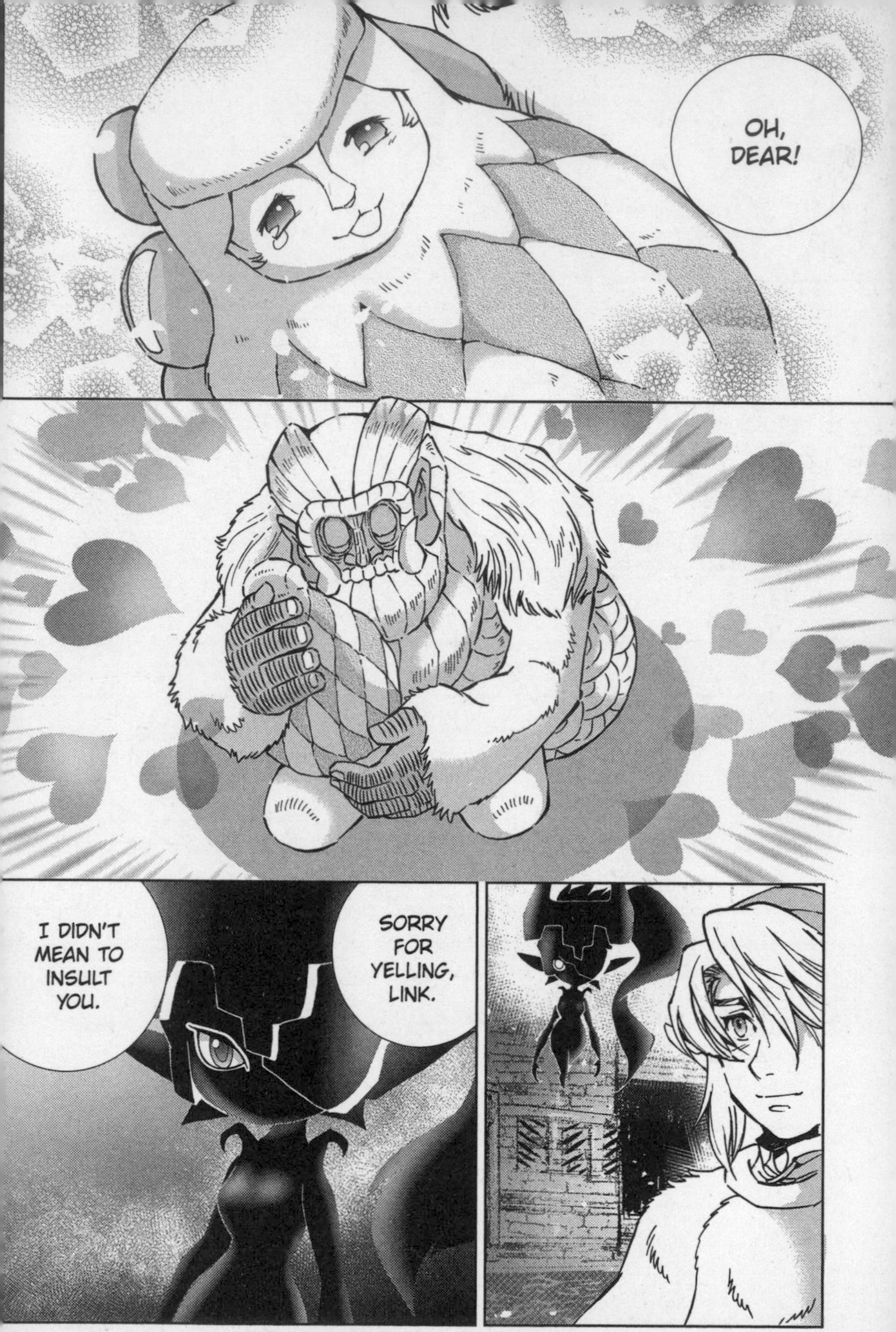
OH, DEAR!
SORRY FOR YELLING, LINK.
I DIDN'T MEAN TO INSULT YOU.

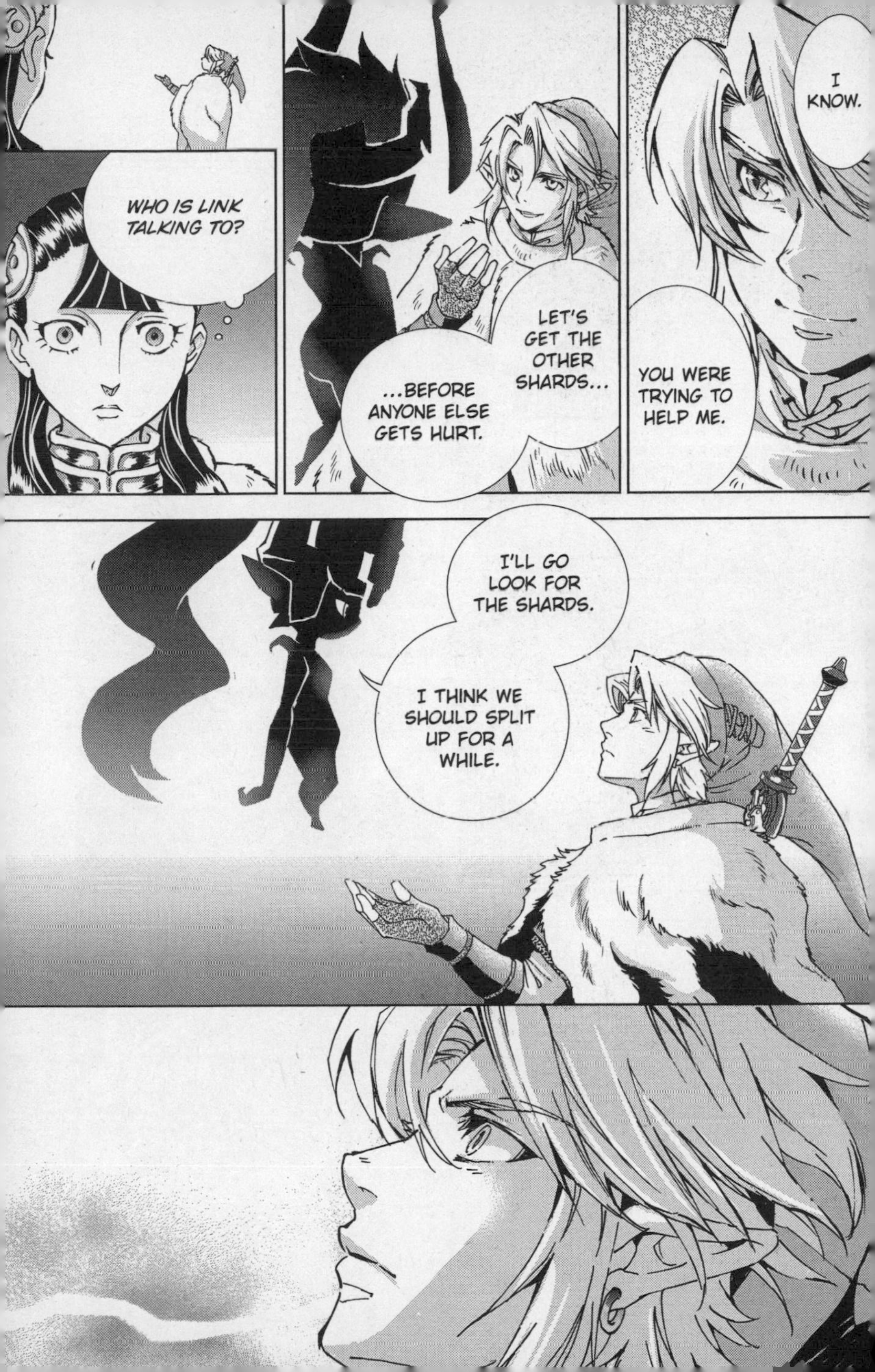
I KNOW.
YOU WERE TRYING TO HELP ME.
LET'S GET THE OTHER SHARDS...
...BEFORE ANYONE ELSE GETS HURT.
WHO IS LINK TALKING TO?
I'LL GO LOOK FOR THE SHARDS.
I THINK WE SHOULD SPLIT UP FOR A WHILE.

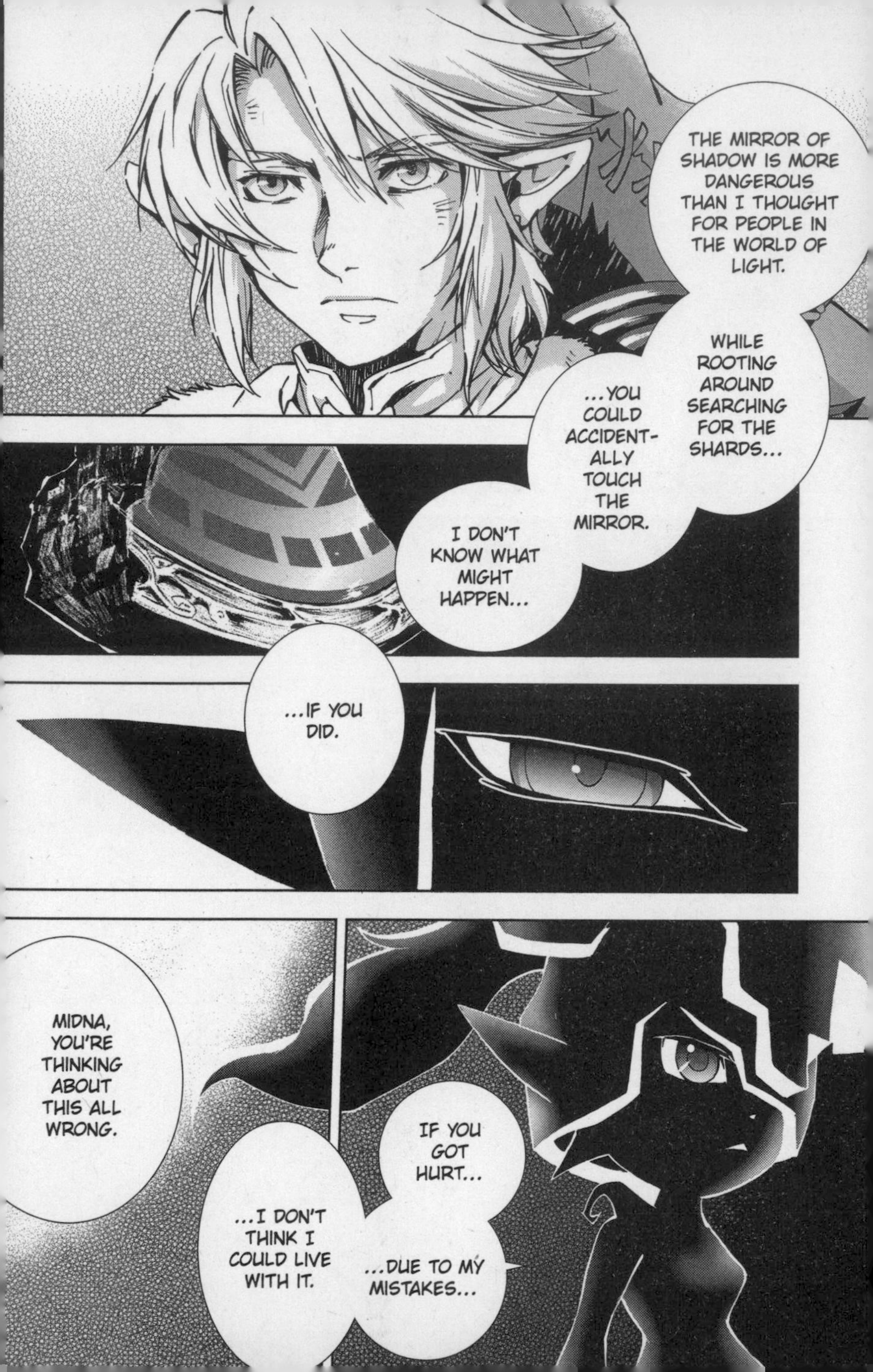
THE MIRROR OF SHADOW IS MORE DANGEROUS THAN I THOUGHT FOR PEOPLE IN THE WORLD OF LIGHT.
WHILE ROOTING AROUND SEARCHING FOR THE SHARDS...
...YOU COULD ACCIDENT-ALLY TOUCH THE MIRROR.
I DON'T KNOW WHAT MIGHT HAPPEN...
...IF YOU DID.
IF YOU GOT HURT...
...DUE TO MY MISTAKES...
...I DON'T THINK I COULD LIVE WITH IT.
MIDNA, YOU'RE THINKING ABOUT THIS ALL WRONG.

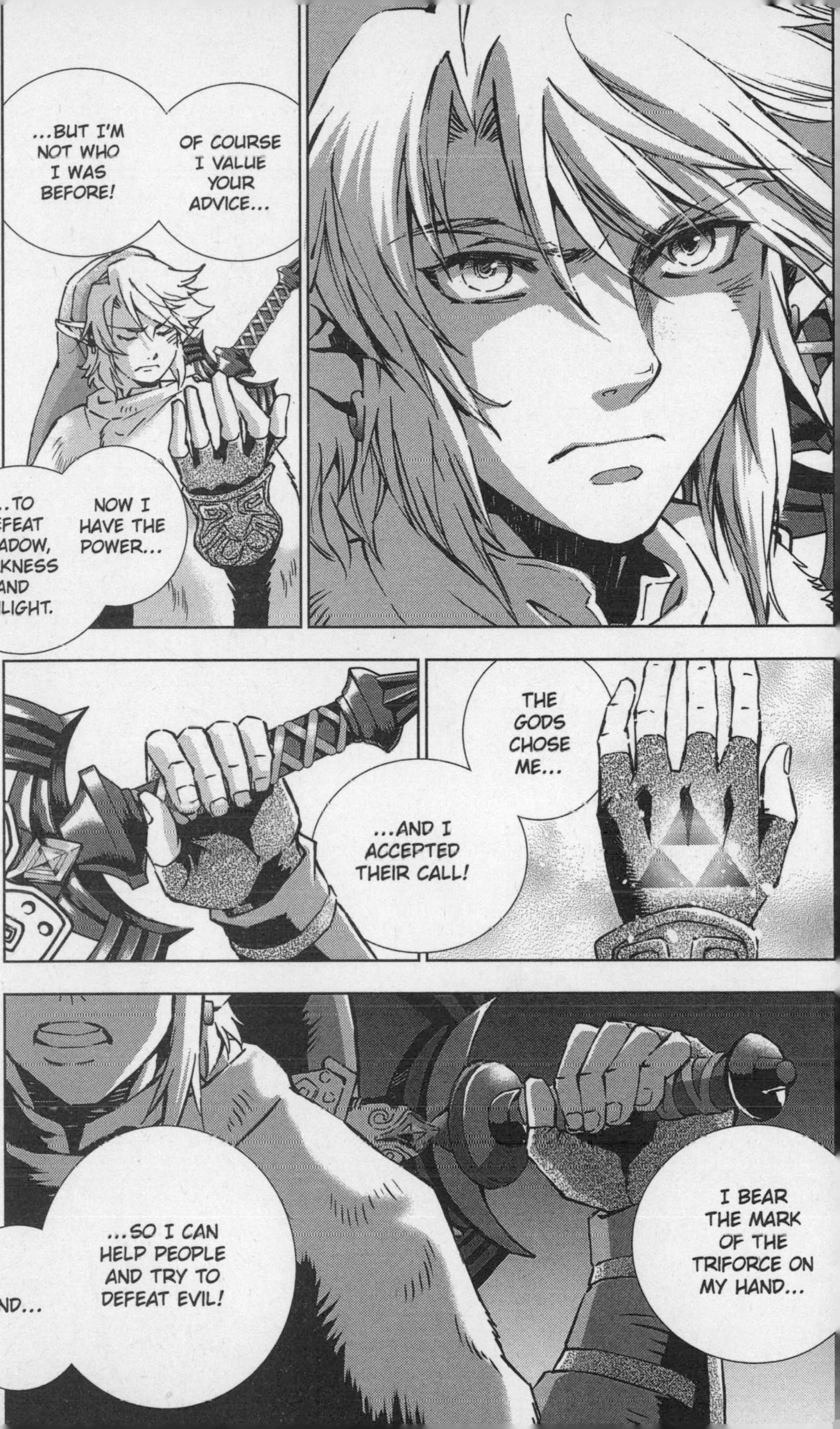
OF COURSE I VALUE YOUR ADVICE...
...BUT I'M NOT WHO I WAS BEFORE!
NOW I HAVE THE POWER...
...TO DEFEAT SHADOW, DARKNESS AND TWILIGHT.
THE GODS CHOSE ME...
...AND I ACCEPTED THEIR CALL!
I BEAR THE MARK OF THE TRIFORCE ON MY HAND...
...SO I CAN HELP PEOPLE AND TRY TO DEFEAT EVIL!
AND...

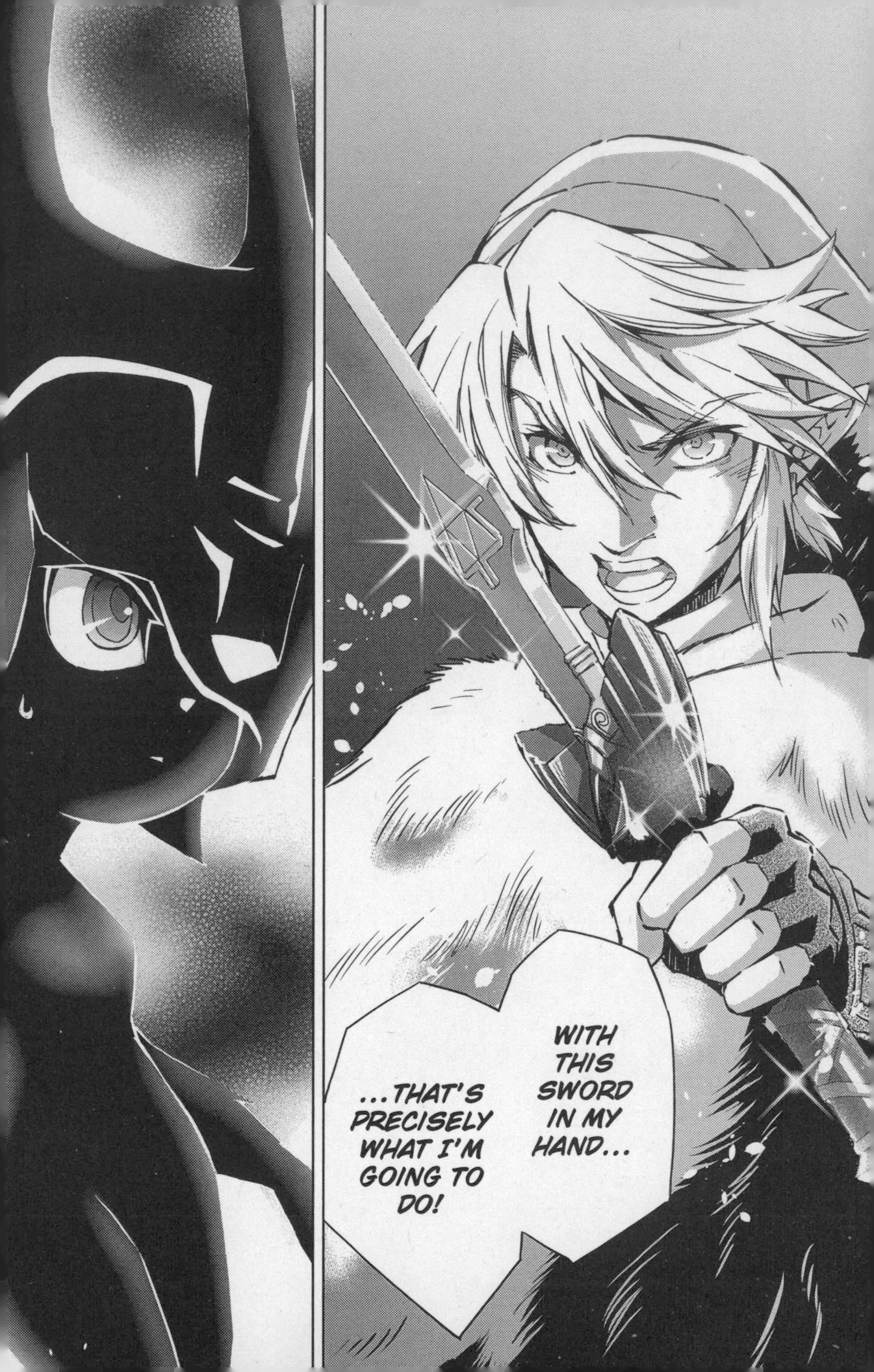
WITH THIS SWORD IN MY HAND...
...THAT'S PRECISELY WHAT I'M GOING TO DO!

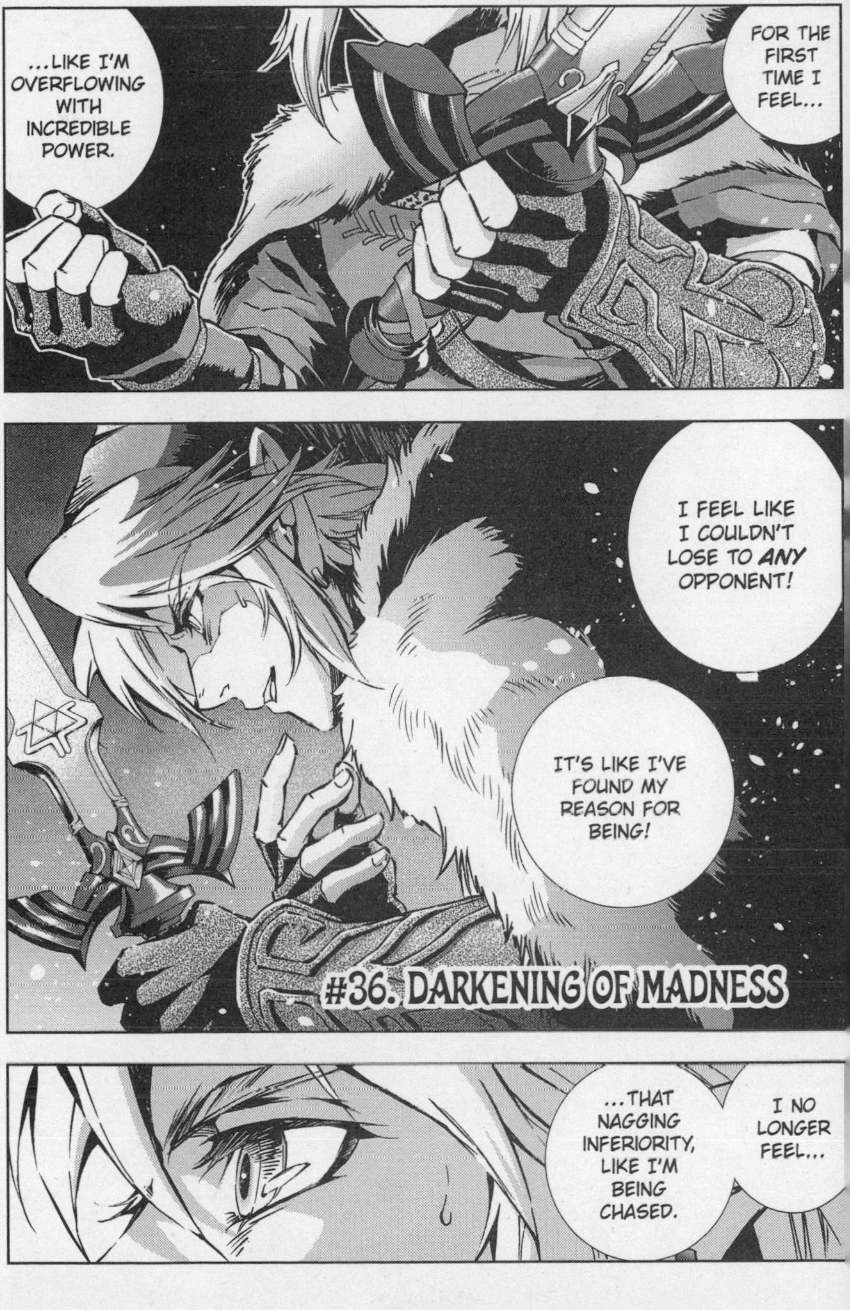
FOR THE FIRST TIME I FEEL...
...LIKE I'M OVERFLOWING WITH INCREDIBLE POWER.
I FEEL LIKE I COULDN'T LOSE TO *ANY* OPPONENT!
IT'S LIKE I'VE FOUND MY REASON FOR BEING!
#36. DARKENING OF MADNESS
I NO LONGER FEEL...
...THAT NAGGING INFERIORITY, LIKE I'M BEING CHASED.

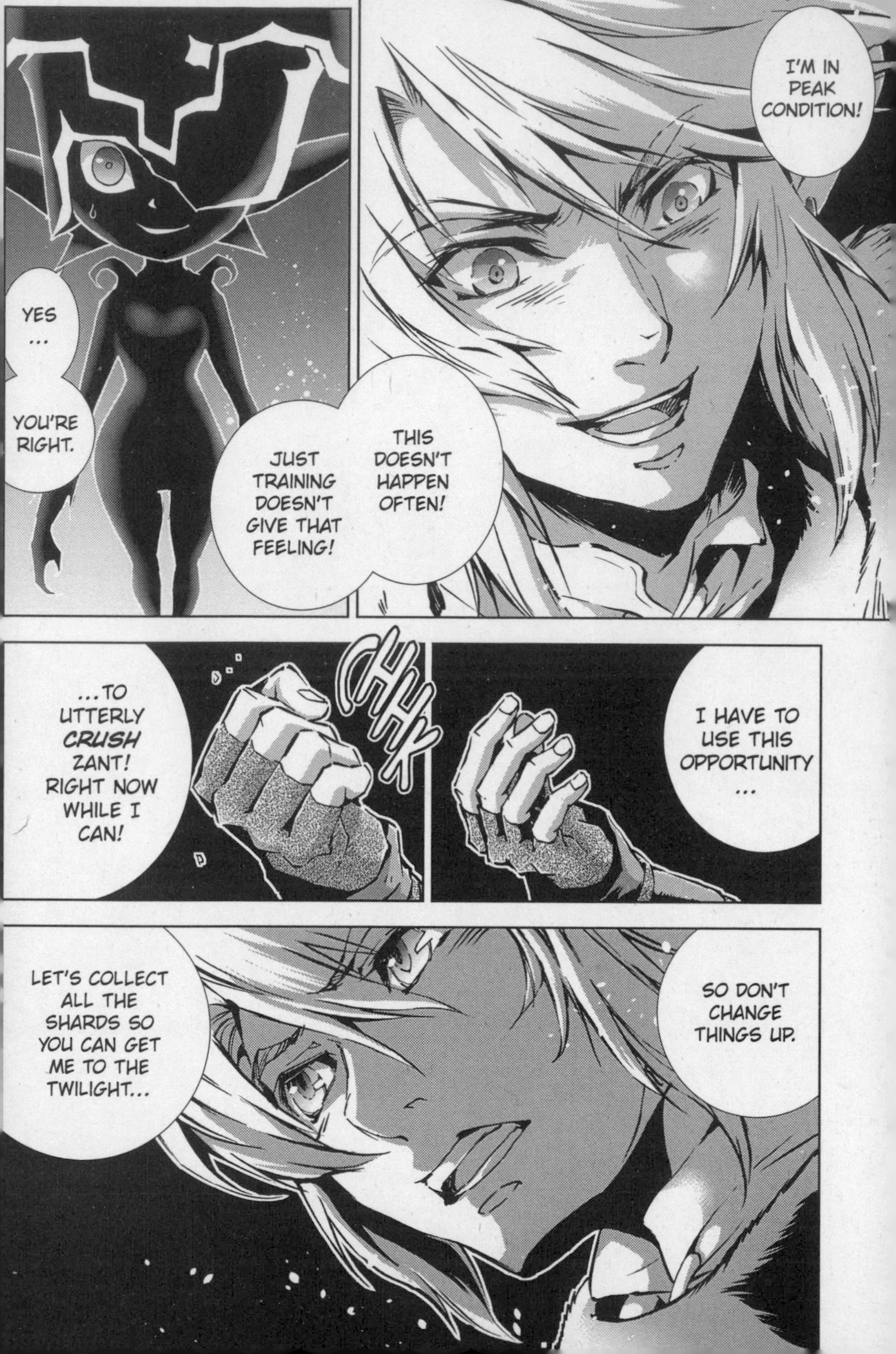
I'M IN PEAK CONDITION!
THIS DOESN'T HAPPEN OFTEN!
JUST TRAINING DOESN'T GIVE THAT FEELING!
YES ...
YOU'RE RIGHT.
I HAVE TO USE THIS OPPORTUNITY ...
CHHK
...TO UTTERLY *CRUSH* ZANT! RIGHT NOW WHILE I CAN!
SO DON'T CHANGE THINGS UP.
LET'S COLLECT ALL THE SHARDS SO YOU CAN GET ME TO THE TWILIGHT...

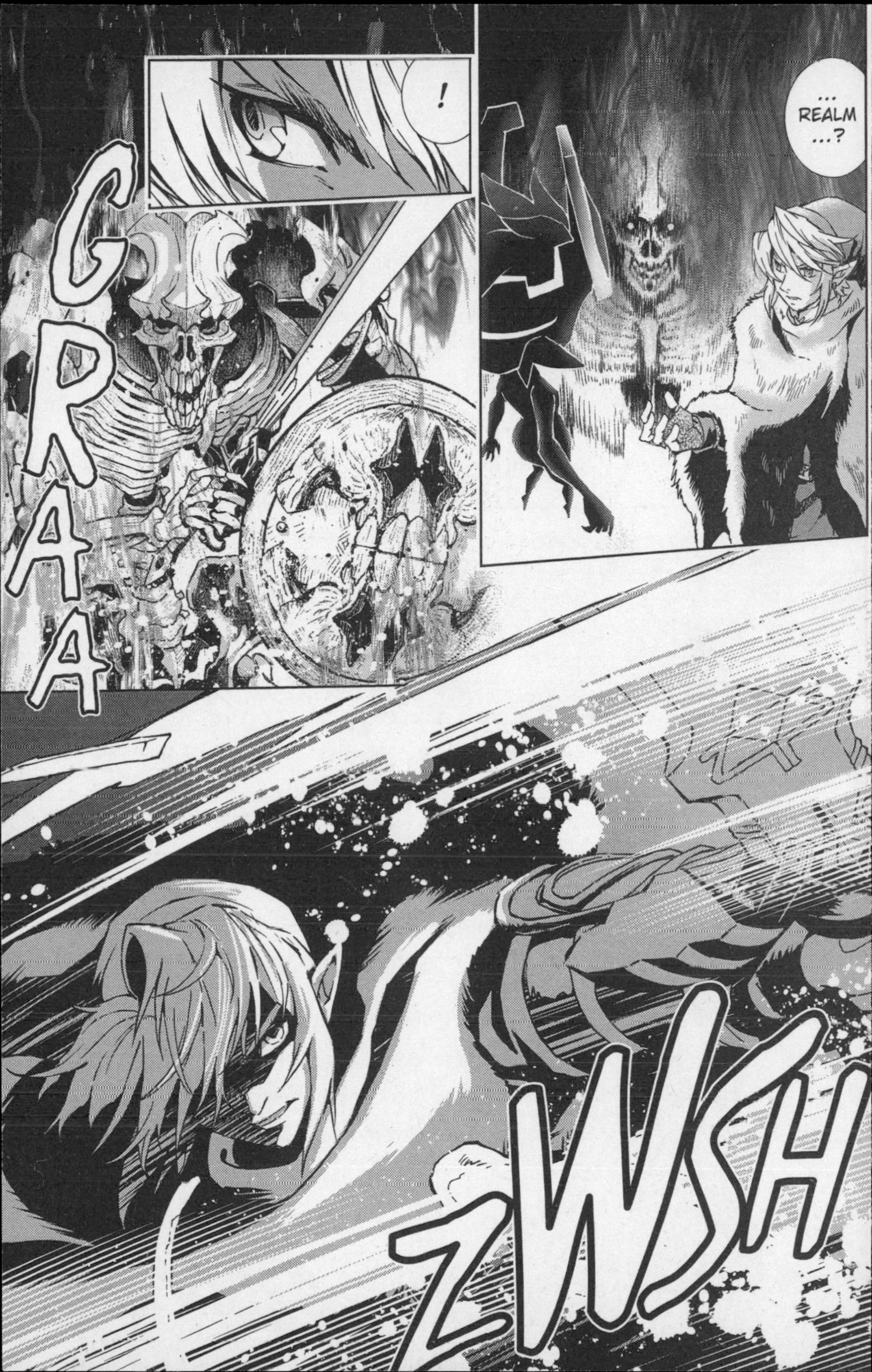
... REALM ...?
!
GRAA
ZWSH

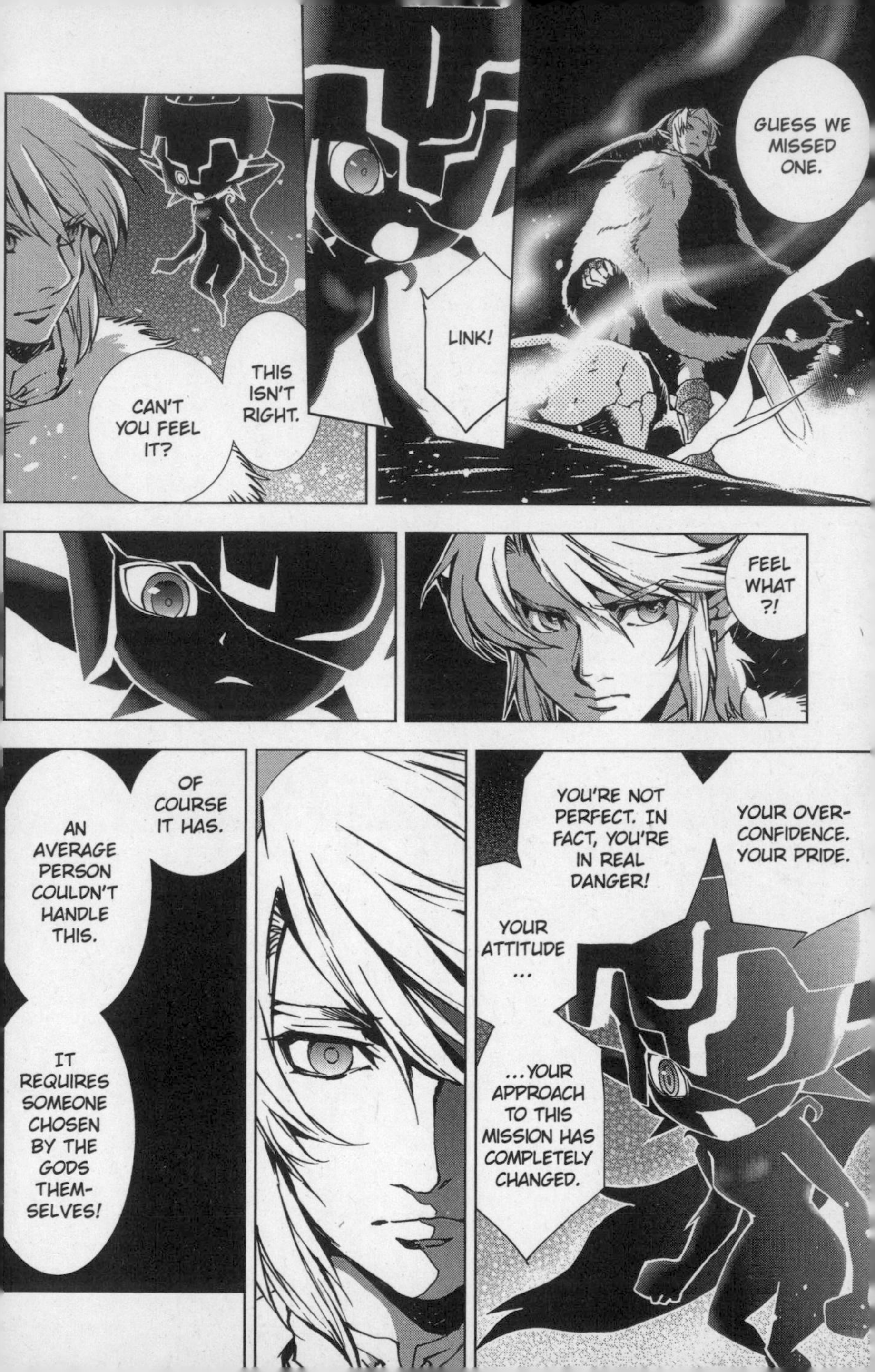
GUESS WE MISSED ONE.
LINK!
THIS ISN'T RIGHT.
CAN'T YOU FEEL IT?
FEEL WHAT?!
YOUR OVER-CONFIDENCE. YOUR PRIDE.
YOU'RE NOT PERFECT. IN FACT, YOU'RE IN REAL DANGER!
YOUR ATTITUDE...
...YOUR APPROACH TO THIS MISSION HAS COMPLETELY CHANGED.
OF COURSE IT HAS.
AN AVERAGE PERSON COULDN'T HANDLE THIS.
IT REQUIRES SOMEONE CHOSEN BY THE GODS THEM-SELVES!

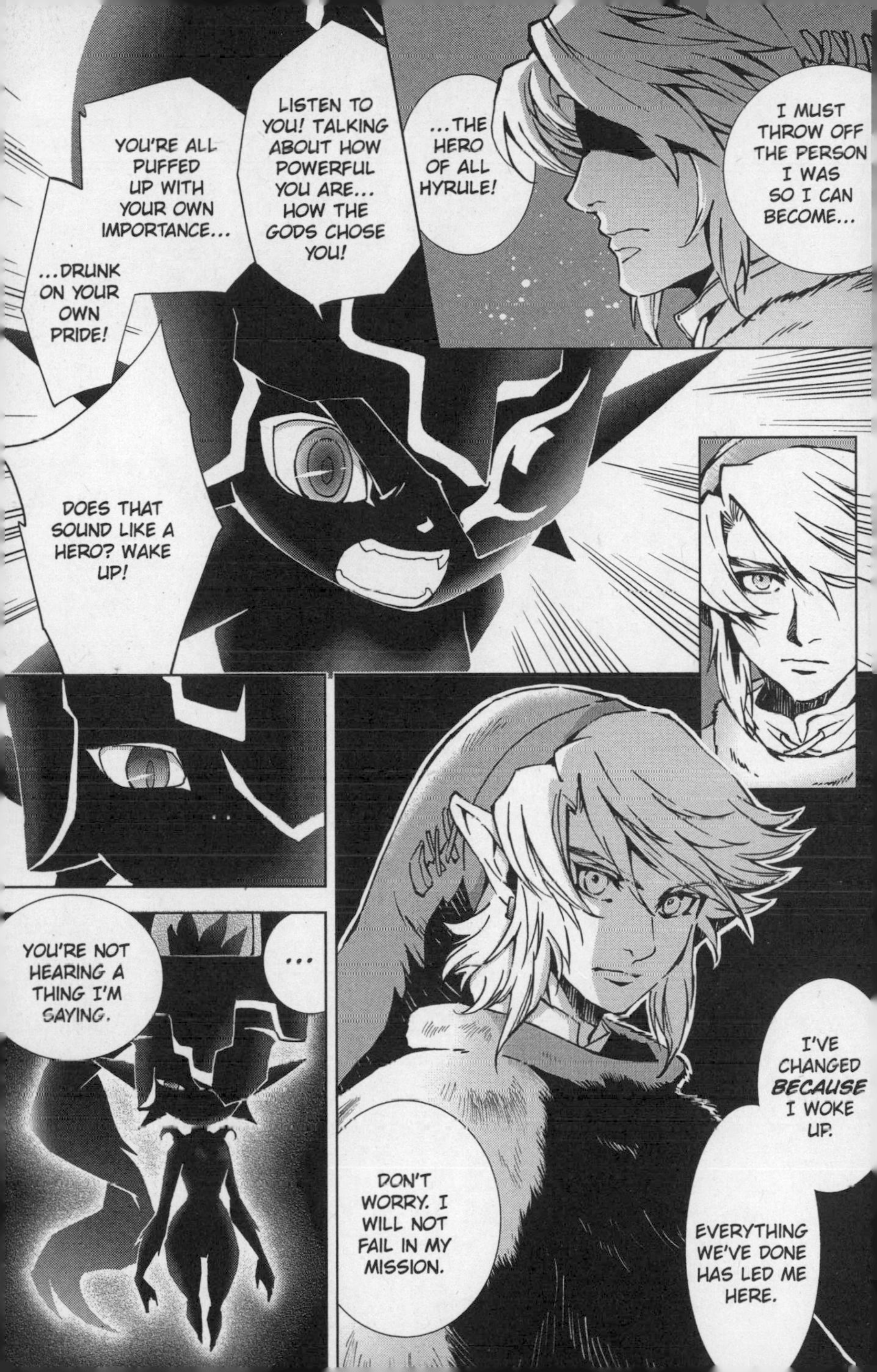

I MUST THROW OFF THE PERSON I WAS SO I CAN BECOME...
...THE HERO OF ALL HYRULE!
LISTEN TO YOU! TALKING ABOUT HOW POWERFUL YOU ARE... HOW THE GODS CHOSE YOU!
YOU'RE ALL PUFFED UP WITH YOUR OWN IMPORTANCE...
...DRUNK ON YOUR OWN PRIDE!
DOES THAT SOUND LIKE A HERO? WAKE UP!
I'VE CHANGED *BECAUSE* I WOKE UP.
EVERYTHING WE'VE DONE HAS LED ME HERE.
DON'T WORRY. I WILL NOT FAIL IN MY MISSION.
...
YOU'RE NOT HEARING A THING I'M SAYING.

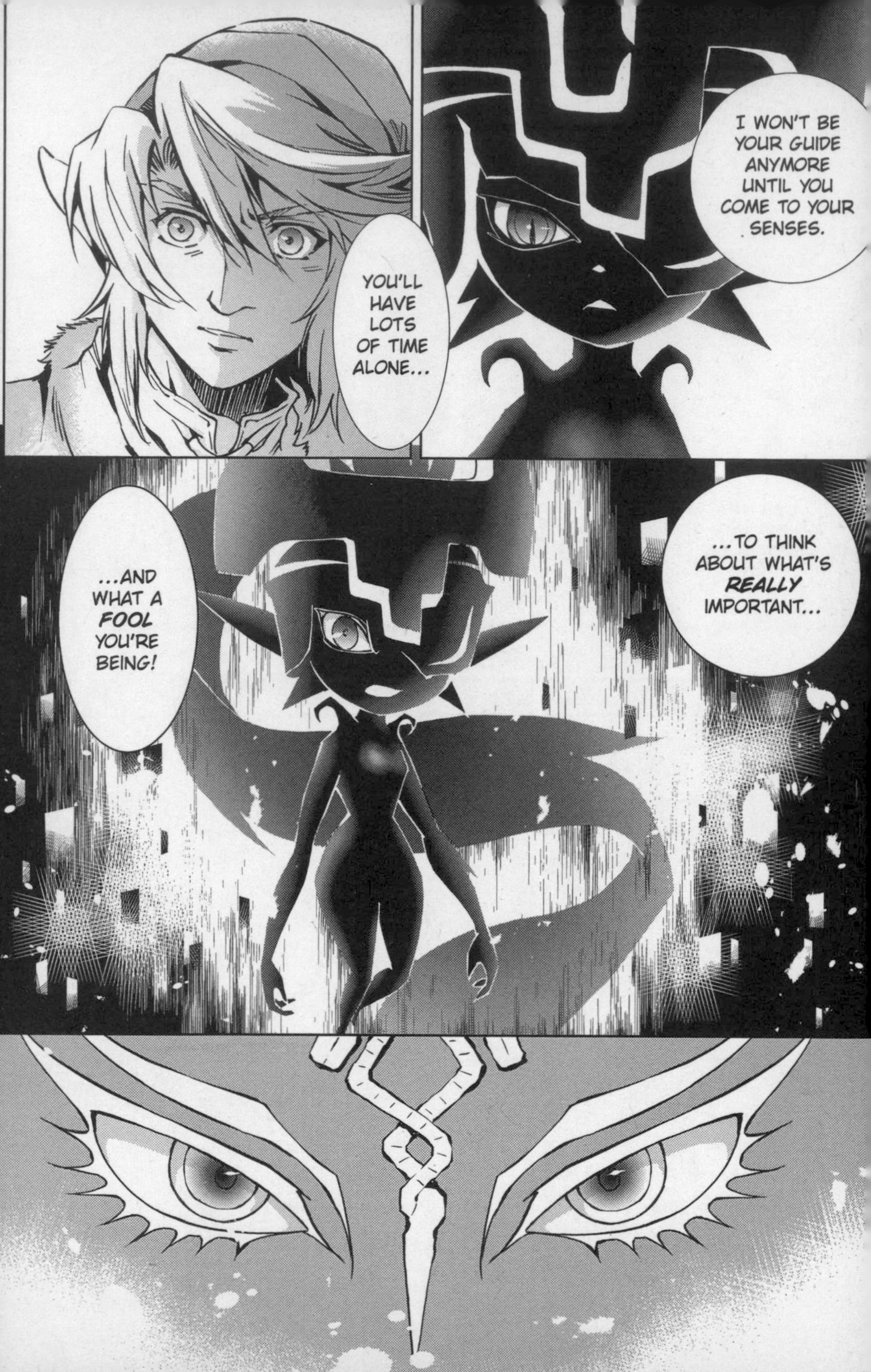
I WON'T BE YOUR GUIDE ANYMORE UNTIL YOU COME TO YOUR SENSES.
YOU'LL HAVE LOTS OF TIME ALONE...
...TO THINK ABOUT WHAT'S *REALLY* IMPORTANT...
...AND WHAT A *FOOL* YOU'RE BEING!

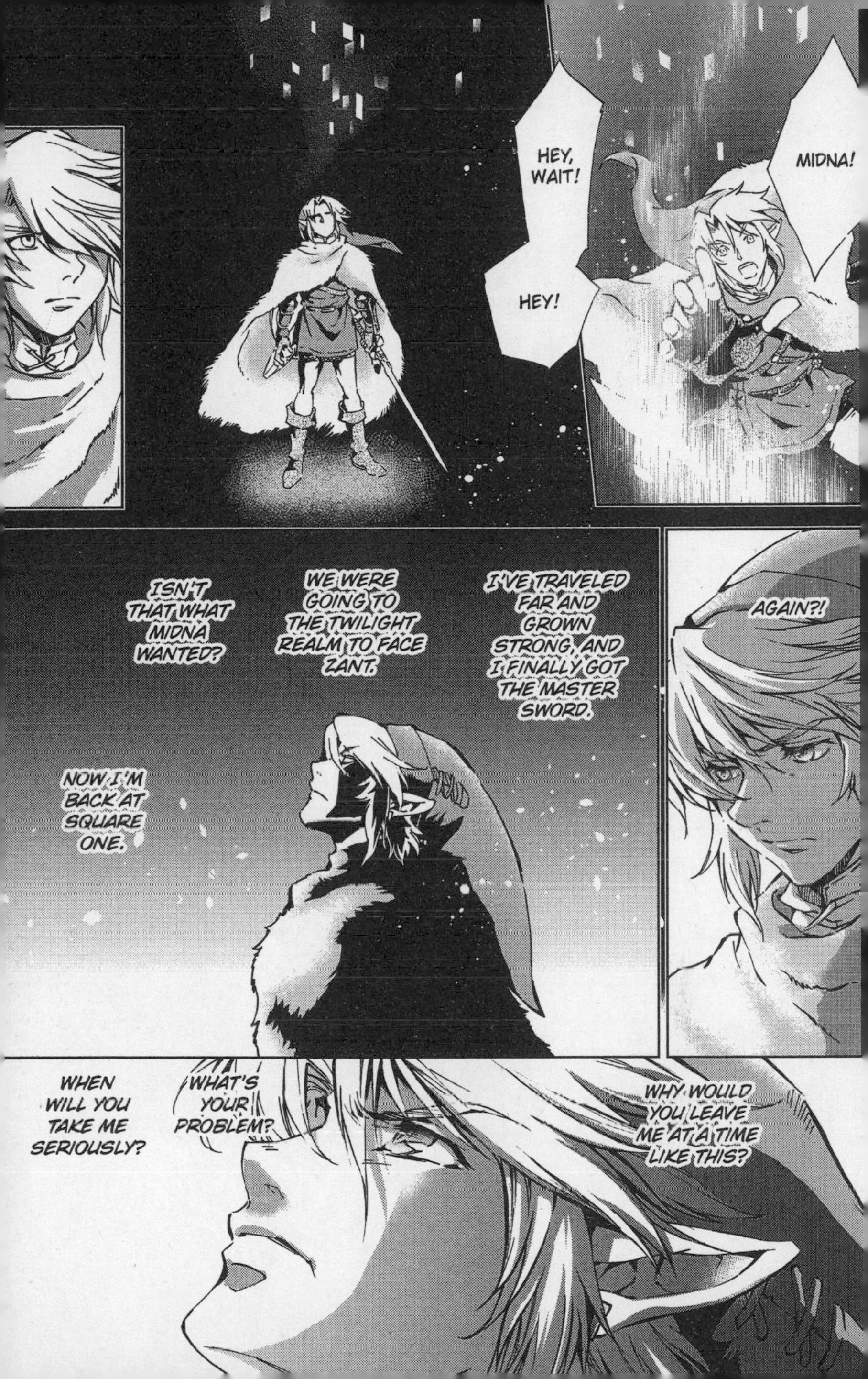
MIDNA!
HEY, WAIT!
HEY!
AGAIN?!
I'VE TRAVELED FAR AND GROWN STRONG, AND I FINALLY GOT THE MASTER SWORD.
WE WERE GOING TO THE TWILIGHT REALM TO FACE ZANT.
ISN'T THAT WHAT MIDNA WANTED?
NOW I'M BACK AT SQUARE ONE.
WHY WOULD YOU LEAVE ME AT A TIME LIKE THIS?
WHAT'S YOUR PROBLEM?
WHEN WILL YOU TAKE ME SERIOUSLY?

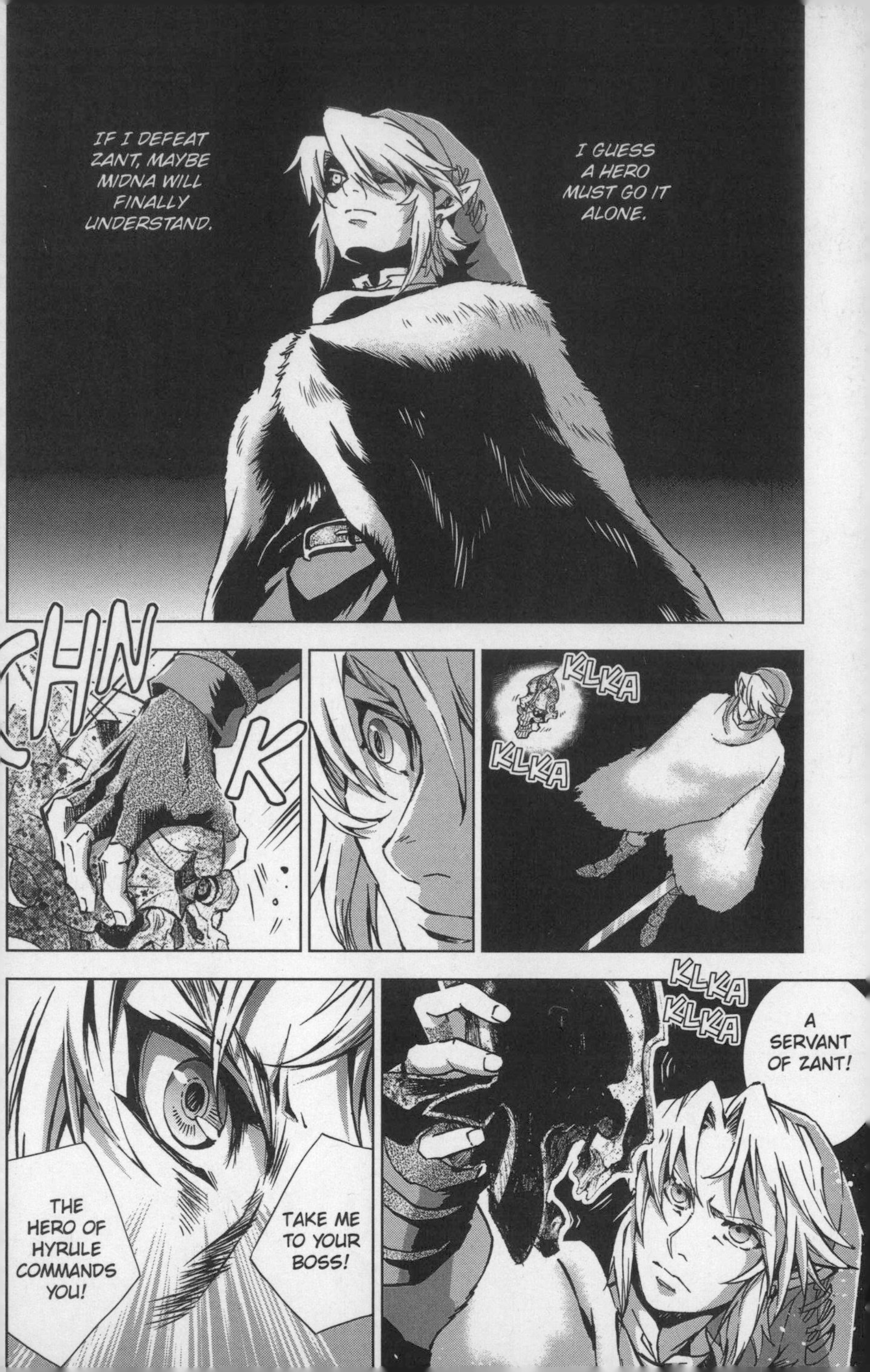
I GUESS A HERO MUST GO IT ALONE.
IF I DEFEAT ZANT, MAYBE MIDNA WILL FINALLY UNDERSTAND.
KLKA
KLKA
CHNK
KLKA KLKA
A SERVANT OF ZANT!
TAKE ME TO YOUR BOSS!
THE HERO OF HYRULE COMMANDS YOU!

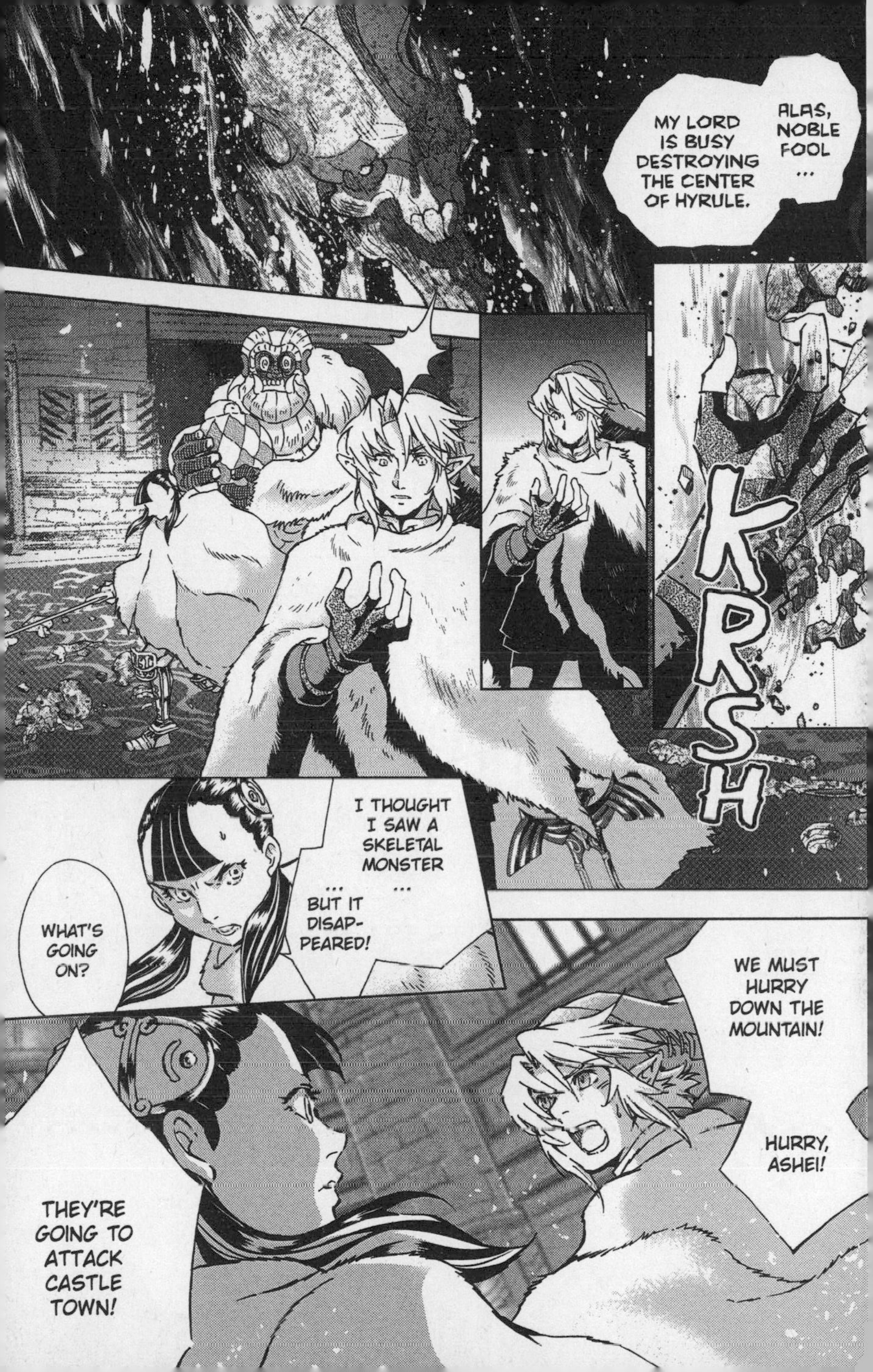
ALAS, NOBLE FOOL ...
MY LORD IS BUSY DESTROYING THE CENTER OF HYRULE.
KRSH
I THOUGHT I SAW A SKELETAL MONSTER ...
... BUT IT DISAP-PEARED!
WHAT'S GOING ON?
WE MUST HURRY DOWN THE MOUNTAIN!
HURRY, ASHEI!
THEY'RE GOING TO ATTACK CASTLE TOWN!

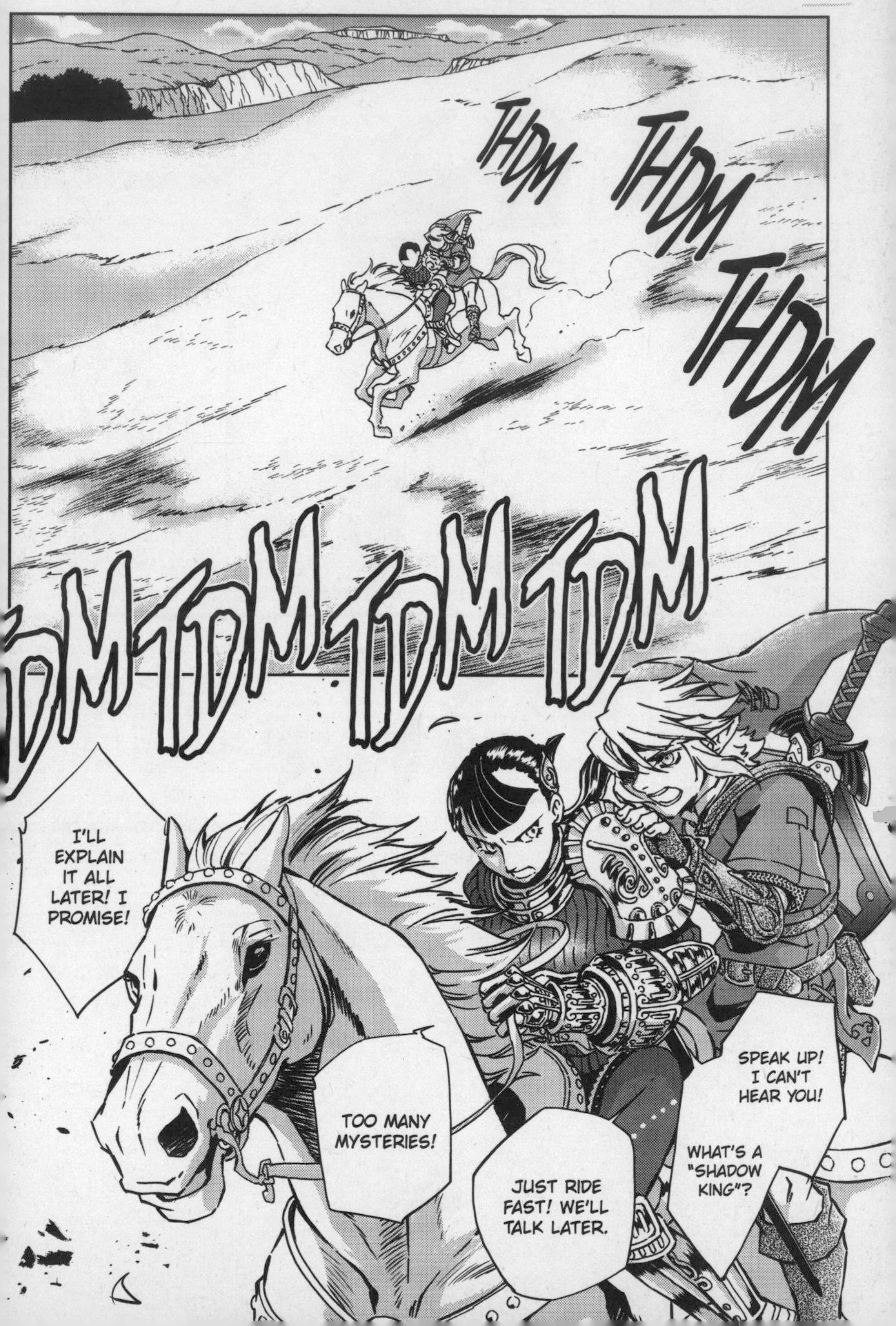
THDM THDM THDM THDM
DM TDM TDM TDM TDM
SPEAK UP! I CAN'T HEAR YOU!
WHAT'S A "SHADOW KING"?
JUST RIDE FAST! WE'LL TALK LATER.
TOO MANY MYSTERIES!
I'LL EXPLAIN IT ALL LATER! I PROMISE!

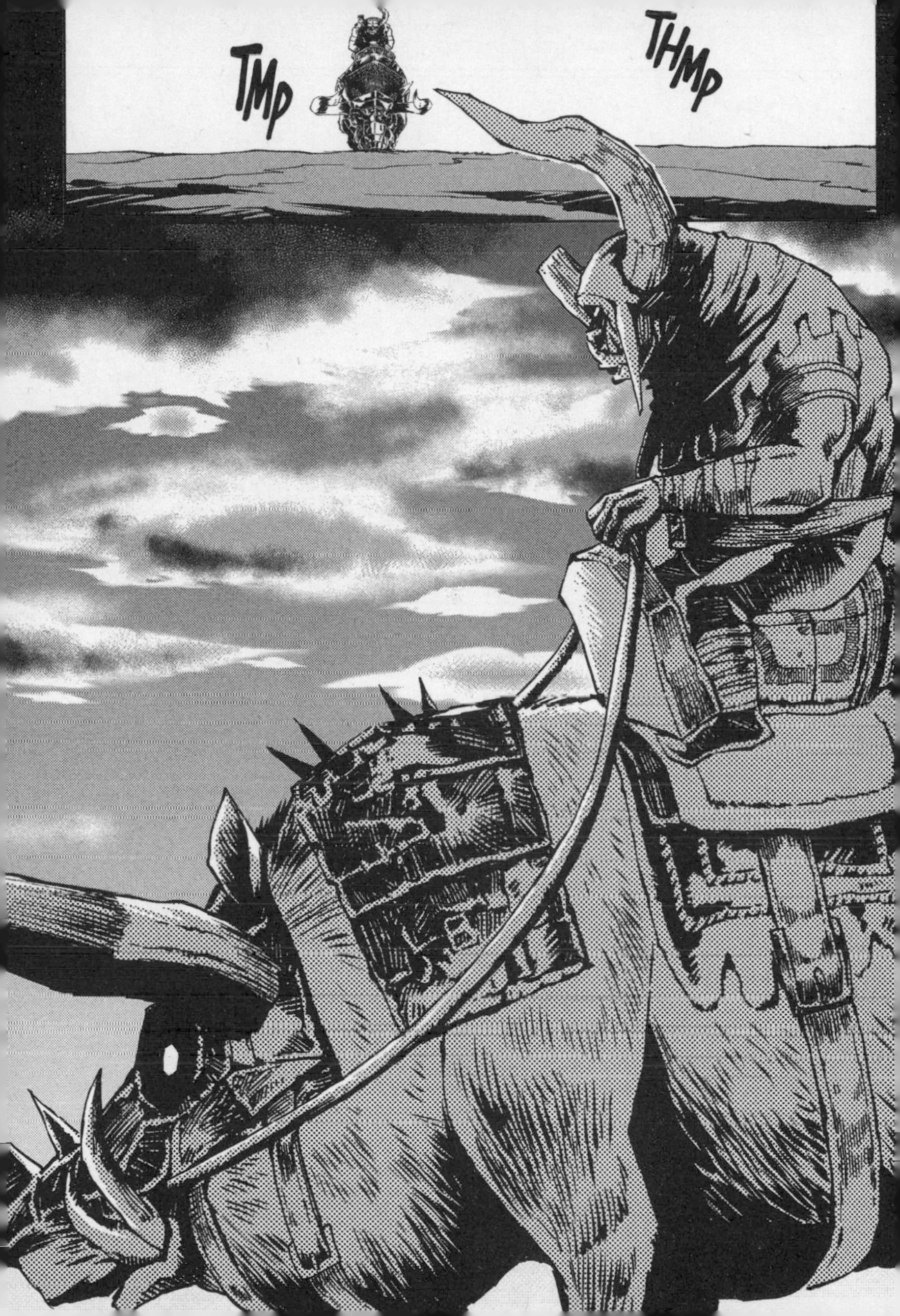
THMP
TMP

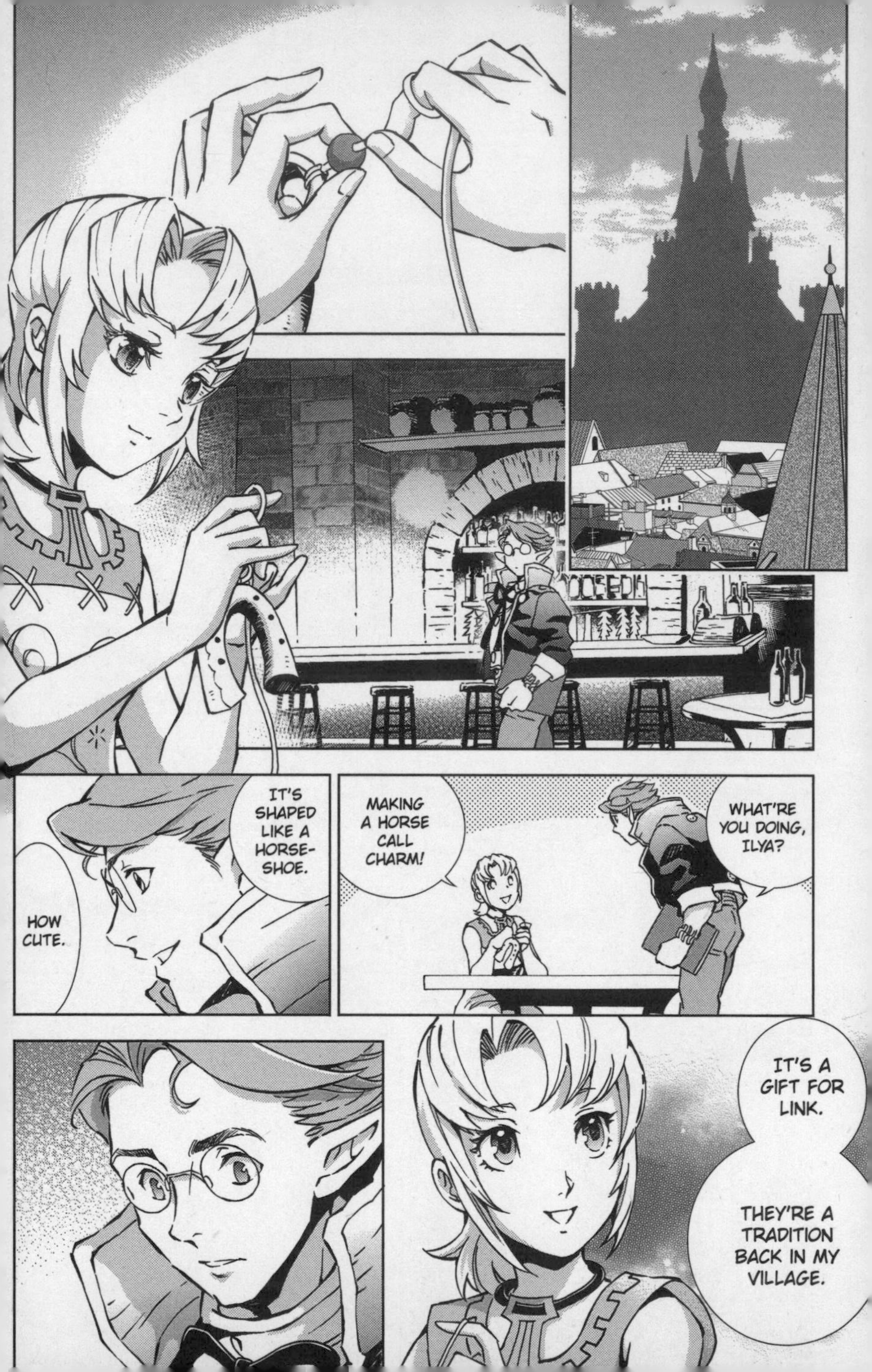
WHAT'RE YOU DOING, ILYA?
MAKING A HORSE CALL CHARM!
IT'S SHAPED LIKE A HORSE-SHOE.
HOW CUTE.
IT'S A GIFT FOR LINK.
THEY'RE A TRADITION BACK IN MY VILLAGE.

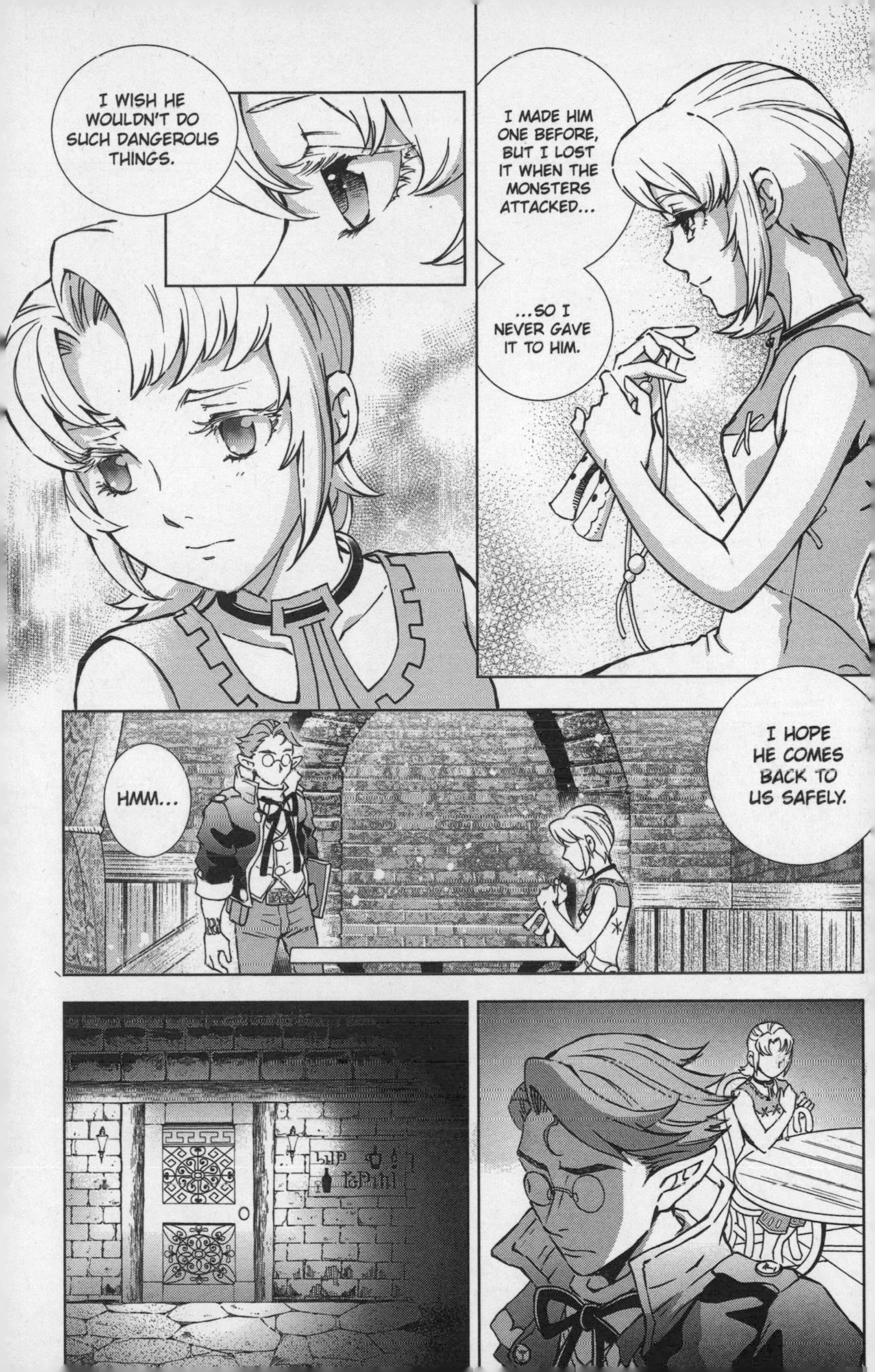
I MADE HIM ONE BEFORE, BUT I LOST IT WHEN THE MONSTERS ATTACKED...
...SO I NEVER GAVE IT TO HIM.
I WISH HE WOULDN'T DO SUCH DANGEROUS THINGS.
I HOPE HE COMES BACK TO US SAFELY.
HMM...

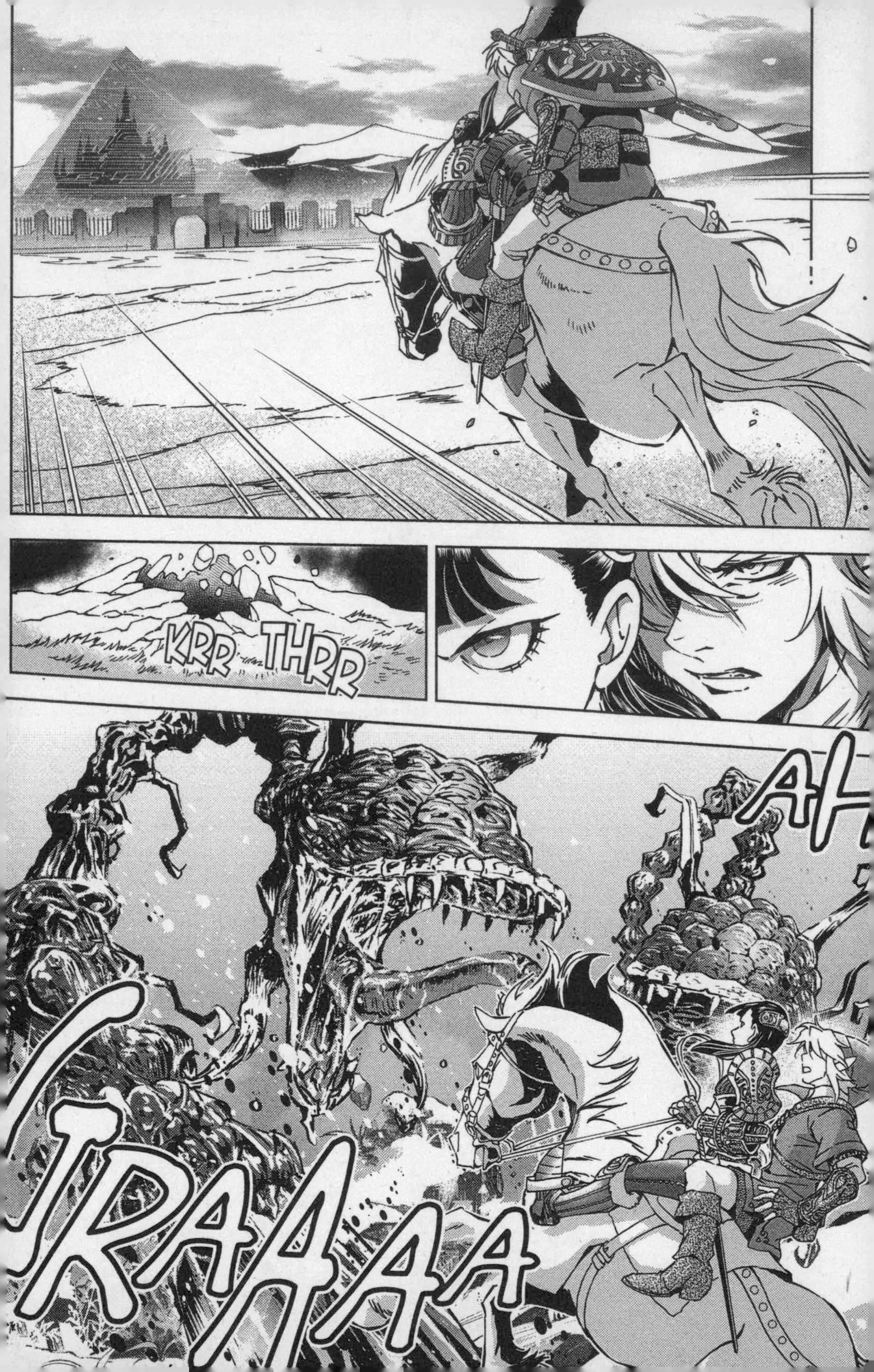
KRR THRR
AH
RAAAA

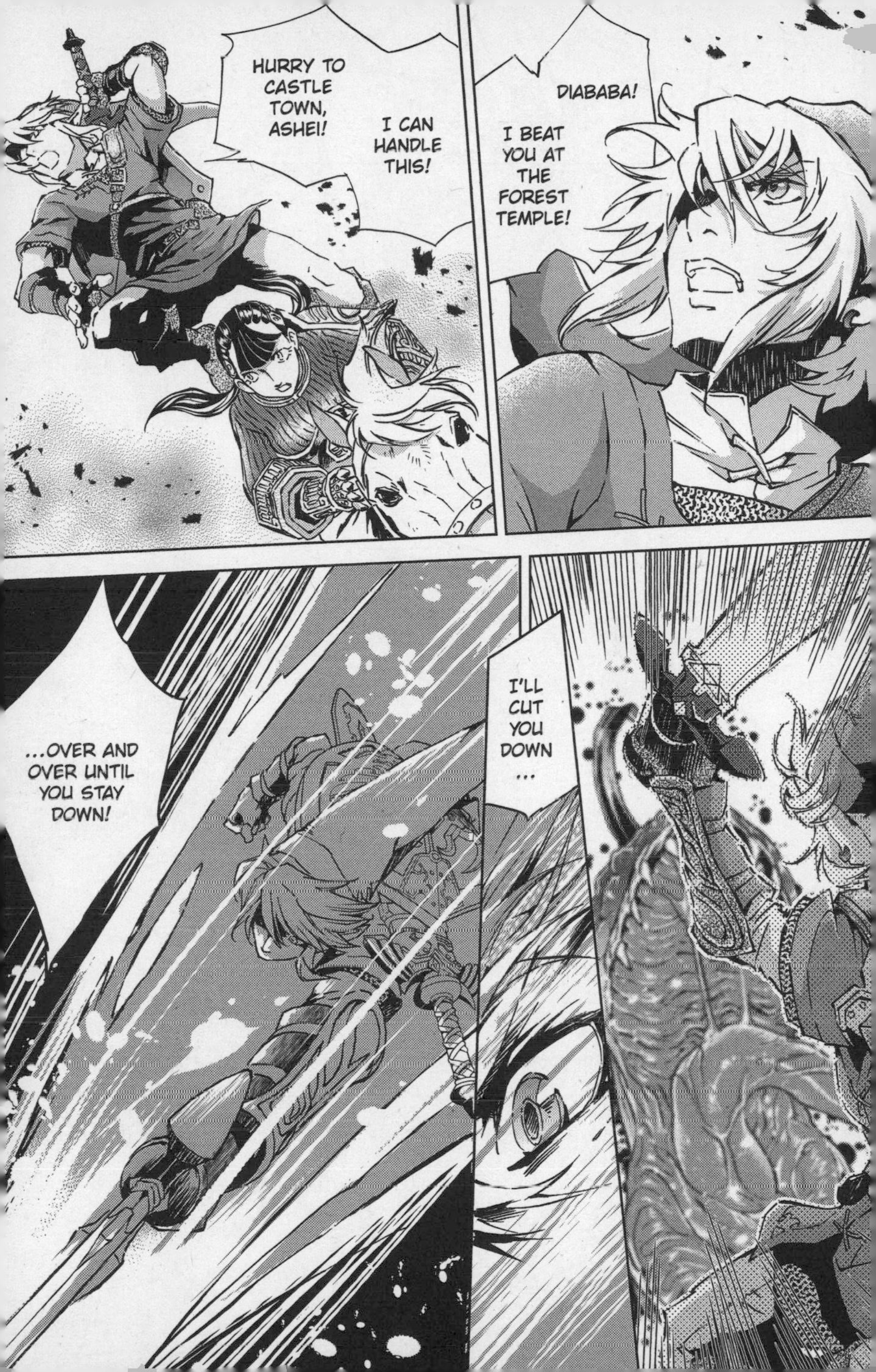
DIABABA!
I BEAT YOU AT THE FOREST TEMPLE!
HURRY TO CASTLE TOWN, ASHEI!
I CAN HANDLE THIS!
I'LL CUT YOU DOWN ...
...OVER AND OVER UNTIL YOU STAY DOWN!

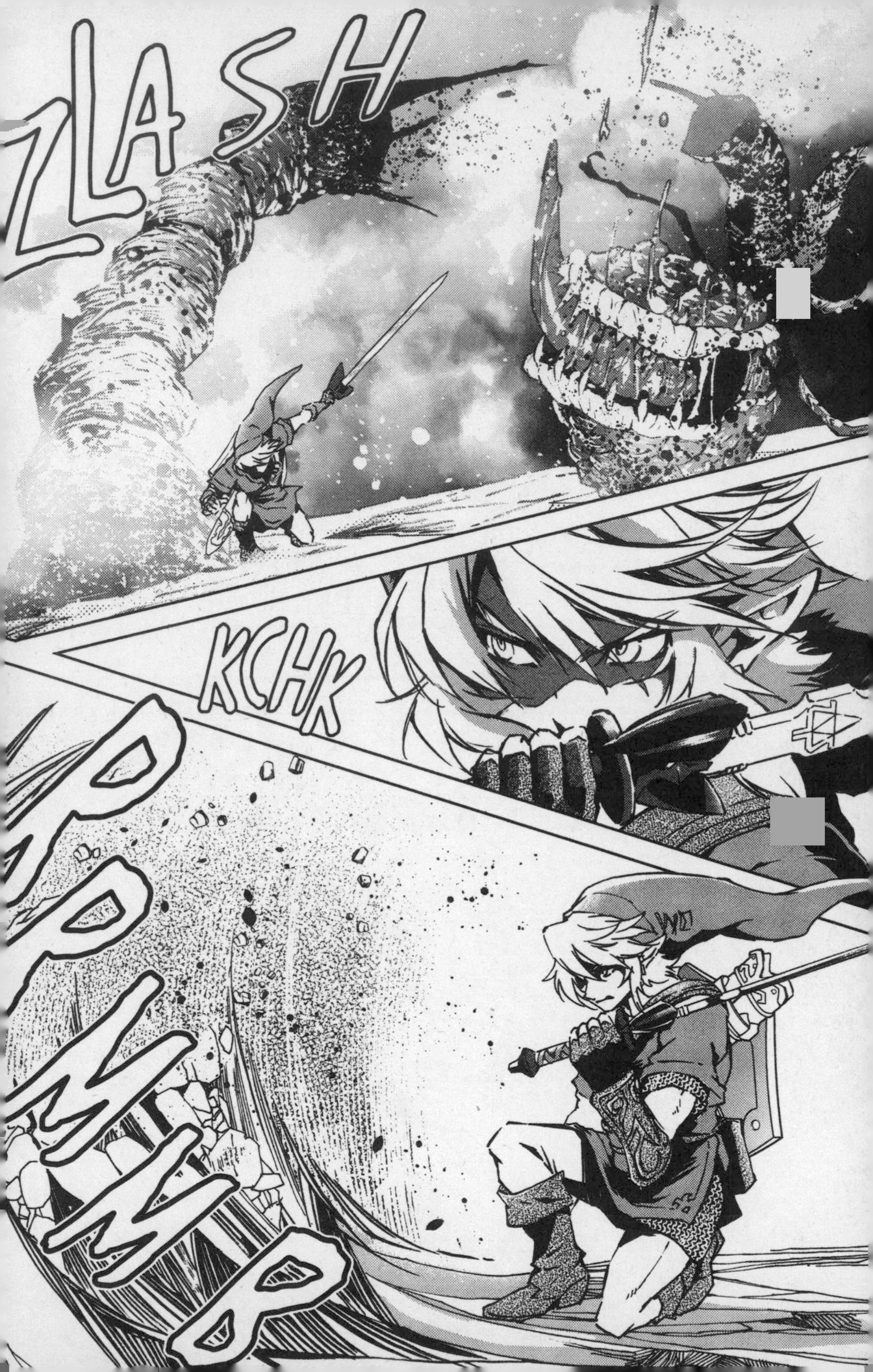
ZLASH
KCHK

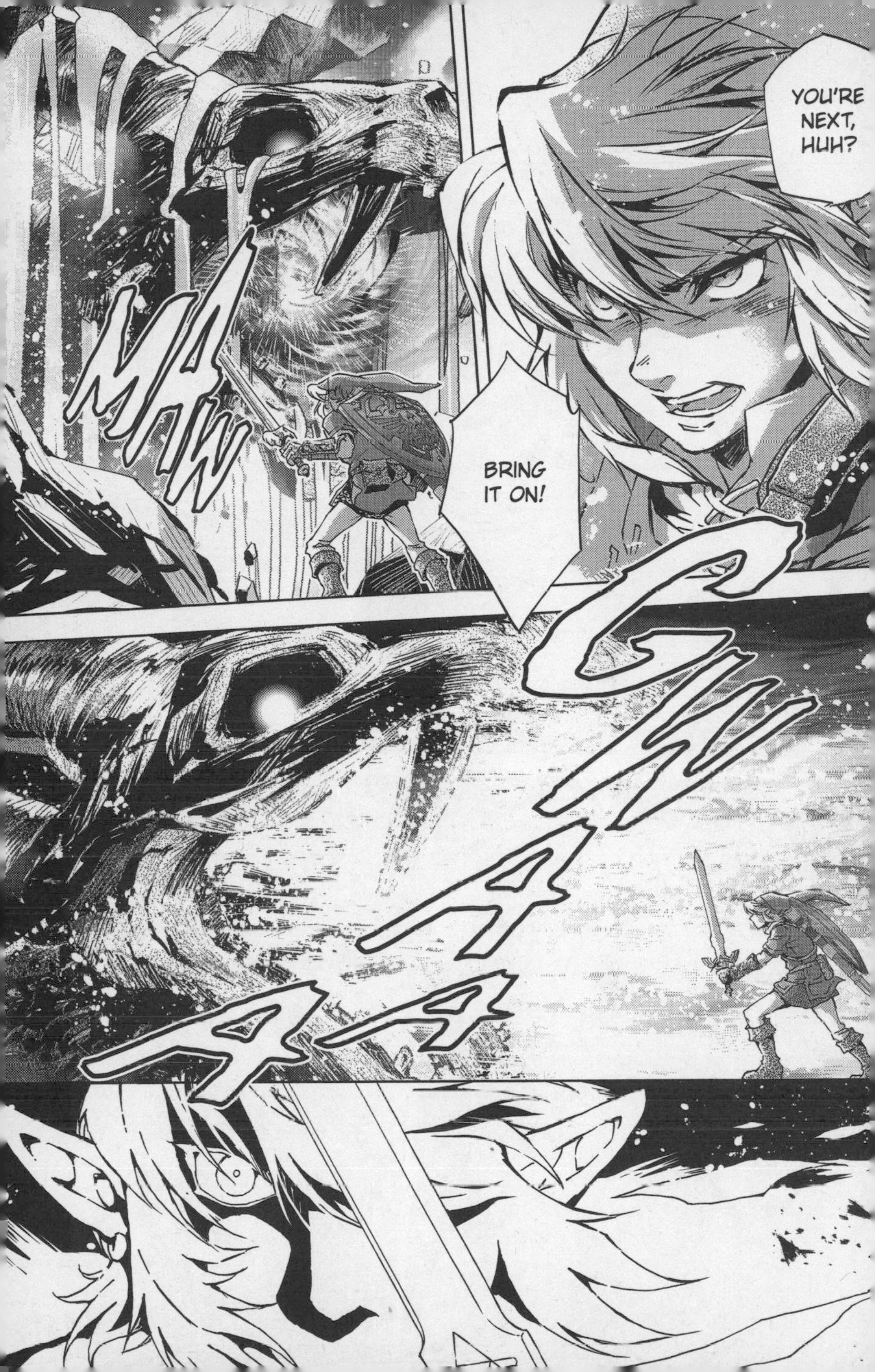
YOU'RE NEXT, HUH?
BRING IT ON!
MAW
GWAAAA

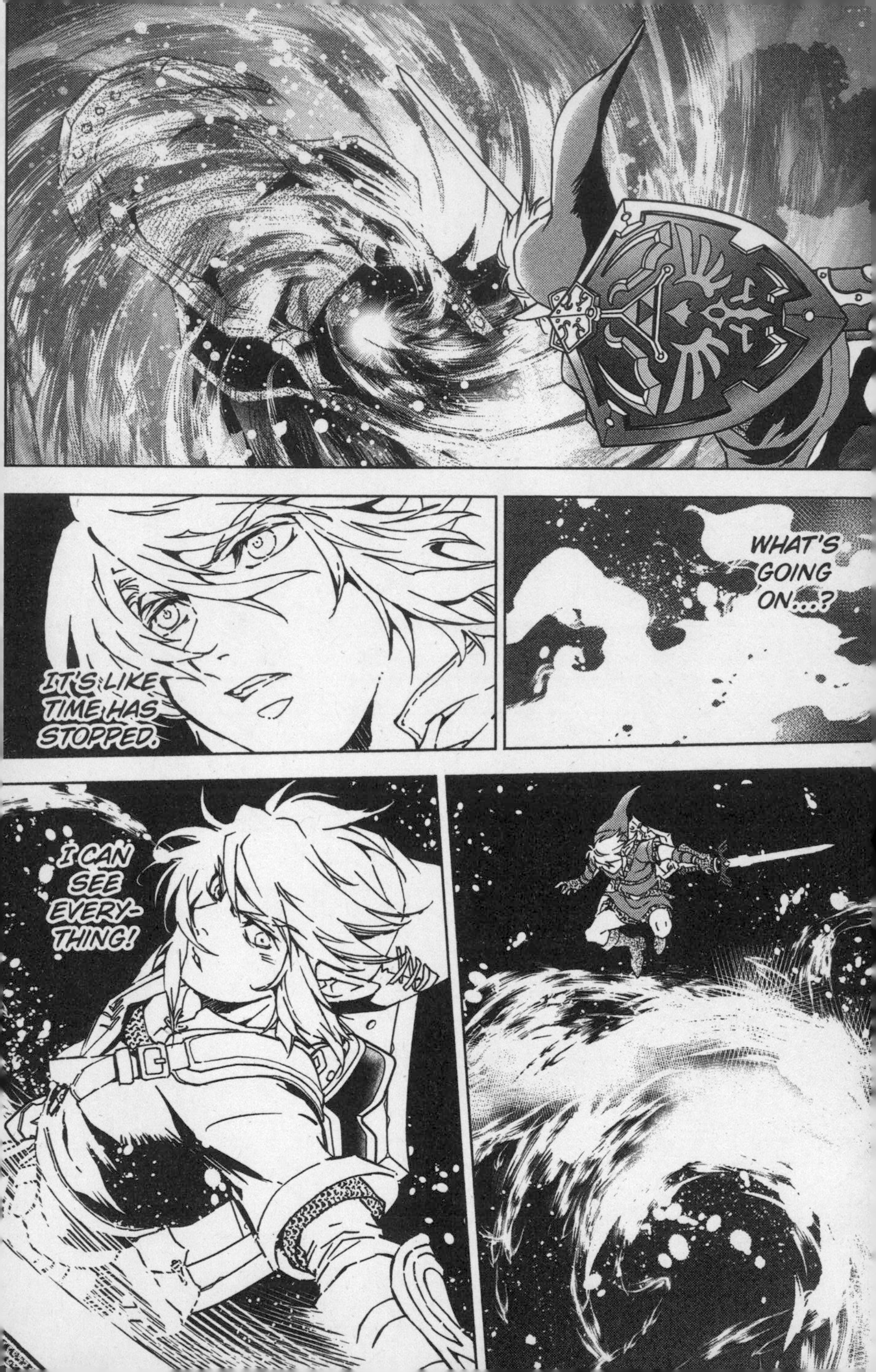
WHAT'S GOING ON...?
IT'S LIKE TIME HAS STOPPED.
I CAN SEE EVERY-THING!

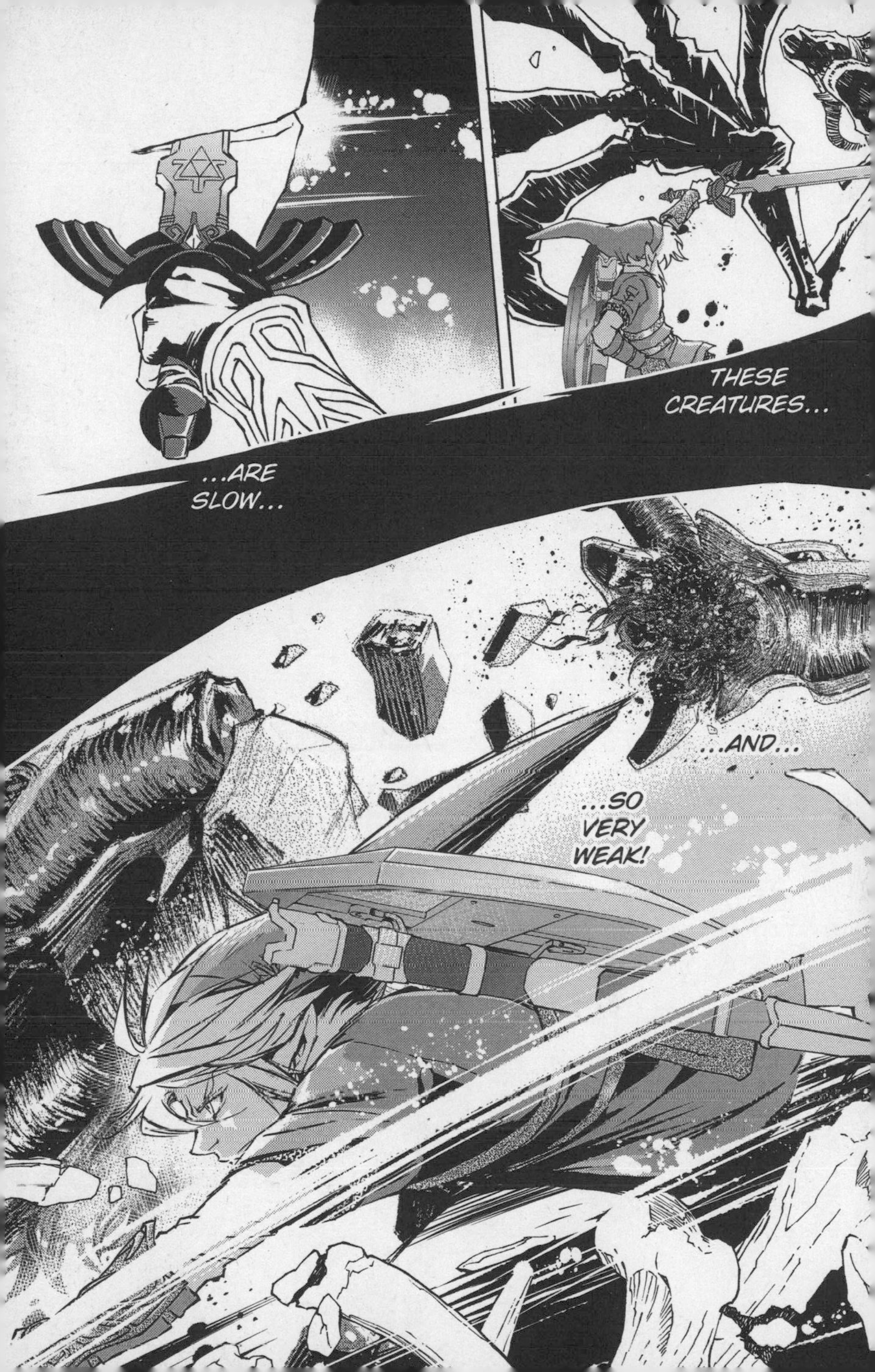
THESE CREATURES...
...ARE SLOW...
...AND...
...SO VERY WEAK!

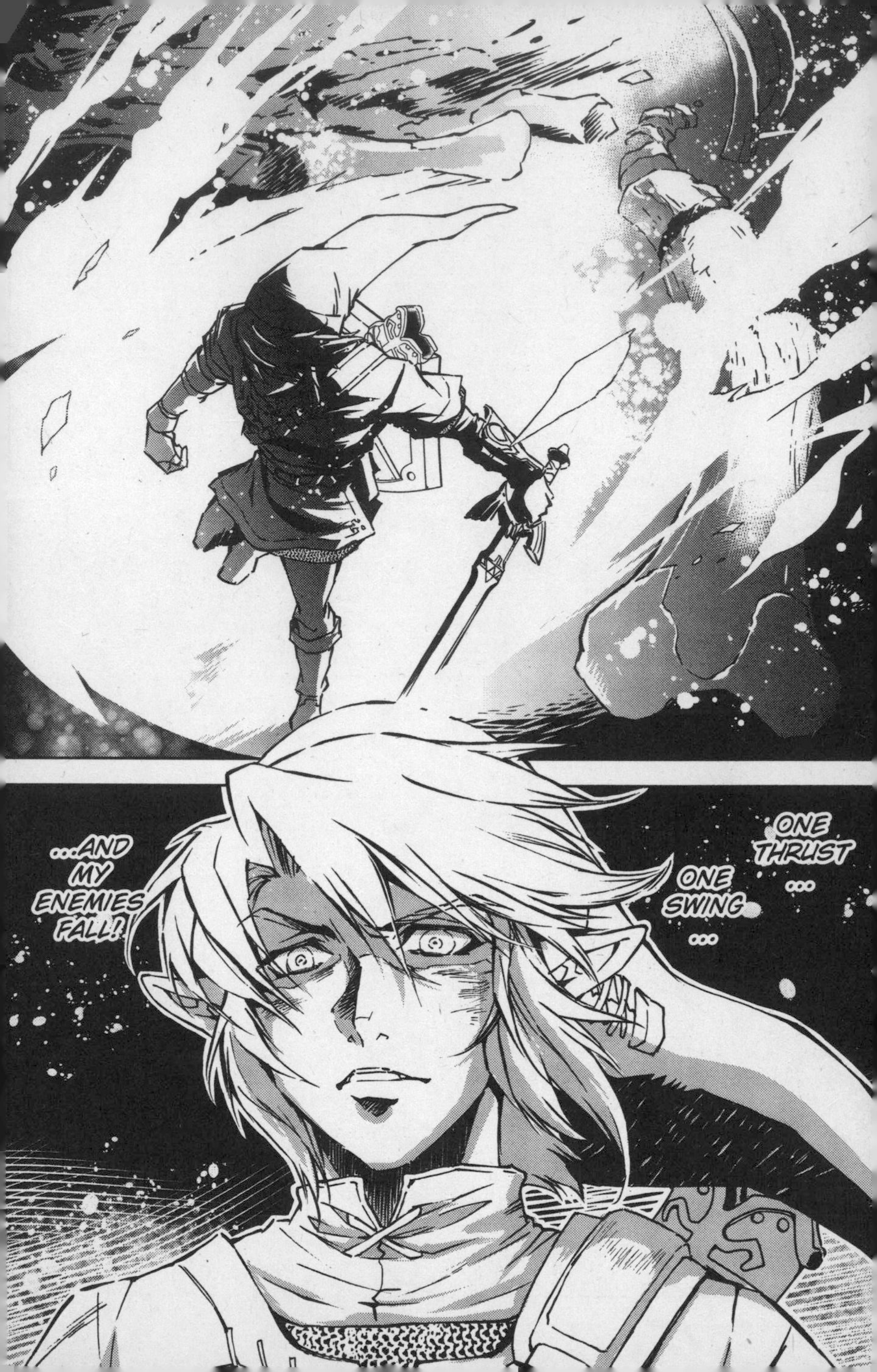

ONE THRUST ...
ONE SWING ...
...AND MY ENEMIES FALL!

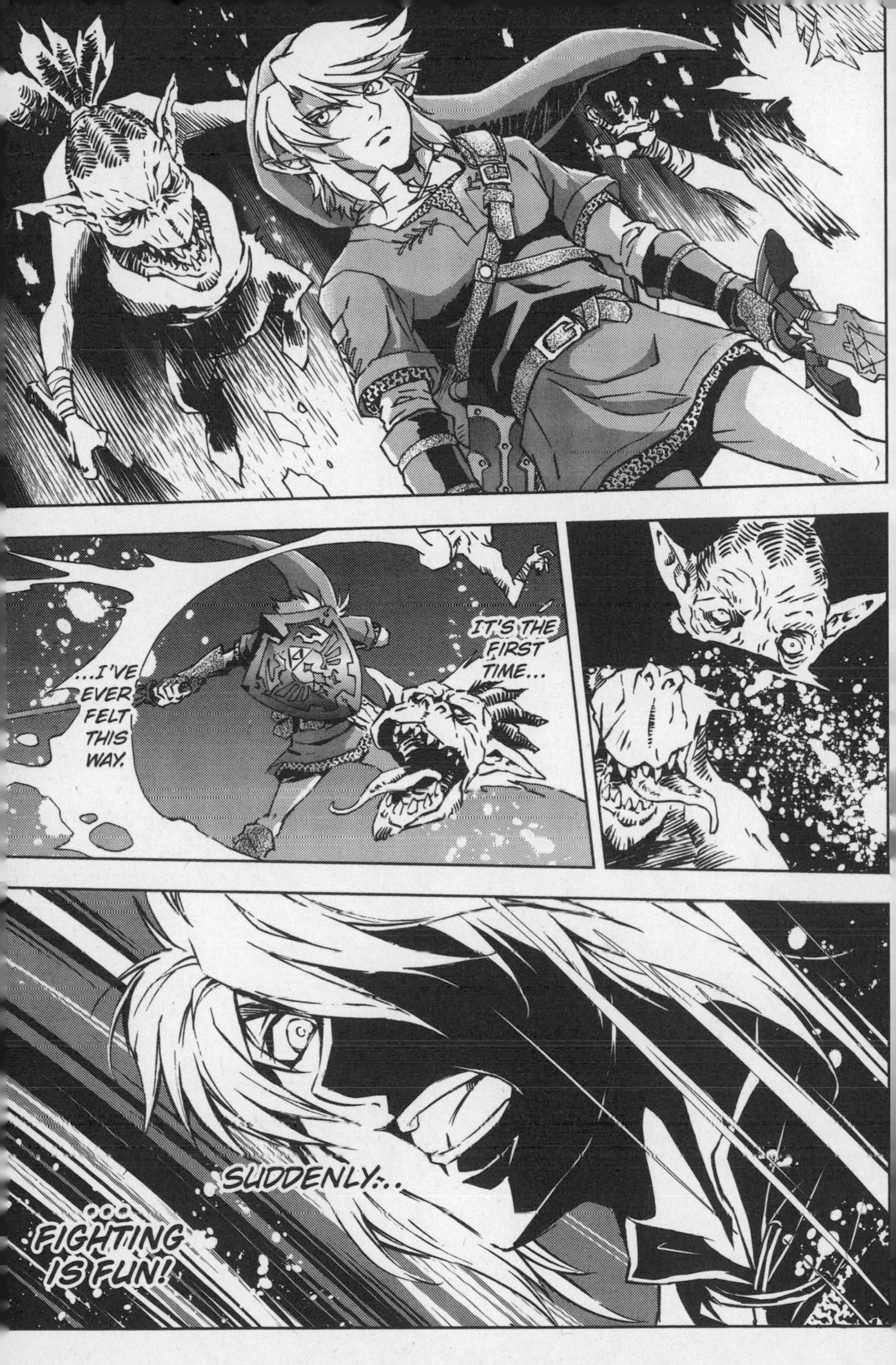
IT'S THE FIRST TIME...
...I'VE EVER FELT THIS WAY.
SUDDENLY...
...FIGHTING IS FUN!

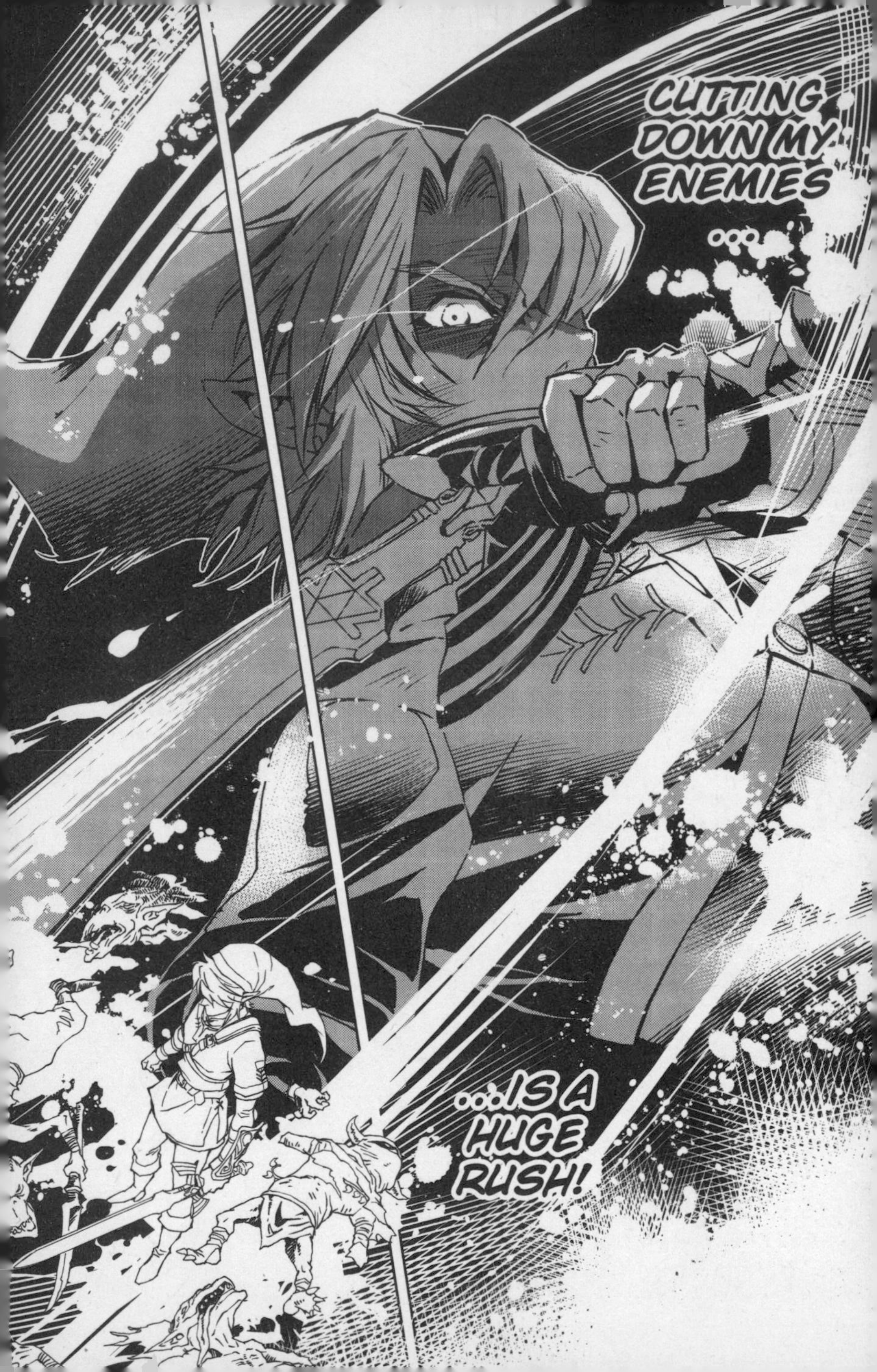
CUTTING DOWN MY ENEMIES...
...IS A HUGE RUSH!

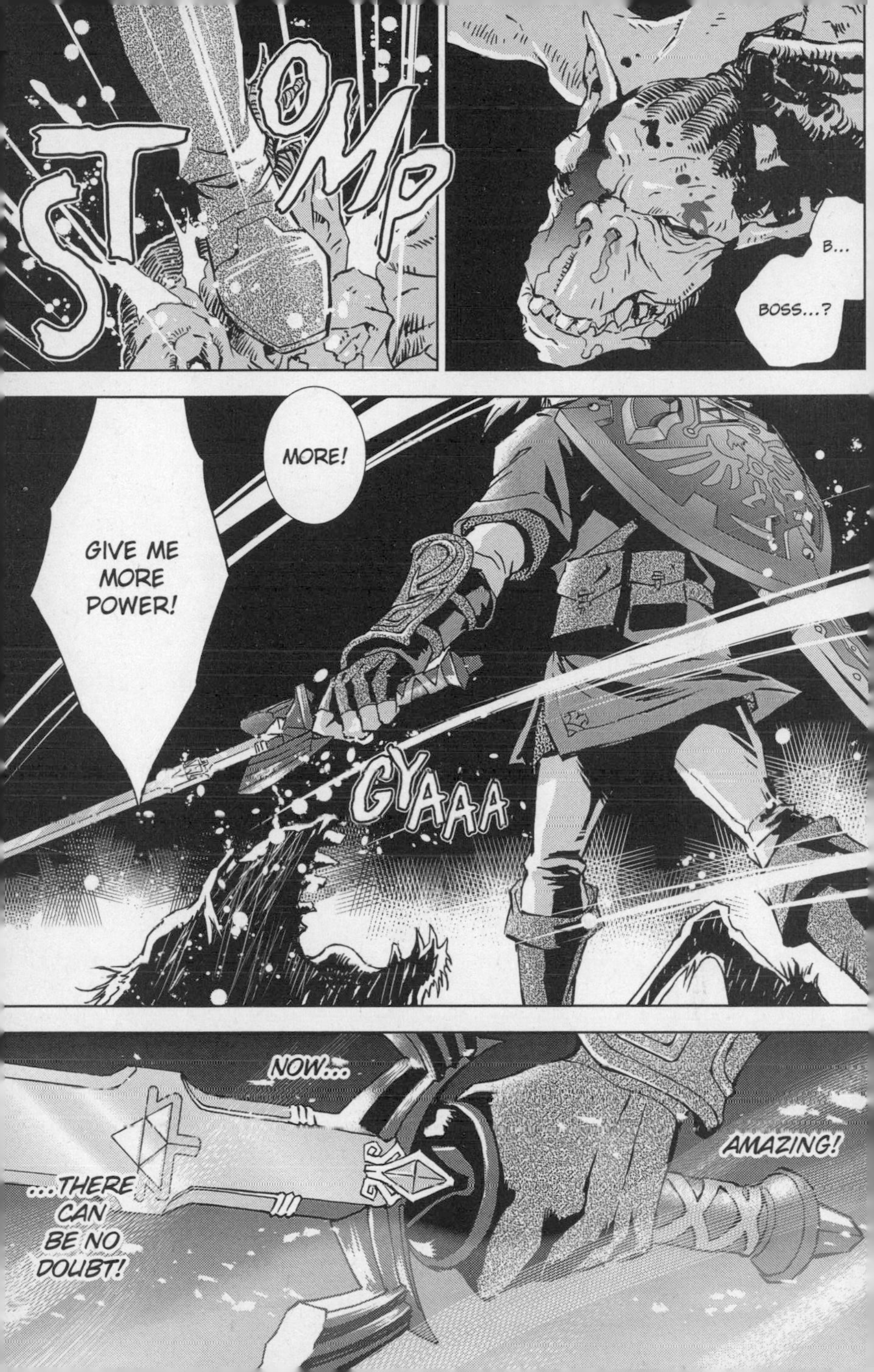
B...
BOSS...?
STOMP
MORE!
GIVE ME MORE POWER!
GYAAA
NOW...
AMAZING!
...THERE CAN BE NO DOUBT!

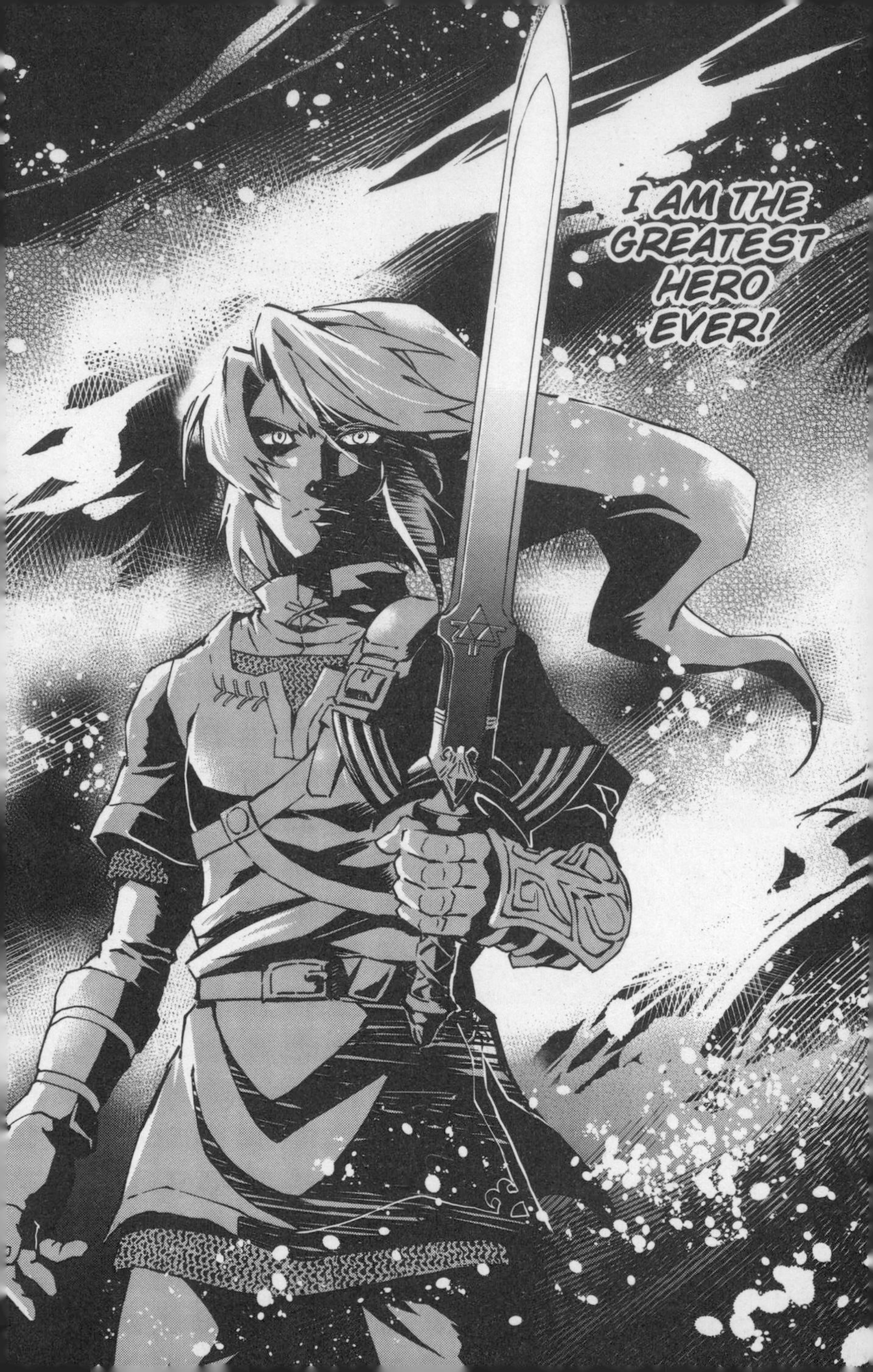
I AM THE GREATEST HERO EVER!

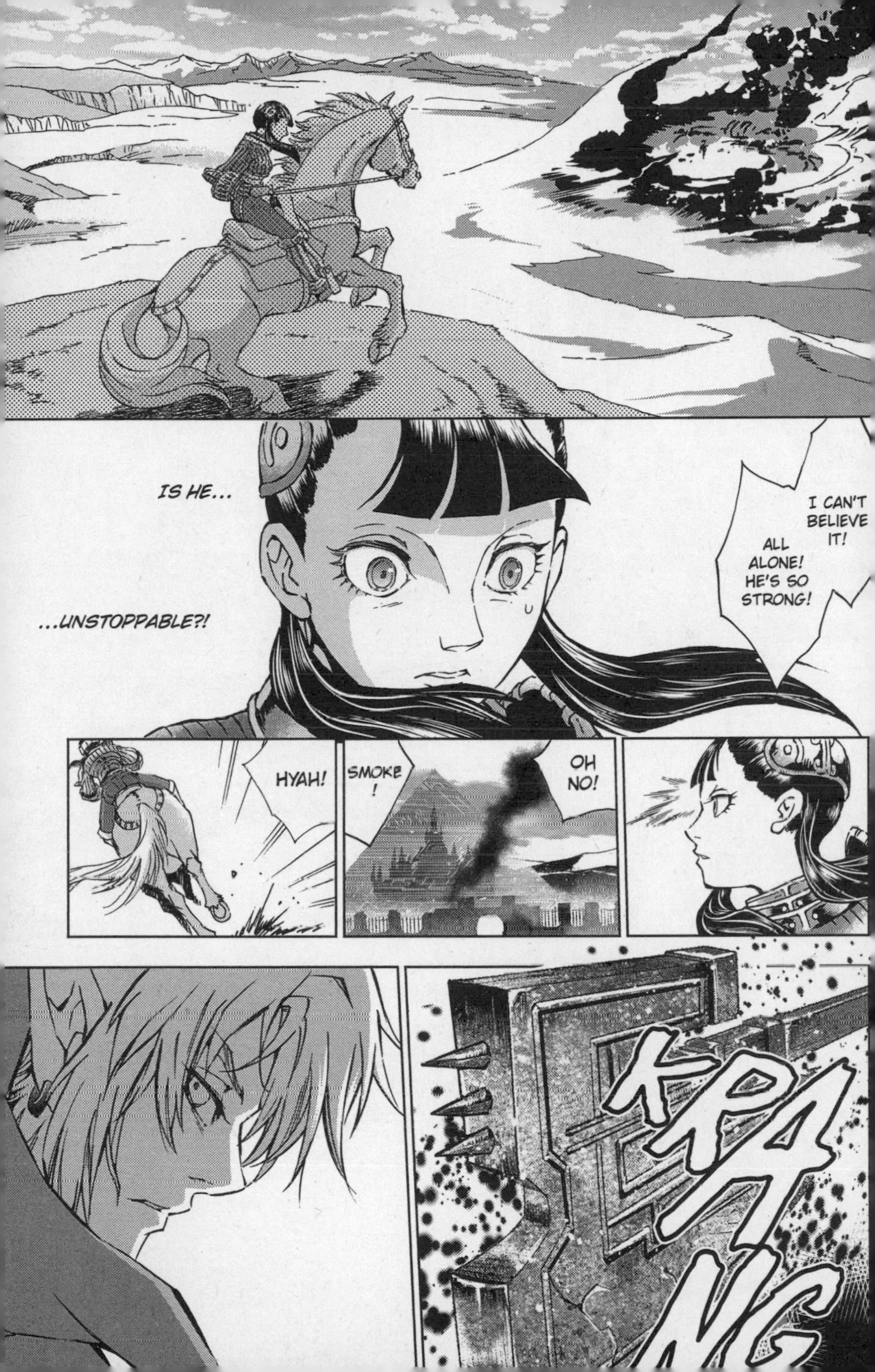
I CAN'T BELIEVE IT!
ALL ALONE! HE'S SO STRONG!
IS HE...
...UNSTOPPABLE?!
OH NO!
SMOKE!
HYAH!
KRANG

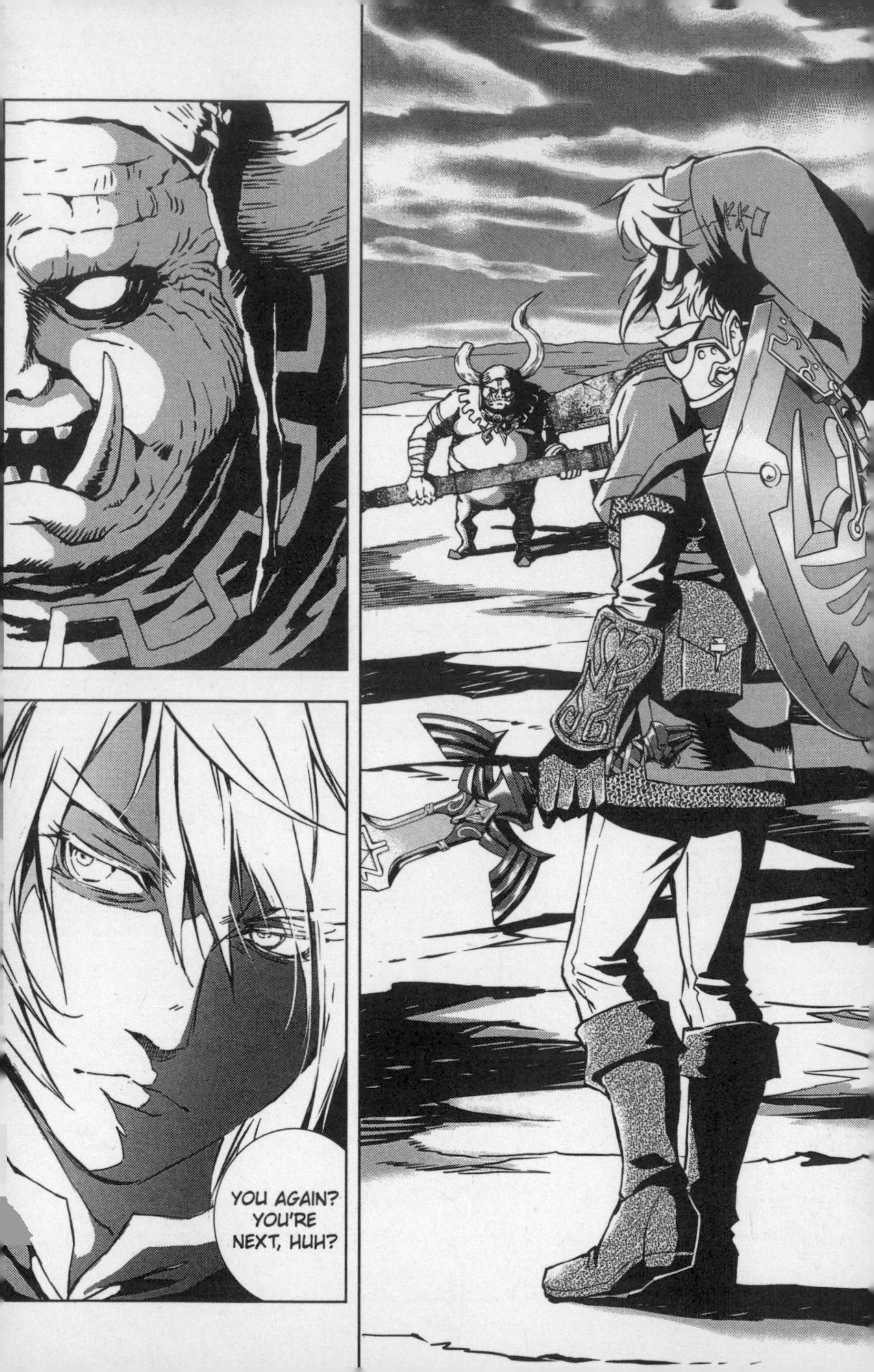
YOU AGAIN? YOU'RE NEXT, HUH?

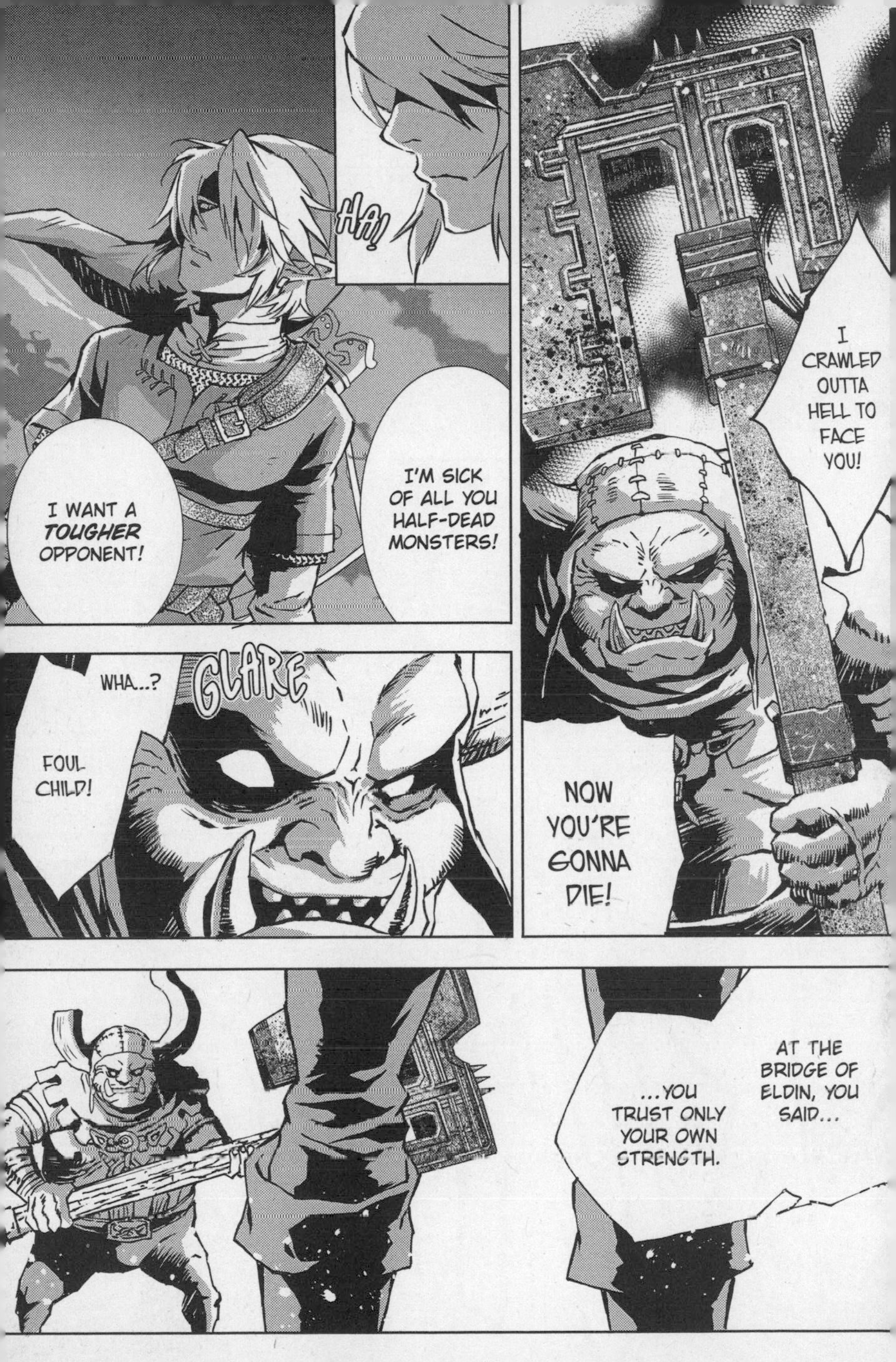
I CRAWLED OUTTA HELL TO FACE YOU!
NOW YOU'RE GONNA DIE!
HA!
I'M SICK OF ALL YOU HALF-DEAD MONSTERS!
I WANT A *TOUGHER* OPPONENT!
GLARE
WHA...?
FOUL CHILD!
AT THE BRIDGE OF ELDIN, YOU SAID...
...YOU TRUST ONLY YOUR OWN STRENGTH.

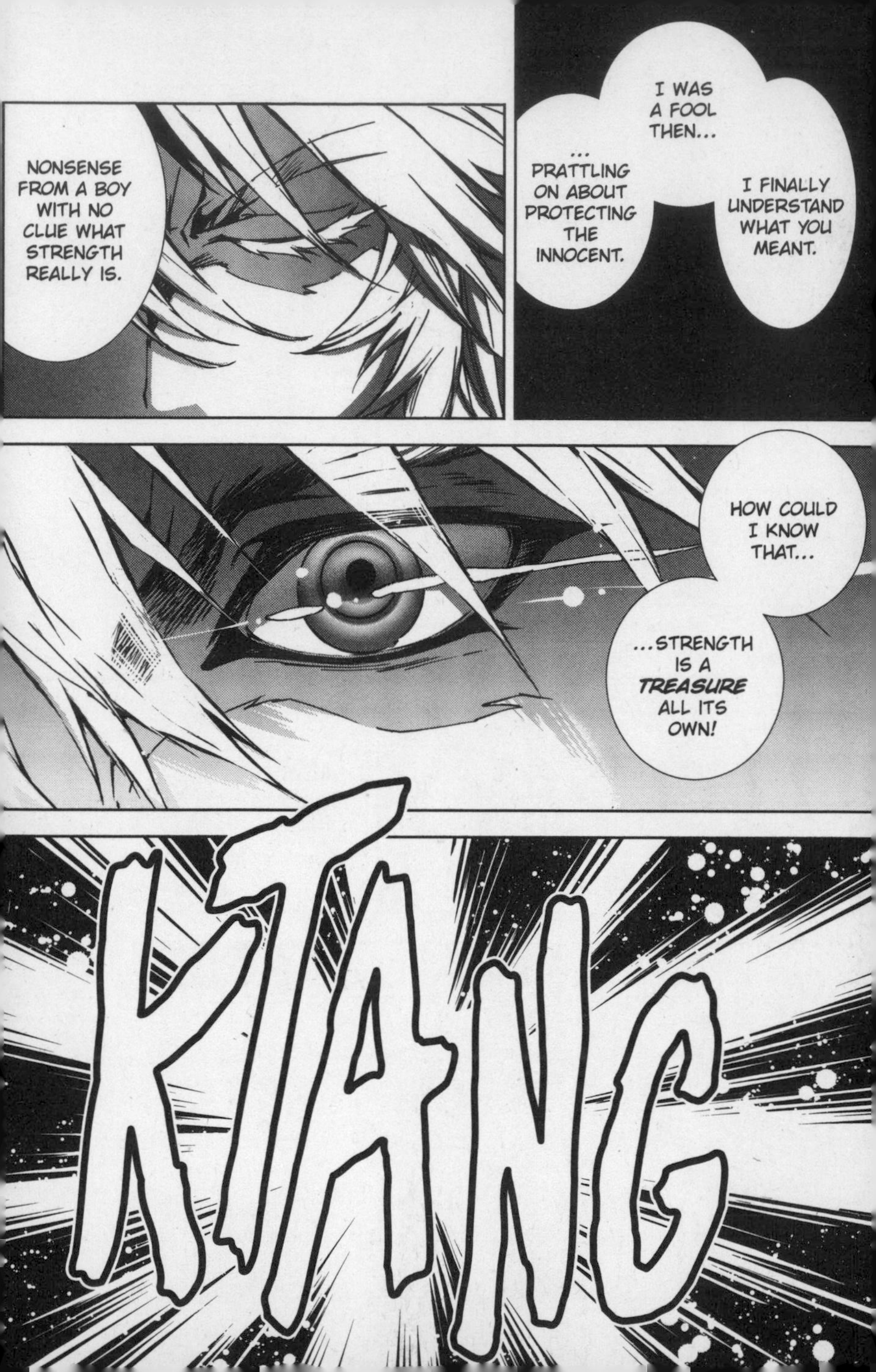
I WAS A FOOL THEN...
...PRATTLING ON ABOUT PROTECTING THE INNOCENT.
I FINALLY UNDERSTAND WHAT YOU MEANT.
NONSENSE FROM A BOY WITH NO CLUE WHAT STRENGTH REALLY IS.
HOW COULD I KNOW THAT...
...STRENGTH IS A *TREASURE* ALL ITS OWN!
KTANG

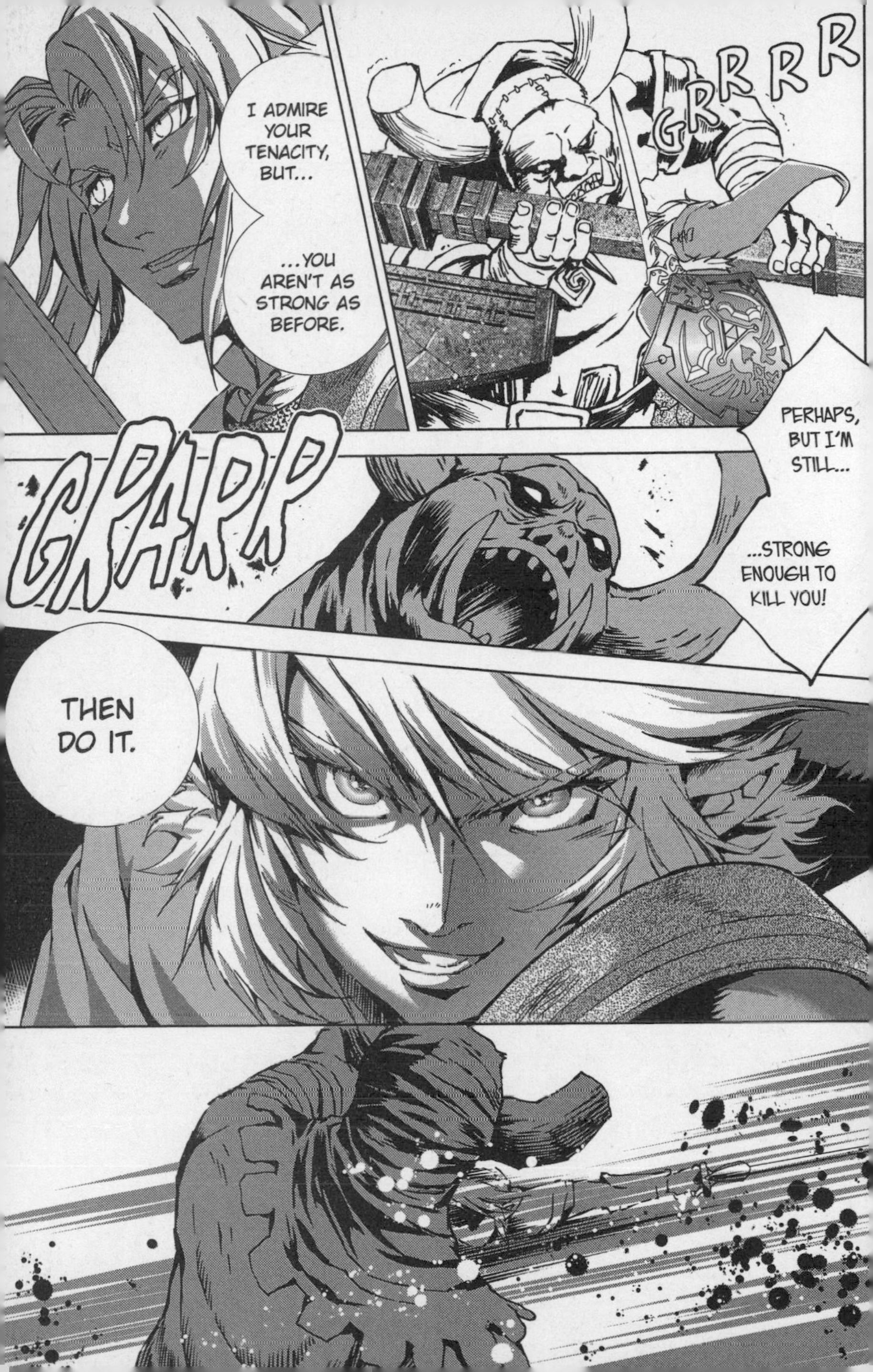
GRRRR
I ADMIRE YOUR TENACITY, BUT...
...YOU AREN'T AS STRONG AS BEFORE.
PERHAPS, BUT I'M STILL...
...STRONG ENOUGH TO KILL YOU!
GRAPP
THEN DO IT.

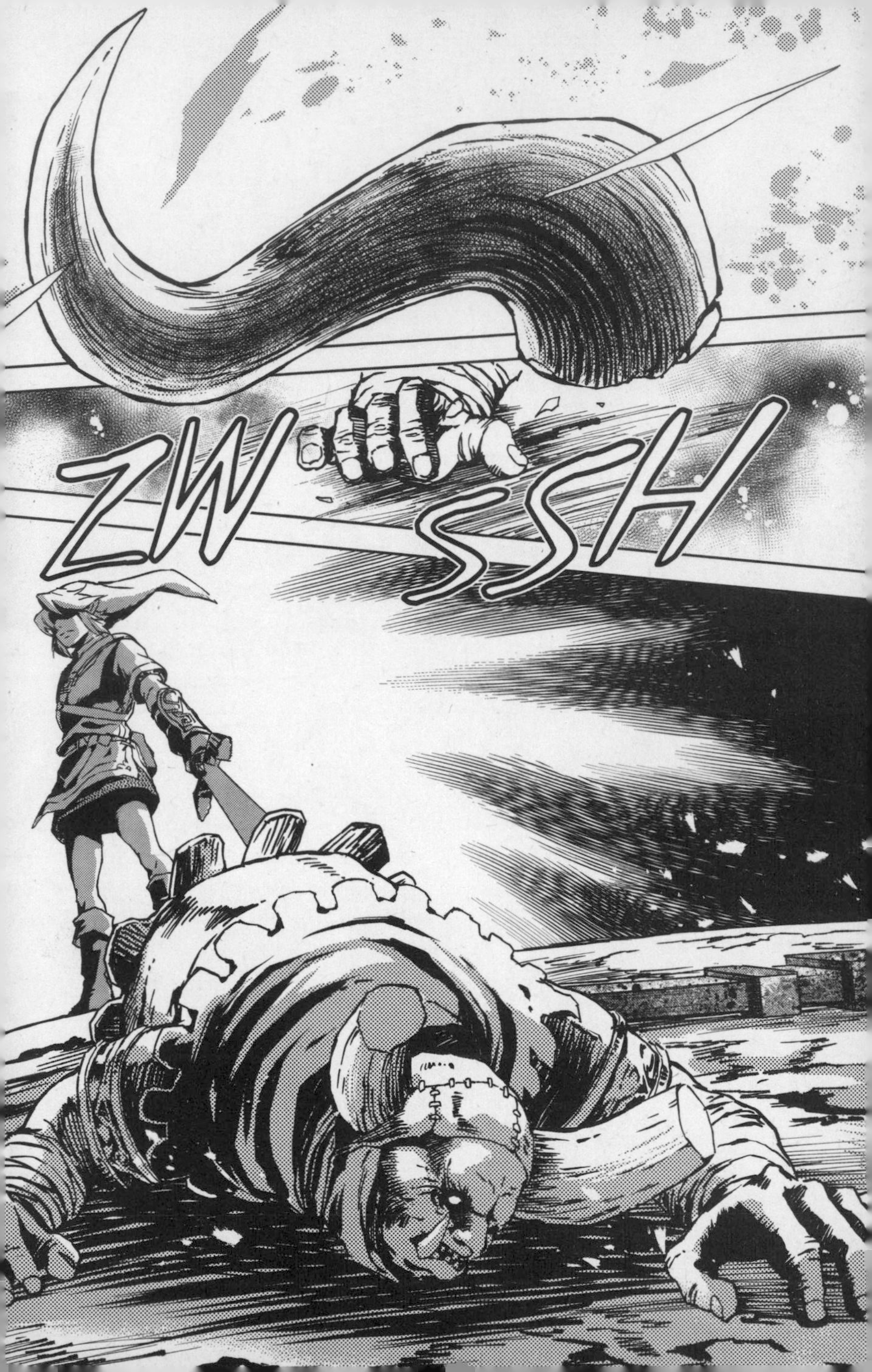
ZWSSH

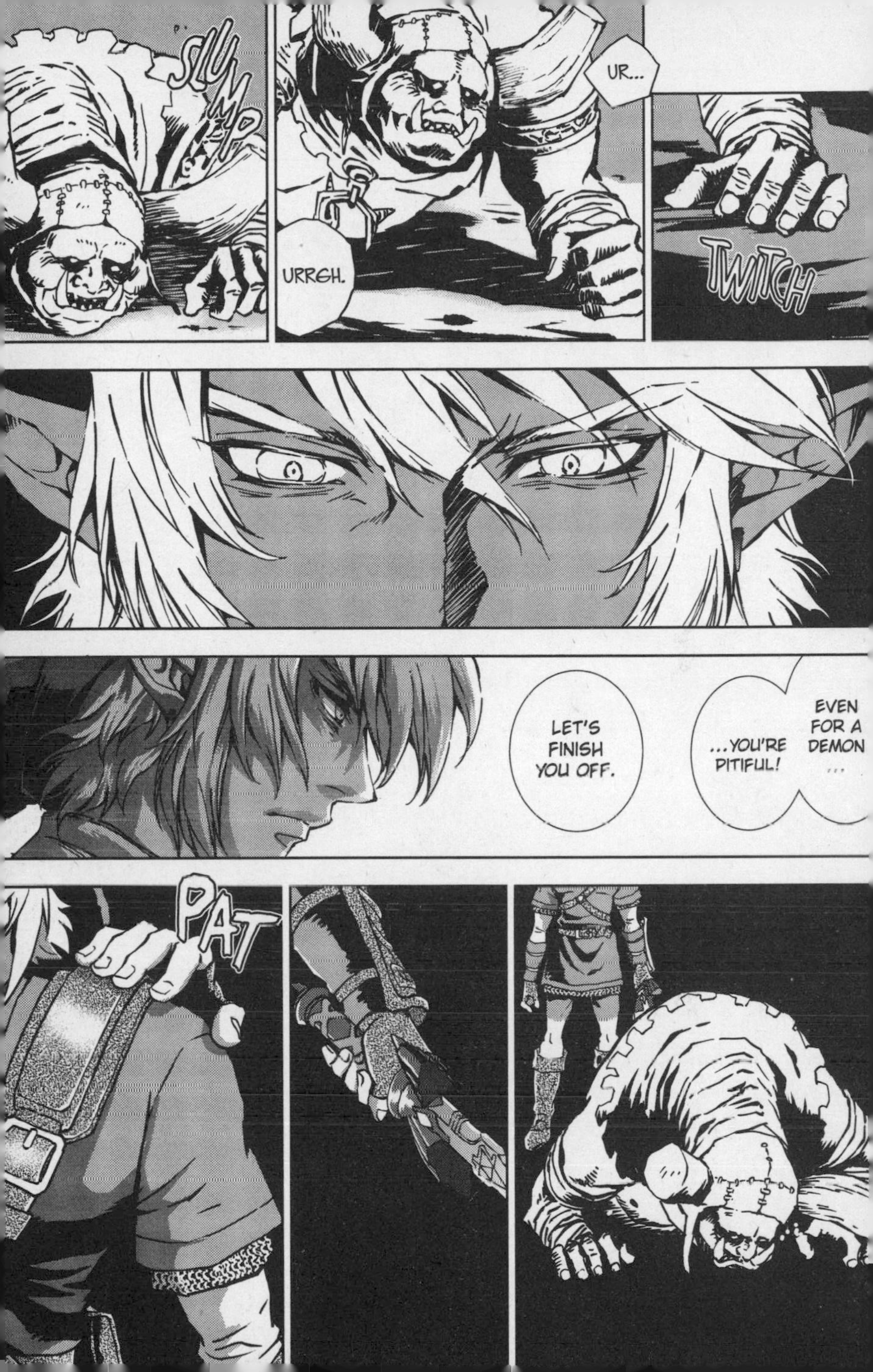
TWITCH
UR...
URRGH.
SLUMP
EVEN FOR A DEMON ...
...YOU'RE PITIFUL!
LET'S FINISH YOU OFF.
PAT

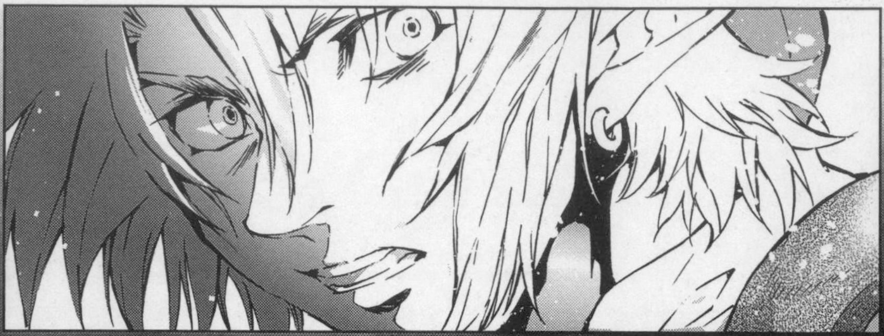
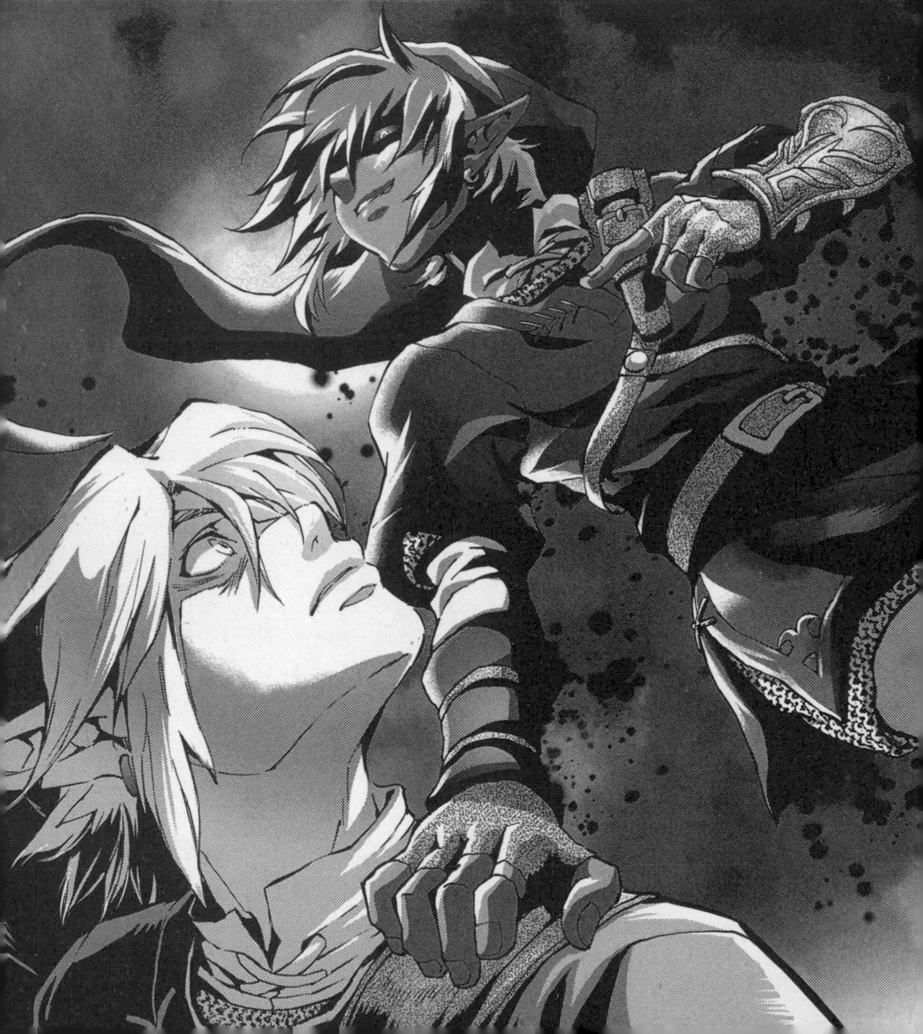

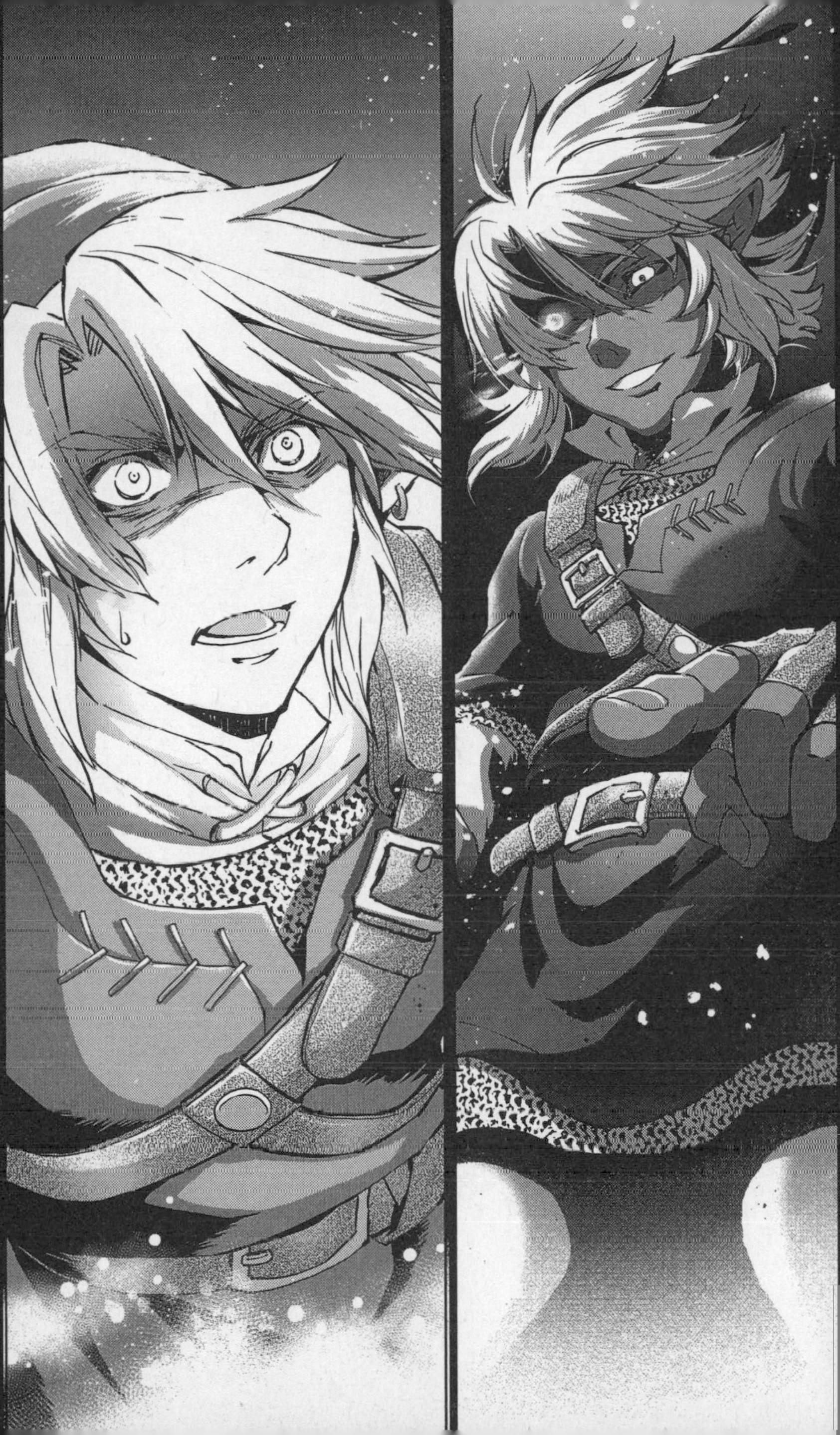

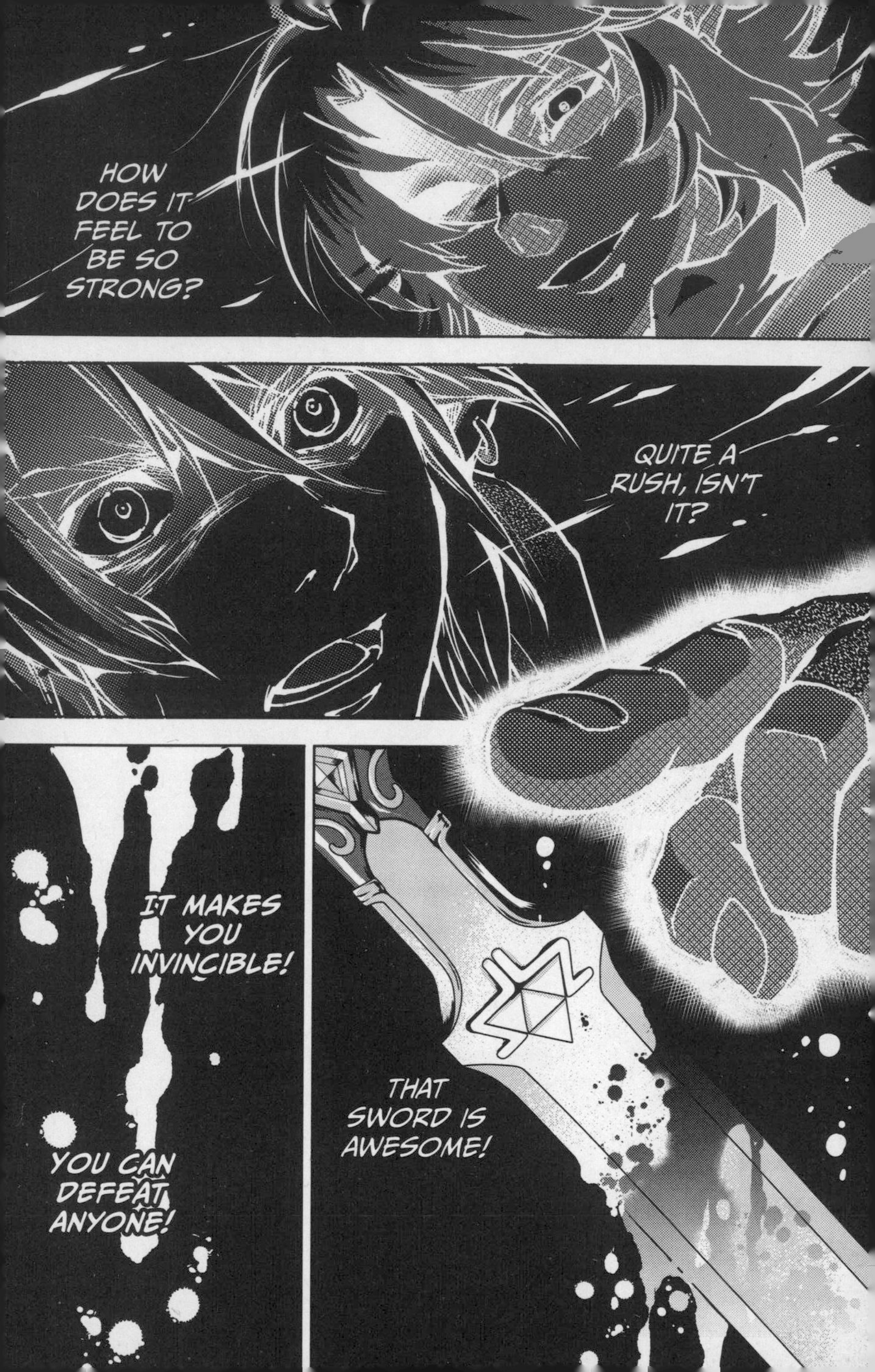
HOW DOES IT FEEL TO BE SO STRONG?
QUITE A RUSH, ISN'T IT?
THAT SWORD IS AWESOME!
IT MAKES YOU INVINCIBLE!
YOU CAN DEFEAT ANYONE!

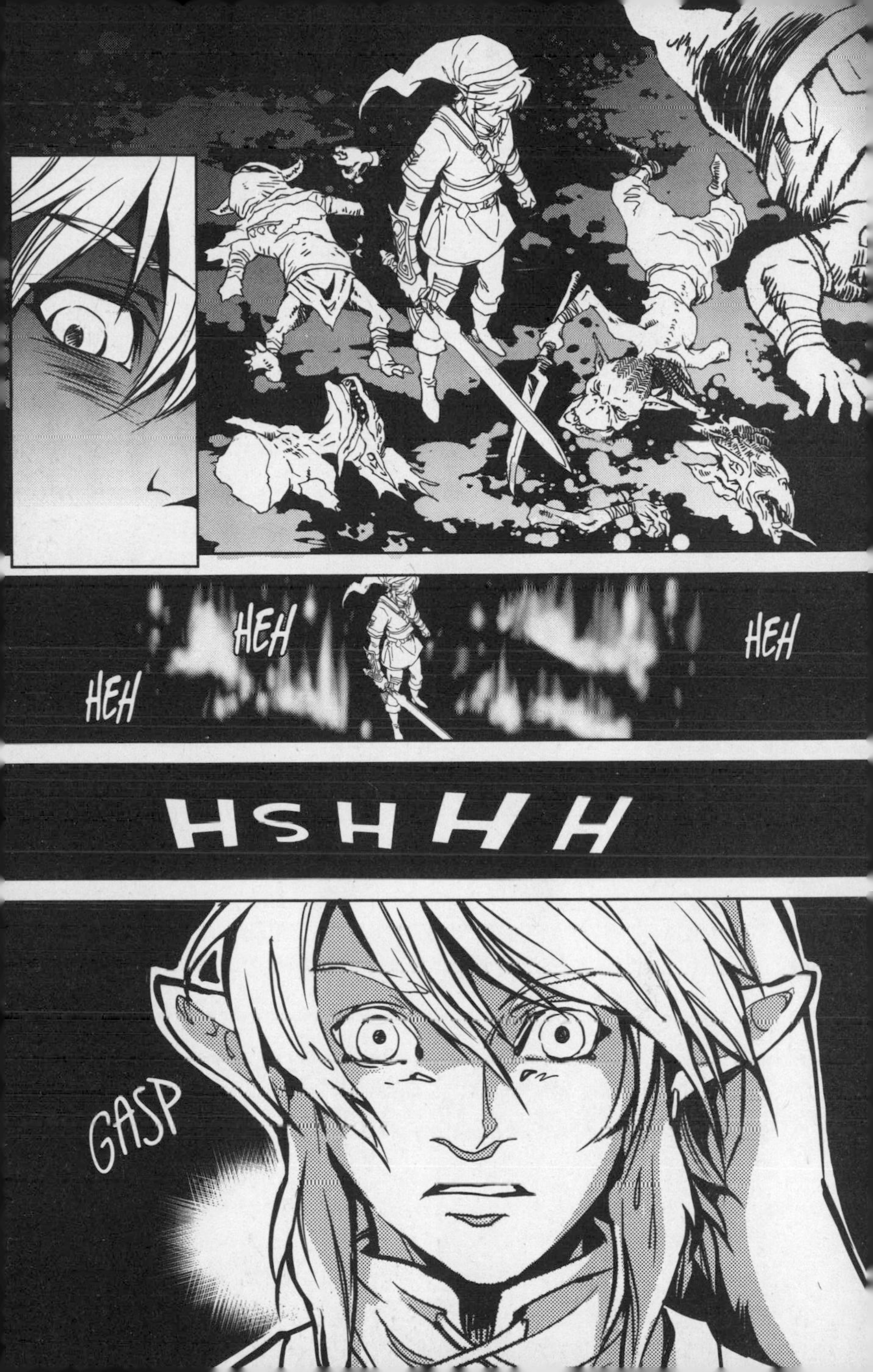
HEH
HEH
HEH
HSHHH
GASP

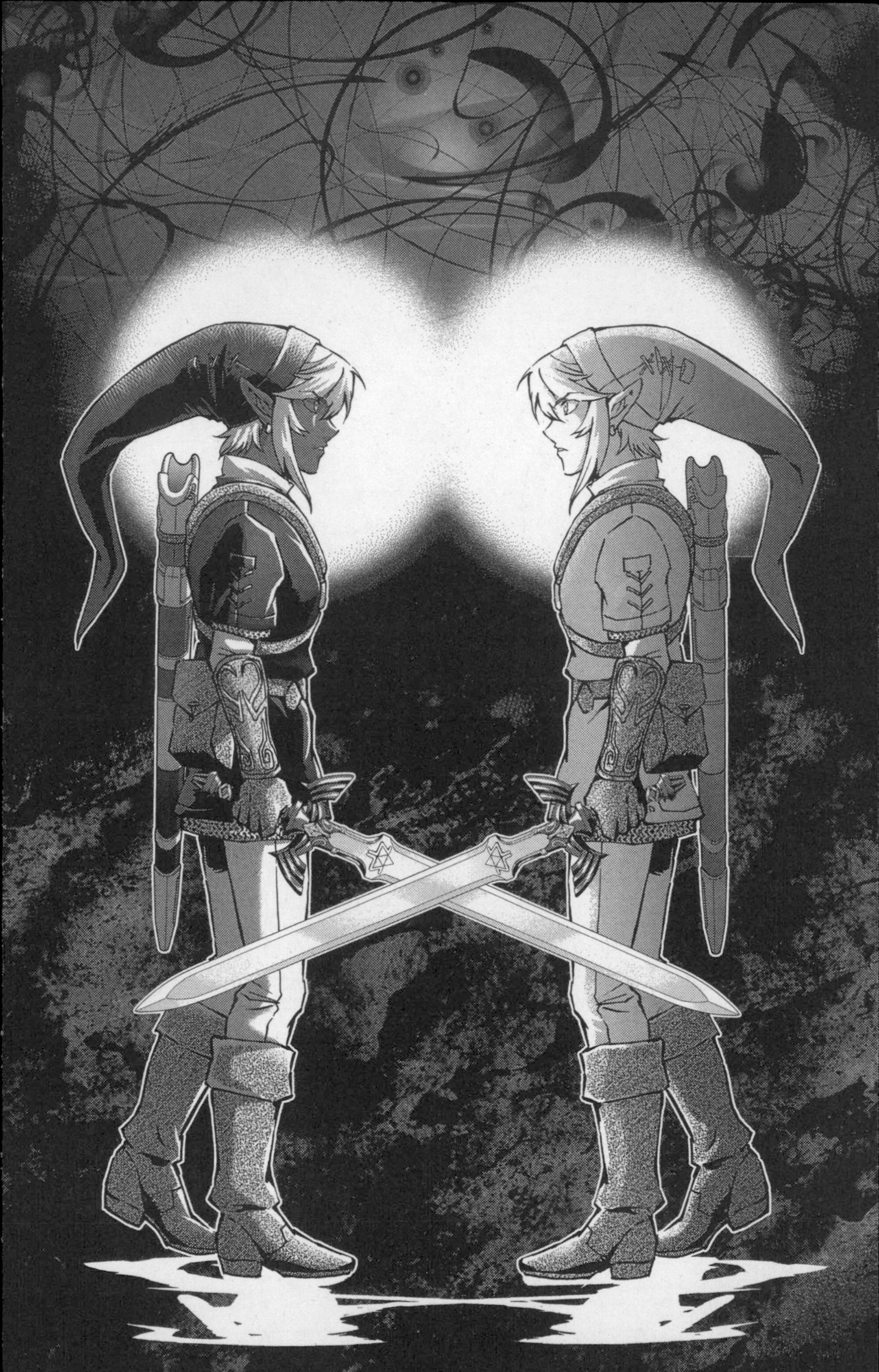

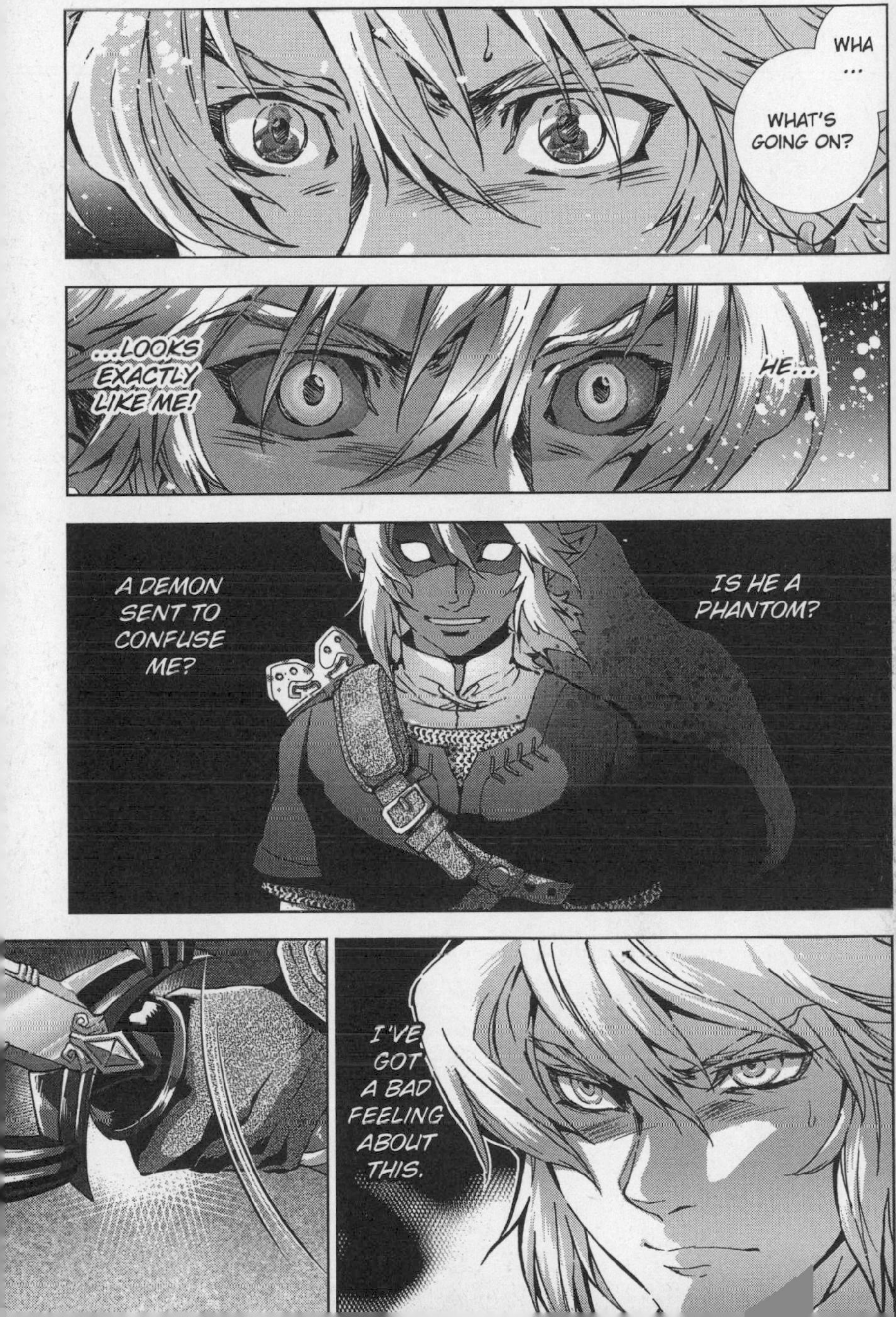
WHA ... WHAT'S GOING ON?
HE...
...LOOKS EXACTLY LIKE ME!
IS HE A PHANTOM?
A DEMON SENT TO CONFUSE ME?
I'VE GOT A BAD FEELING ABOUT THIS.

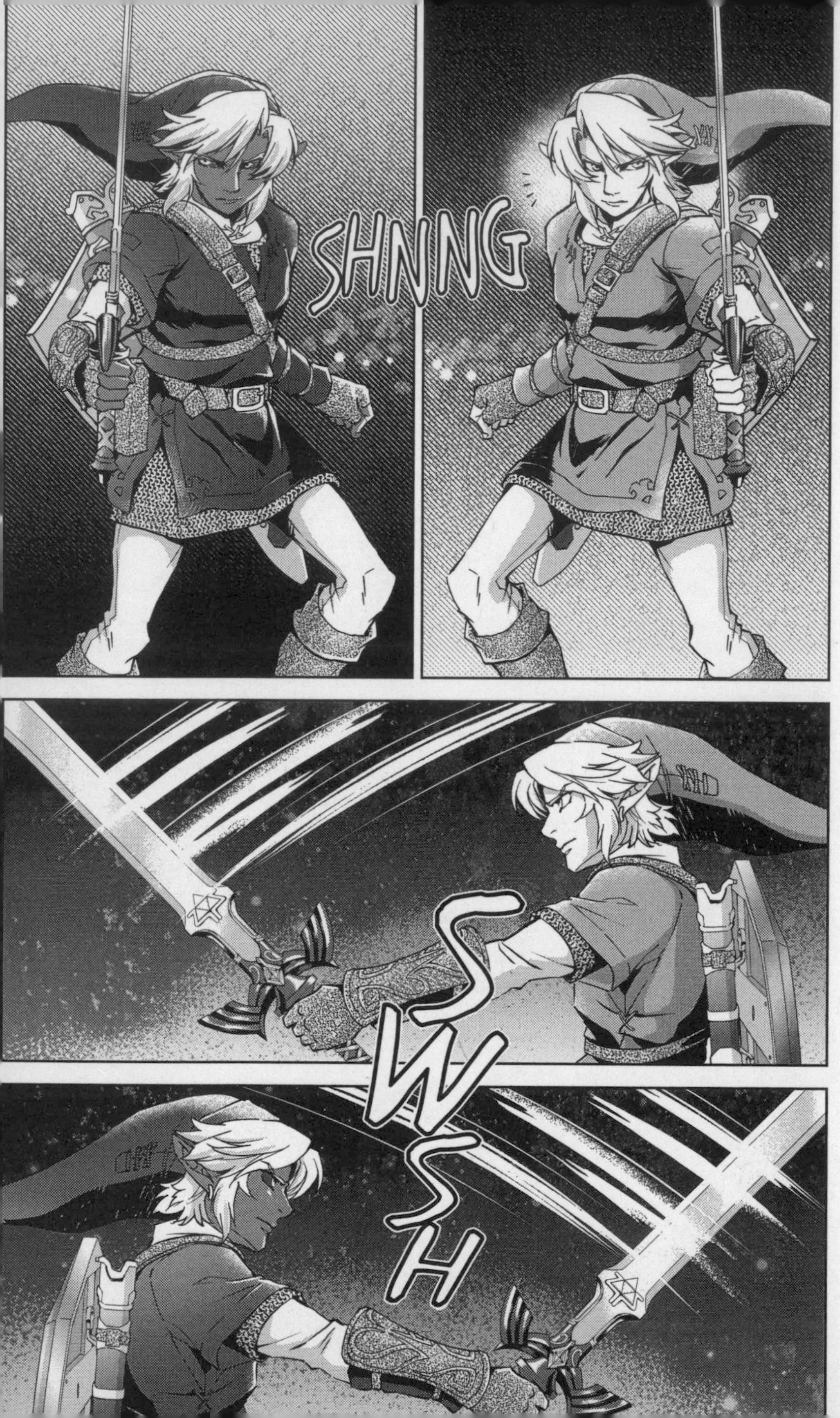
SHNNG
SWISH

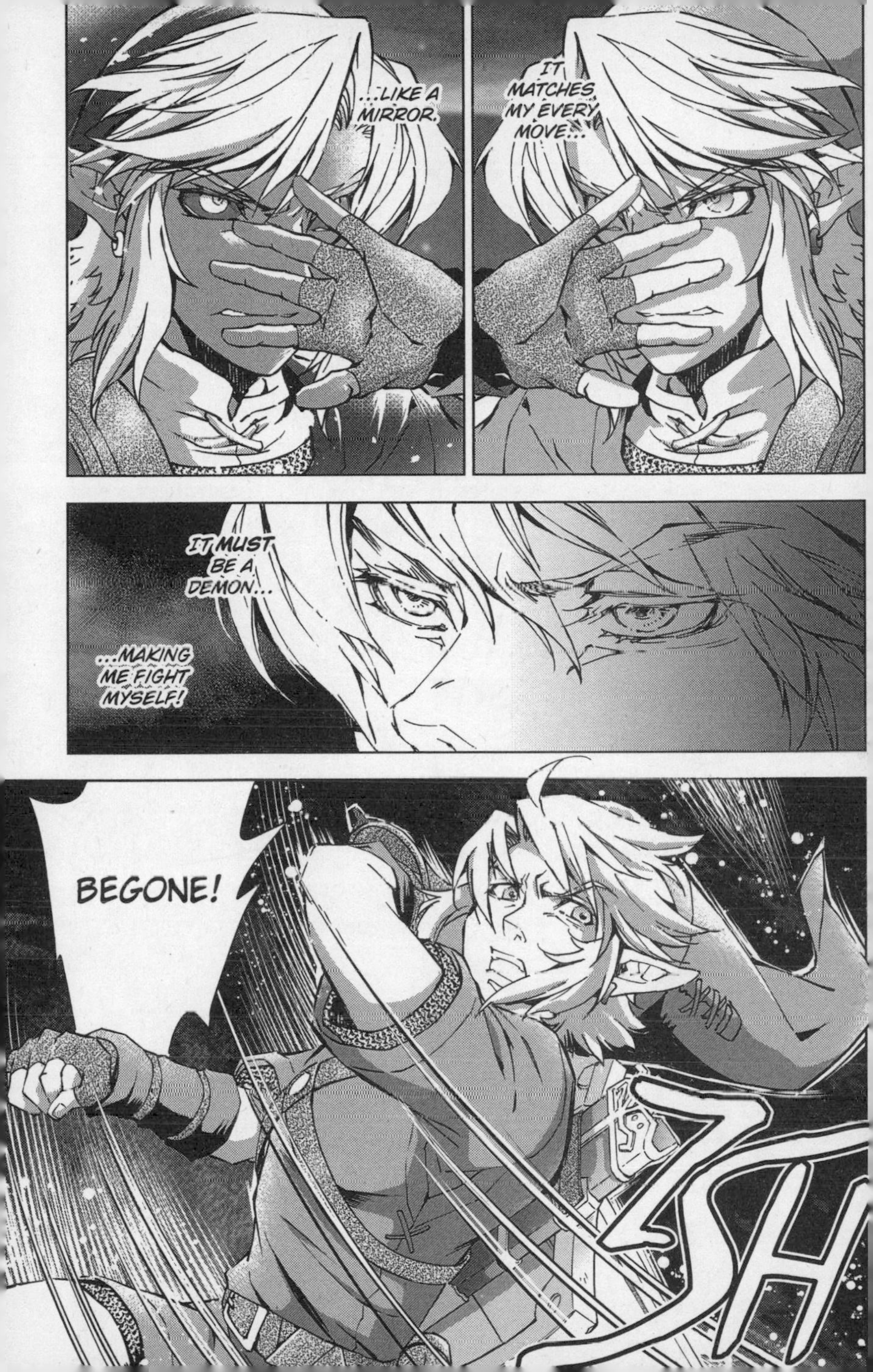
IT MATCHES MY EVERY MOVE...
...LIKE A MIRROR.
IT MUST BE A DEMON...
...MAKING ME FIGHT MYSELF!
BEGONE!
ZSH

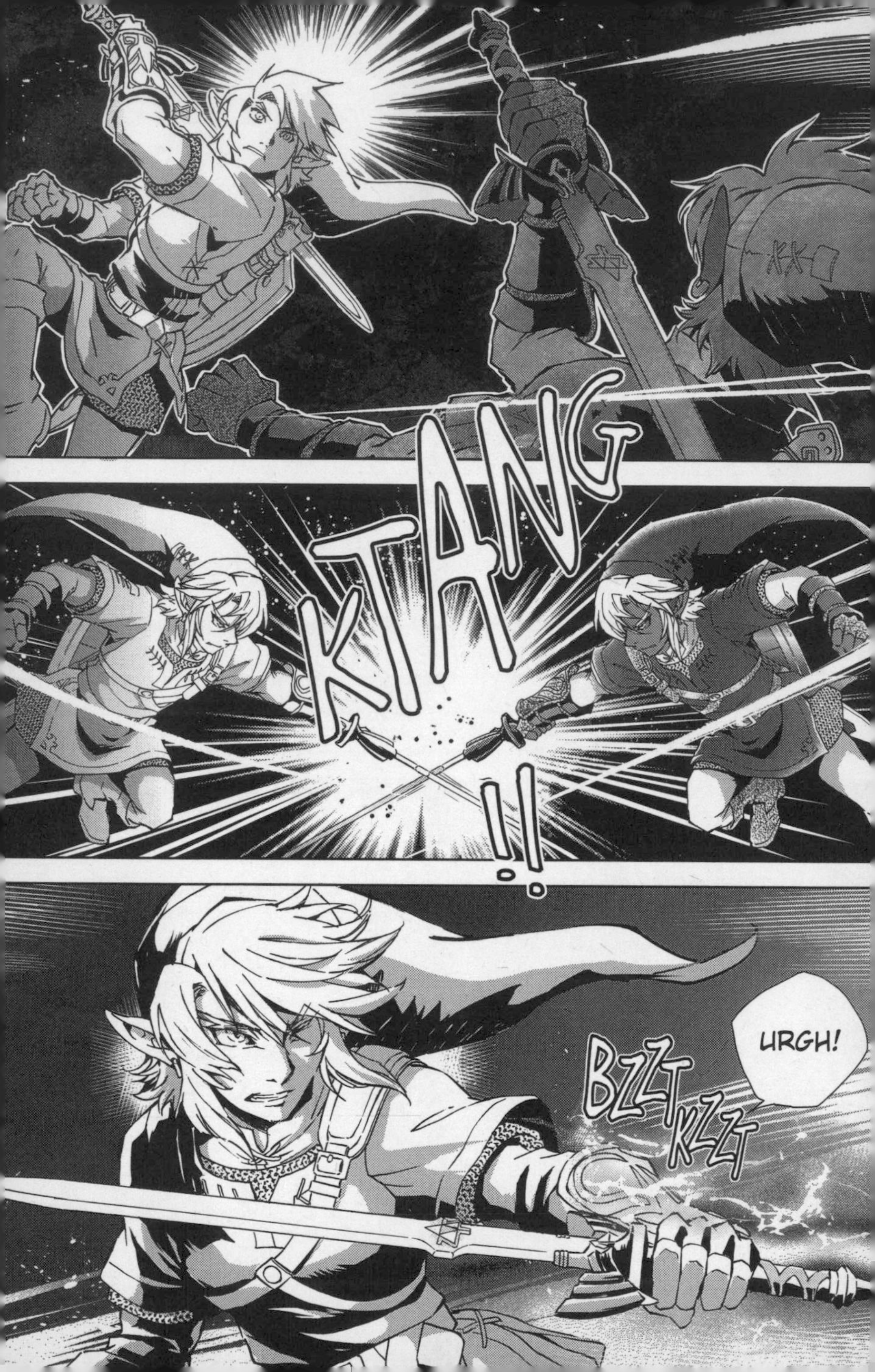
KTANG!!
URGH!
BZZT KZZT

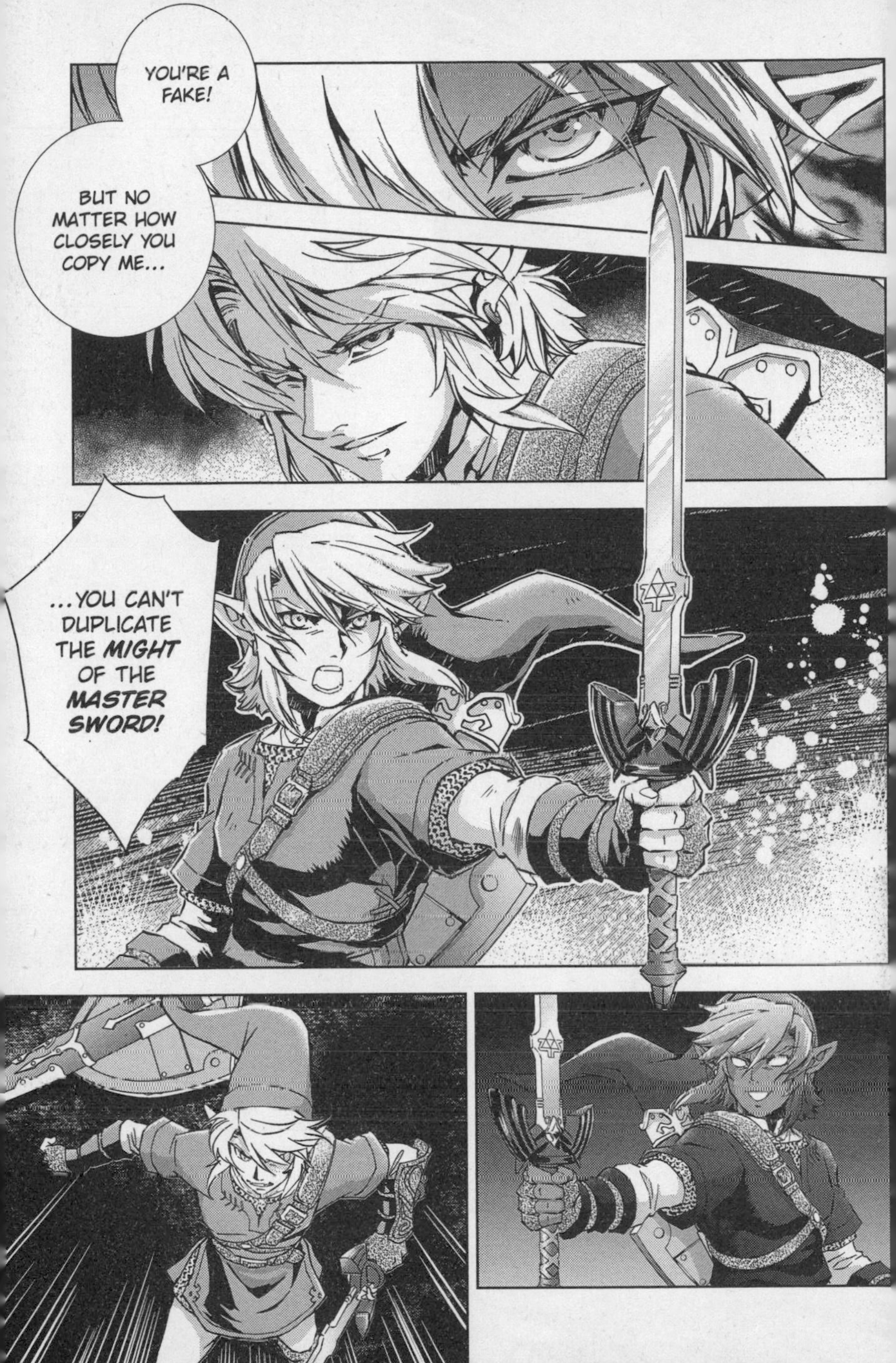
YOU'RE A FAKE!
BUT NO MATTER HOW CLOSELY YOU COPY ME...
...YOU CAN'T DUPLICATE THE *MIGHT* OF THE *MASTER SWORD!*

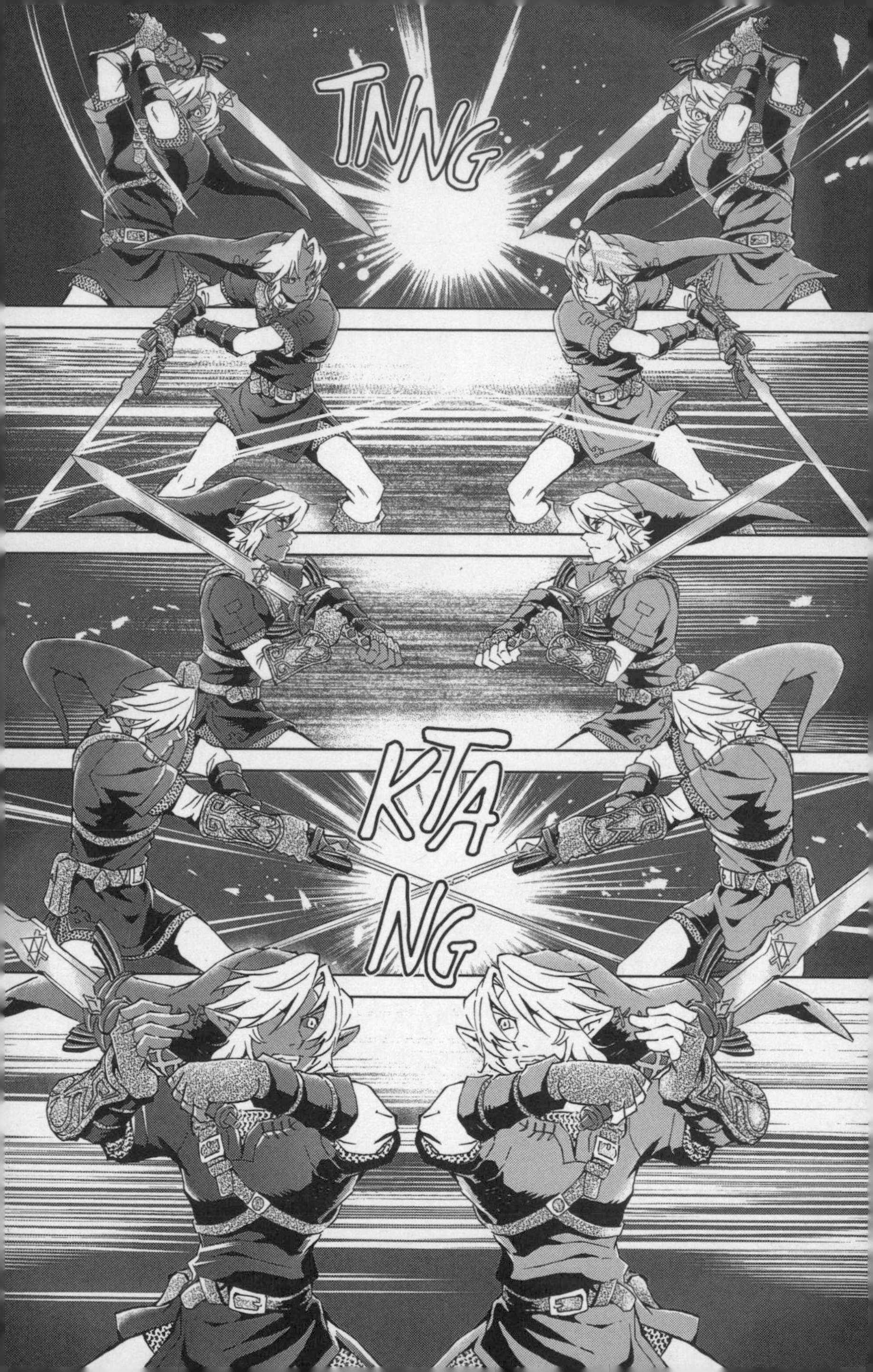
TNNG
KTANG

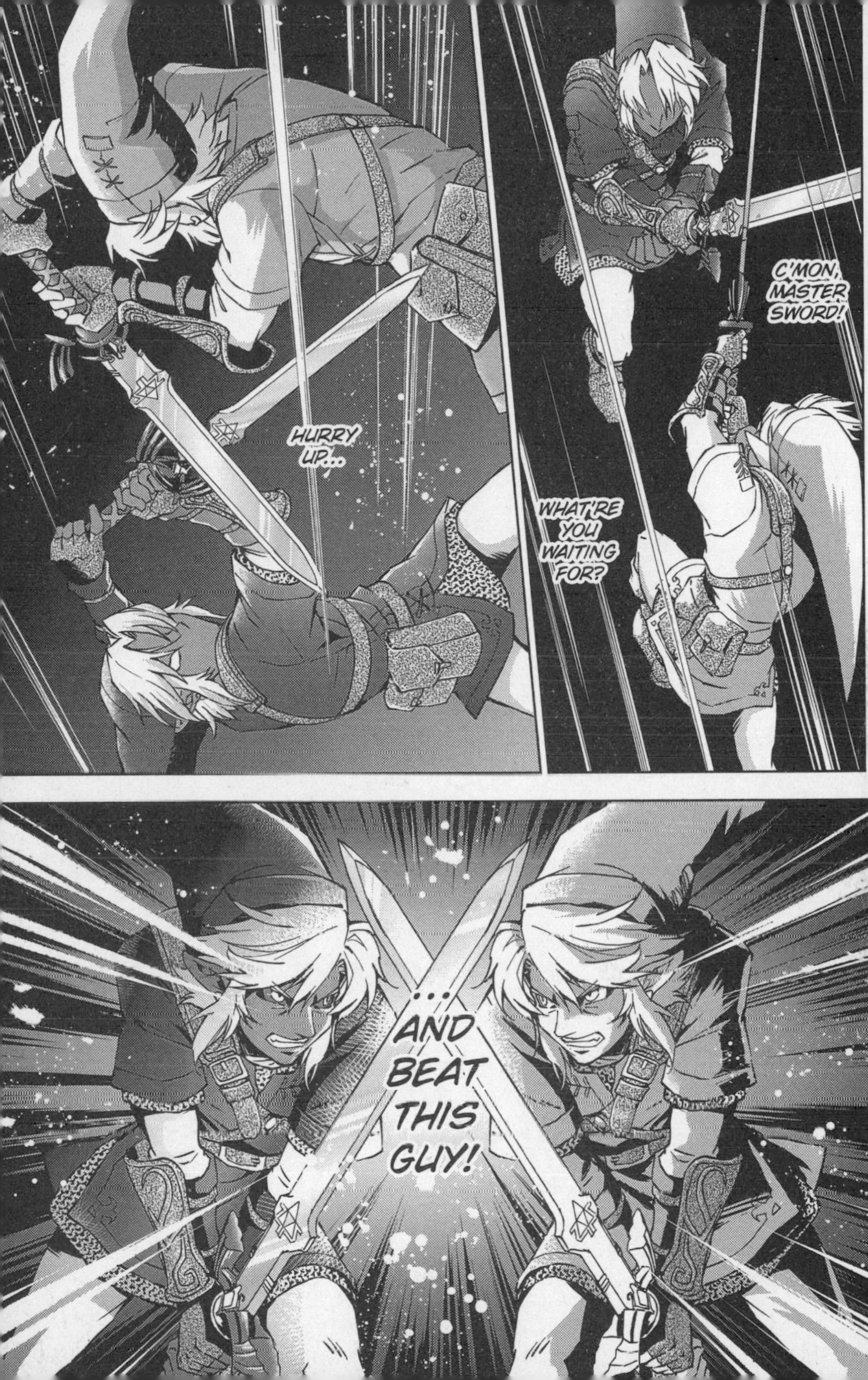
C'MON, MASTER SWORD!
WHAT'RE YOU WAITING FOR?
HURRY UP...
...AND BEAT THIS GUY!

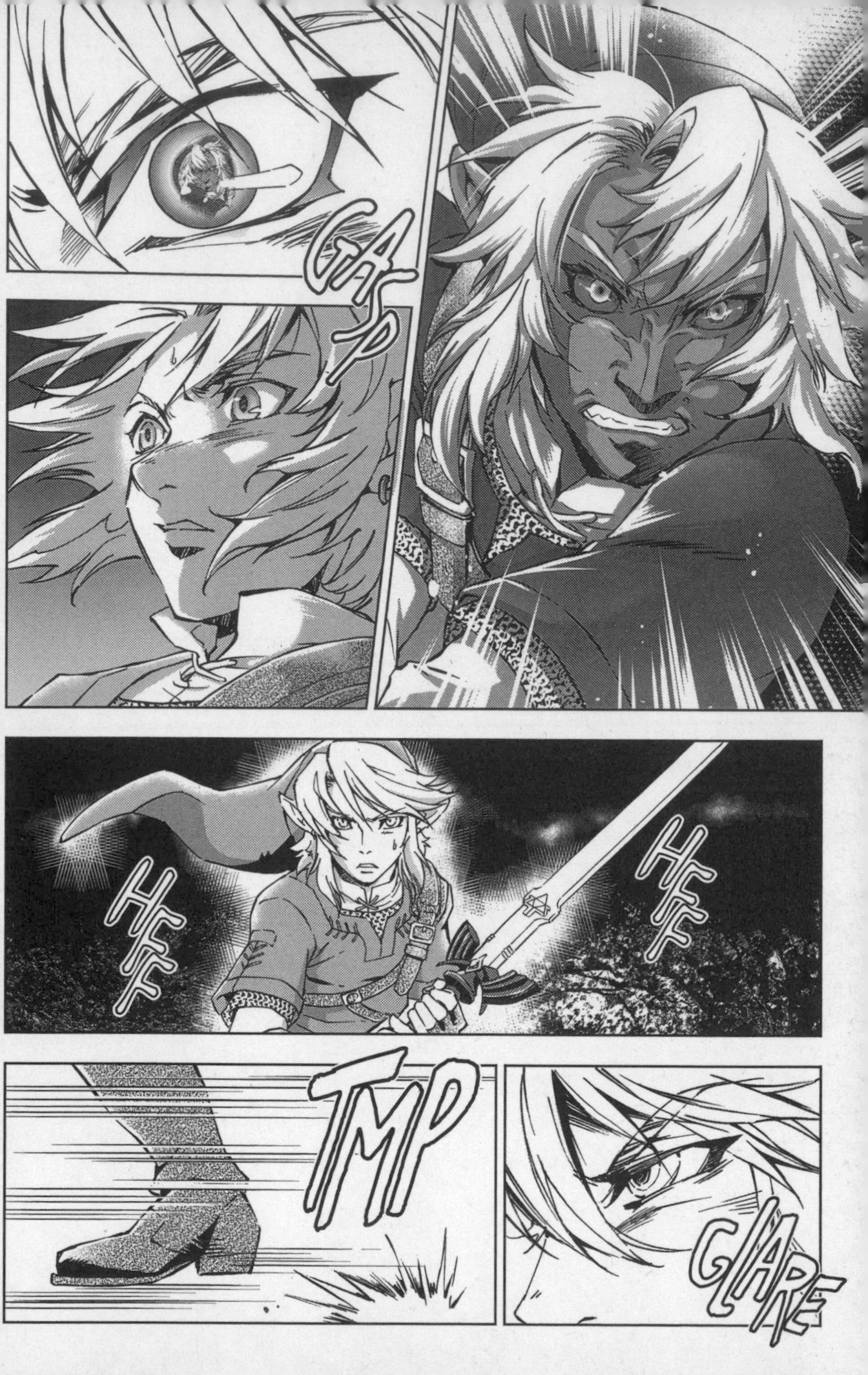
GASP
HUFF
HUFF
GLARE
TMP

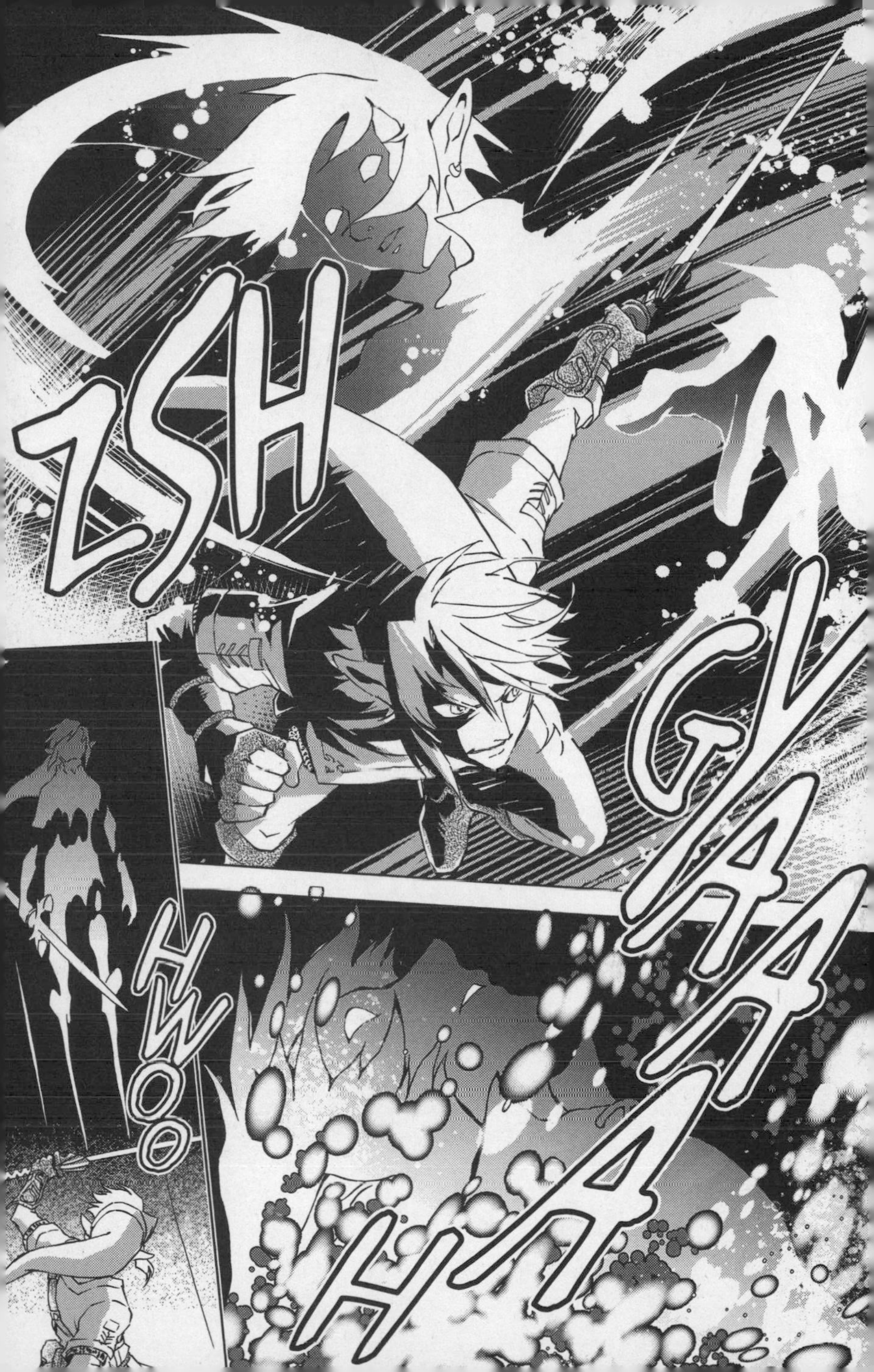
ZSH
GYAAAA
AAH
HWOO

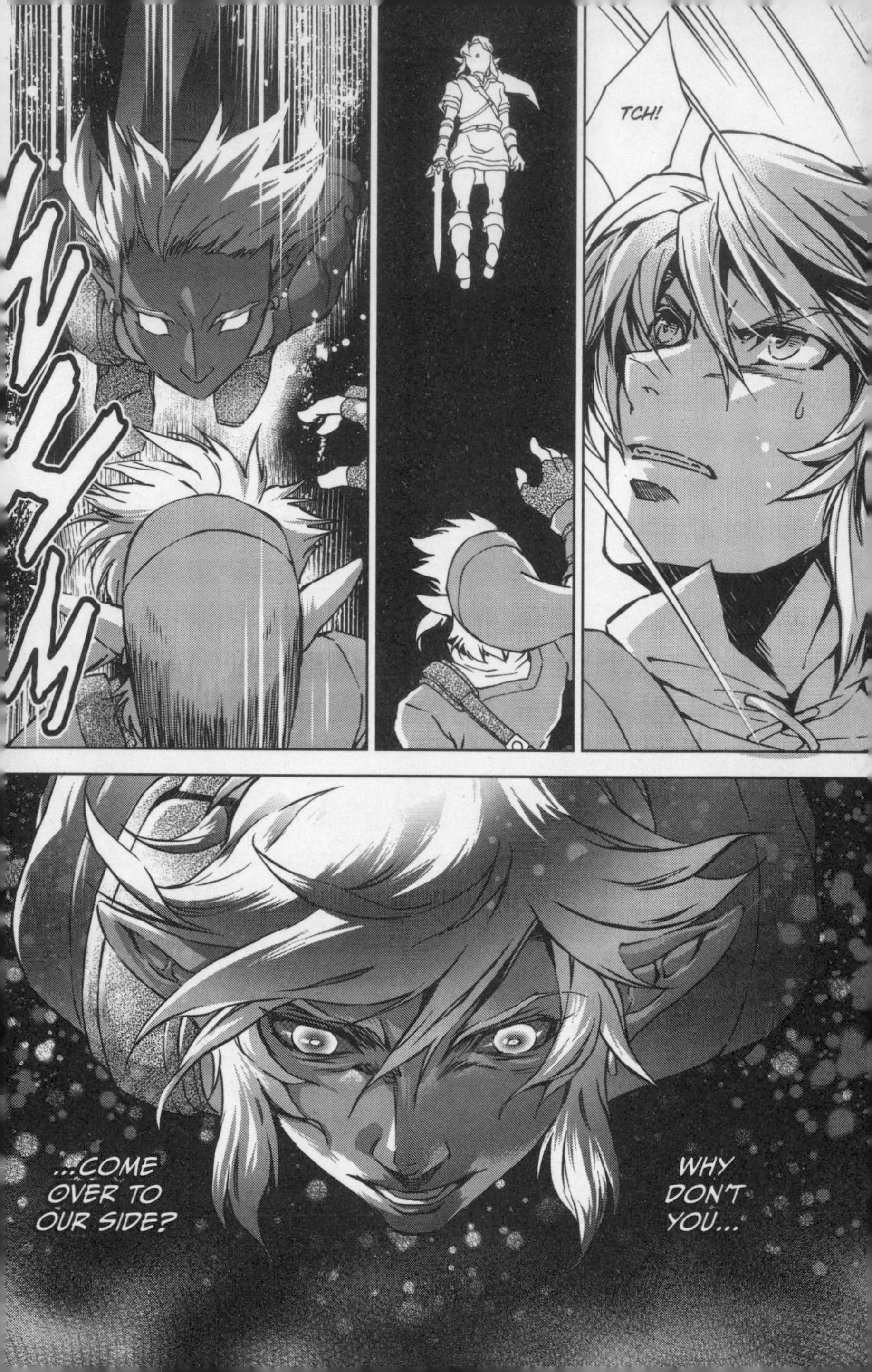
TCH!
WHY DON'T YOU...
...COME OVER TO OUR SIDE?

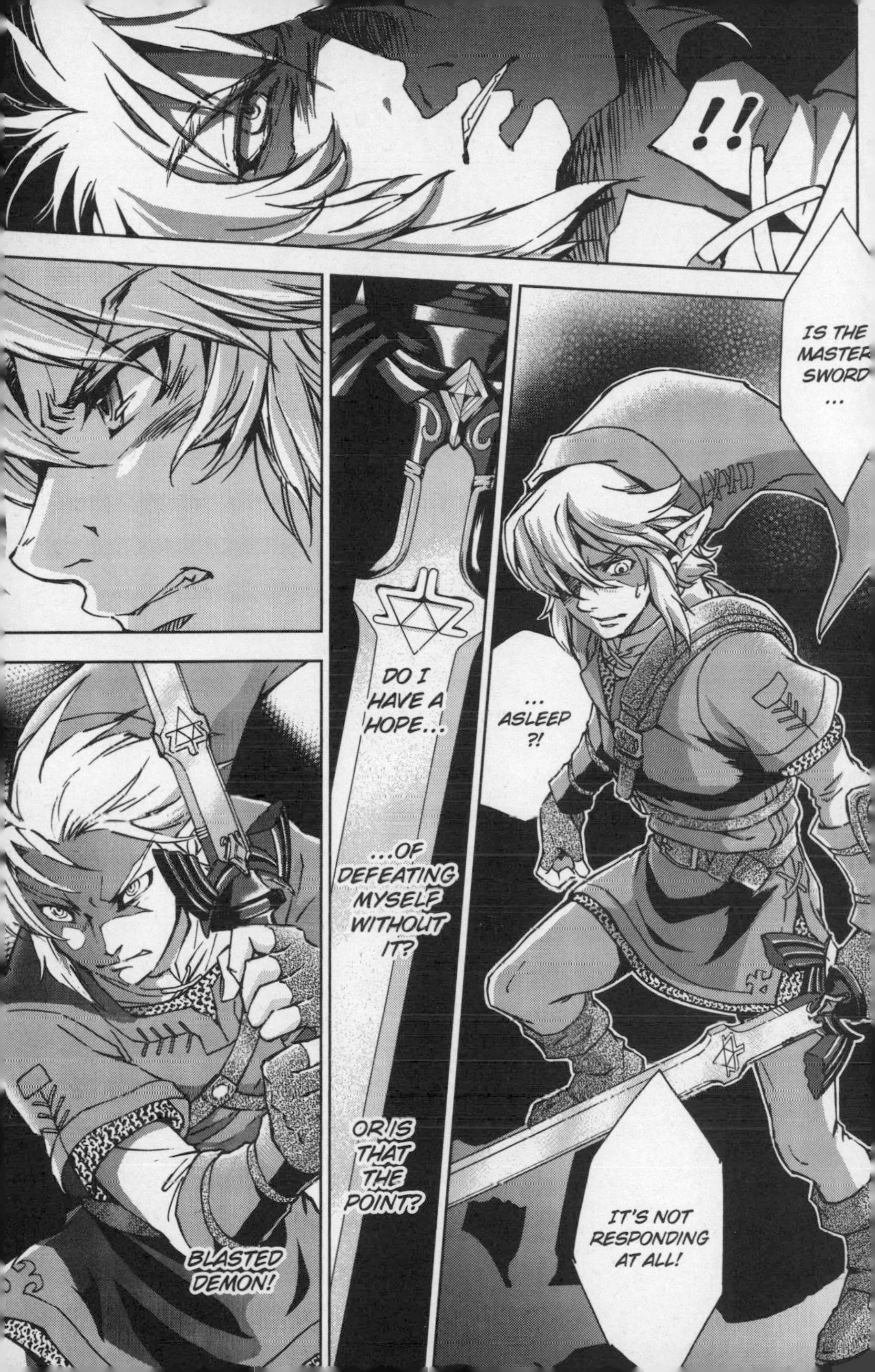
!!
IS THE MASTER SWORD ...
... ASLEEP ?!
IT'S NOT RESPONDING AT ALL!
DO I HAVE A HOPE...
...OF DEFEATING MYSELF WITHOUT IT?
OR IS THAT THE POINT?
BLASTED DEMON!

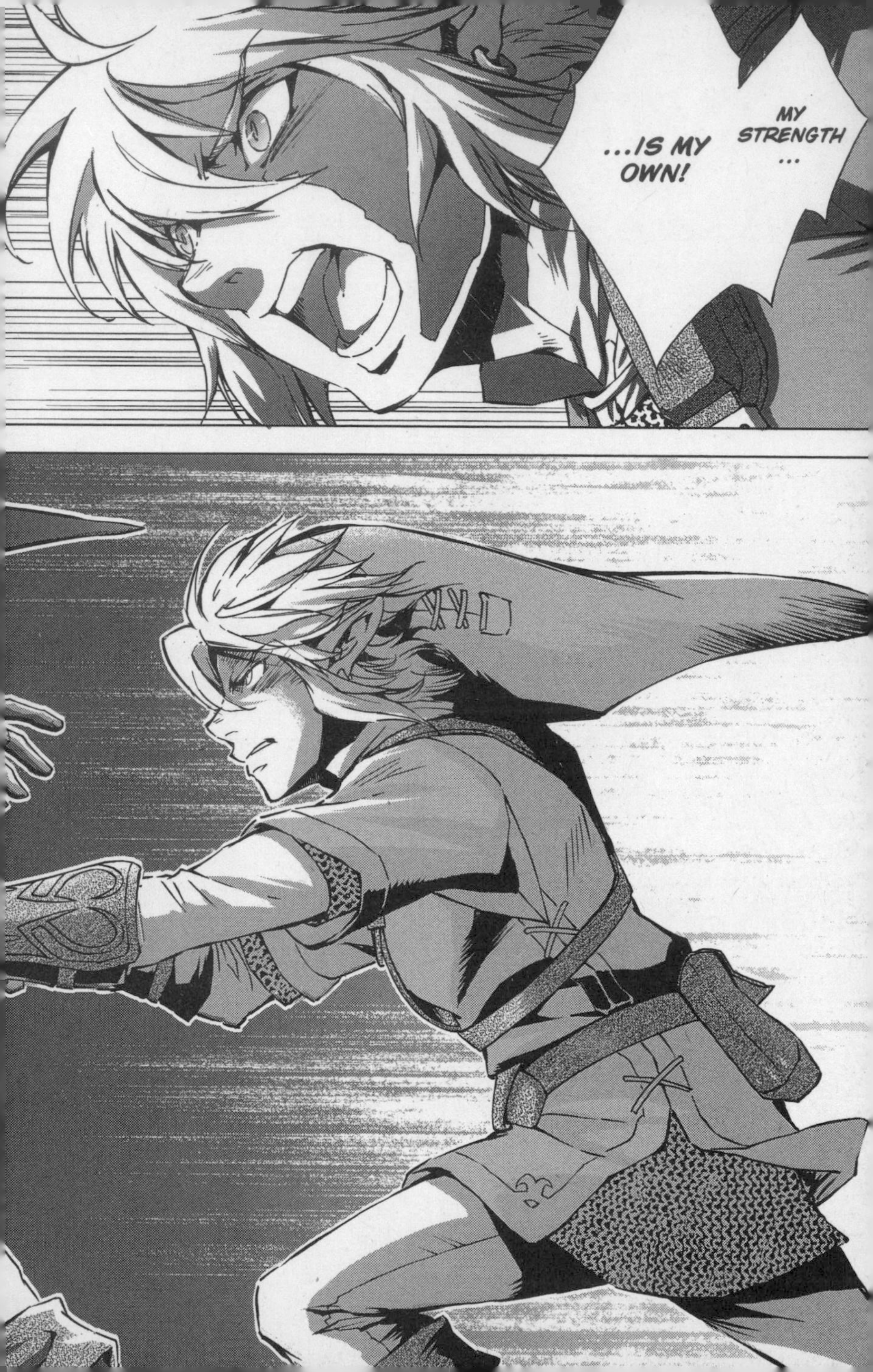
MY STRENGTH ...
...IS MY OWN!

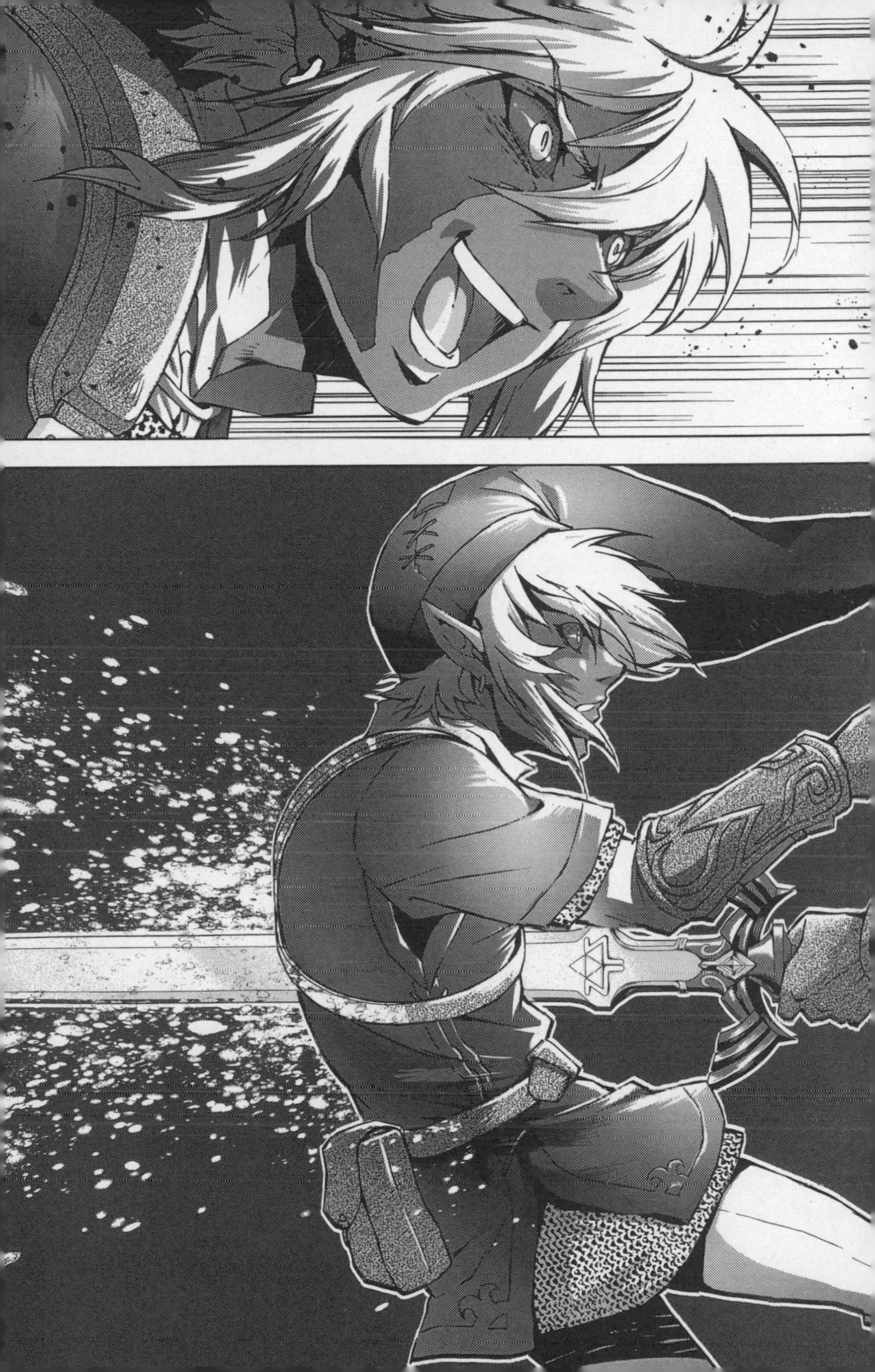

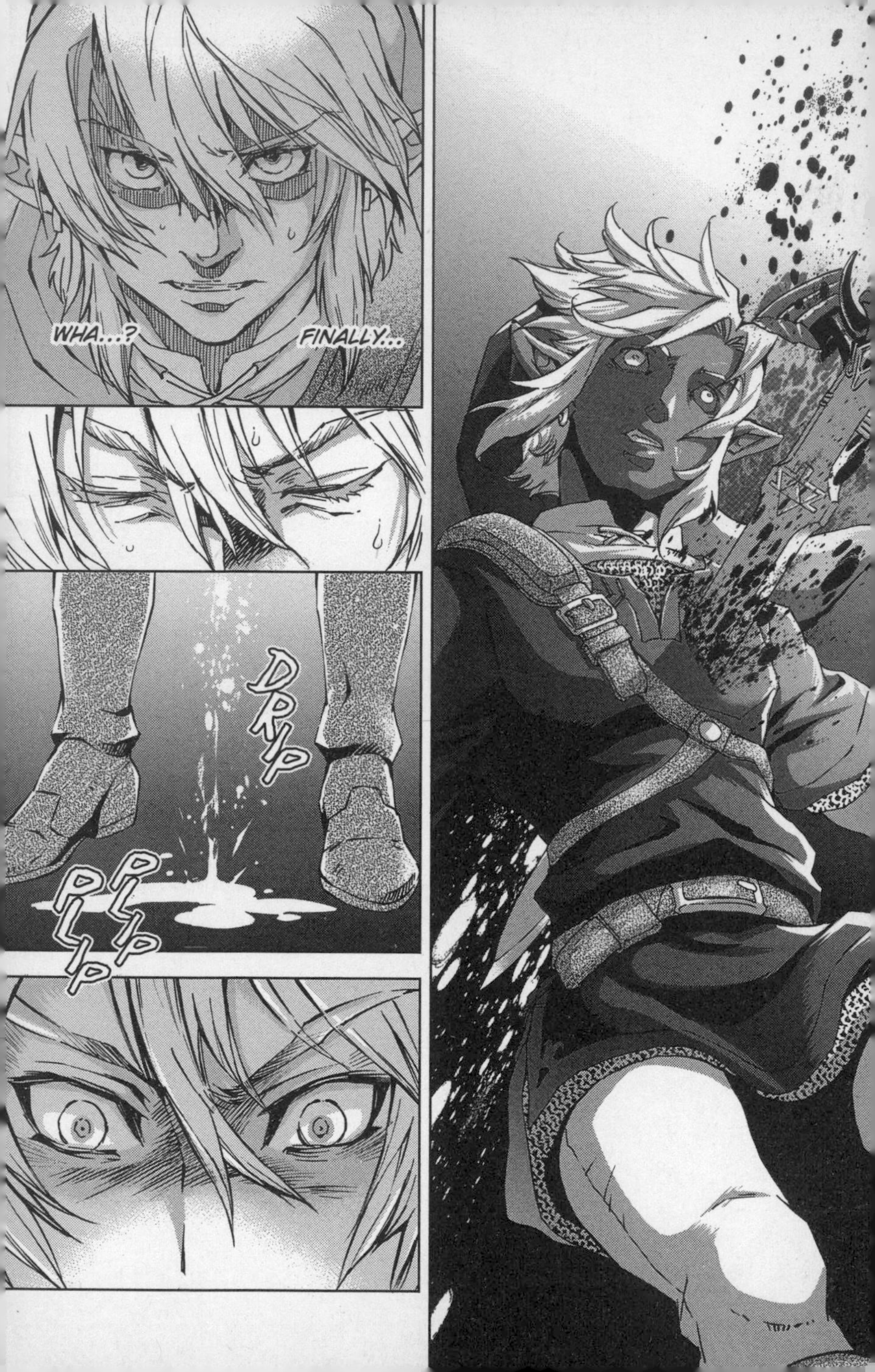
FINALLY...
WHA...?
DRIP
PLIP
PLIP

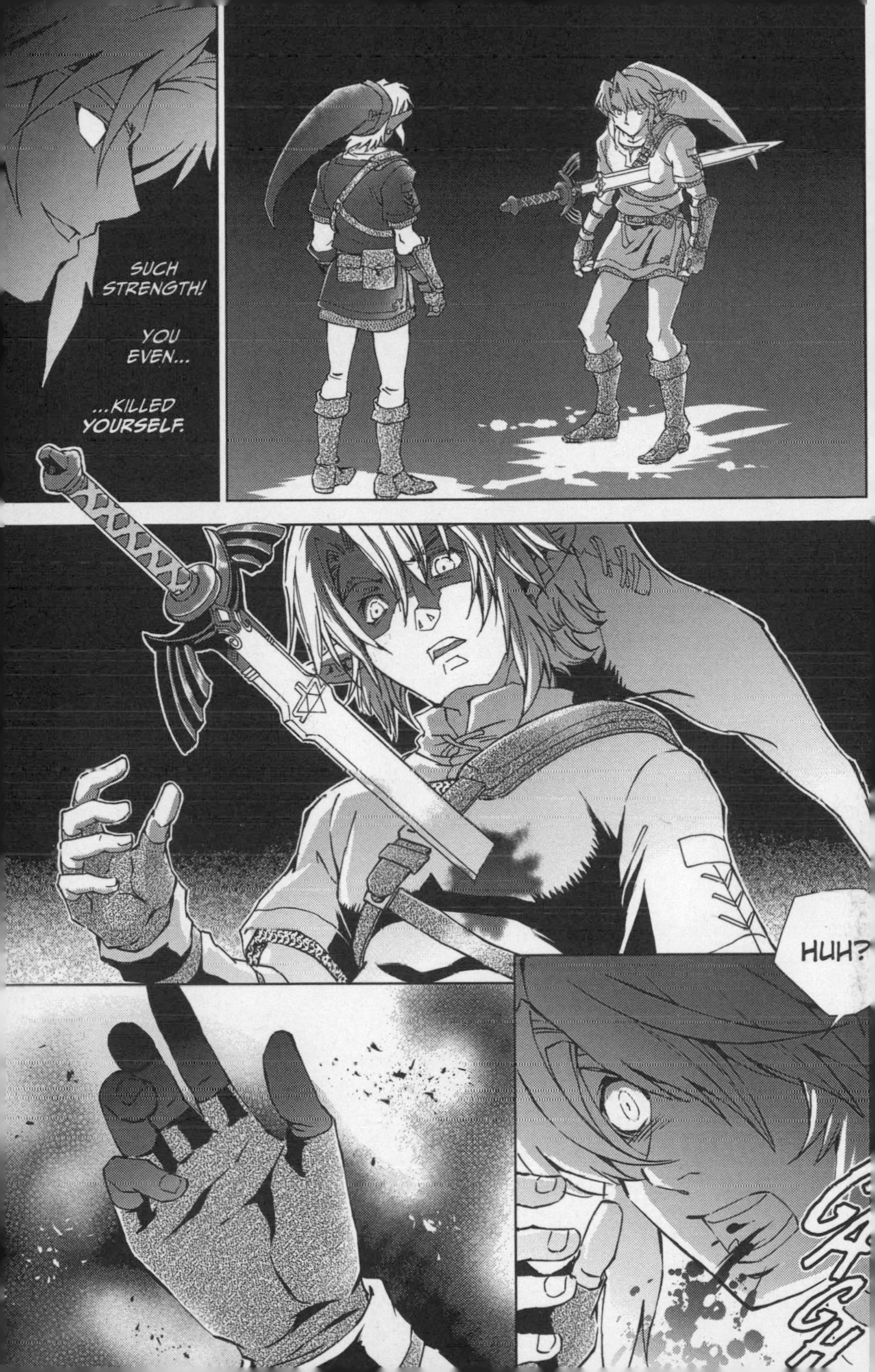
SUCH STRENGTH!
YOU EVEN...
...KILLED YOURSELF.
HUH?
GAHGH

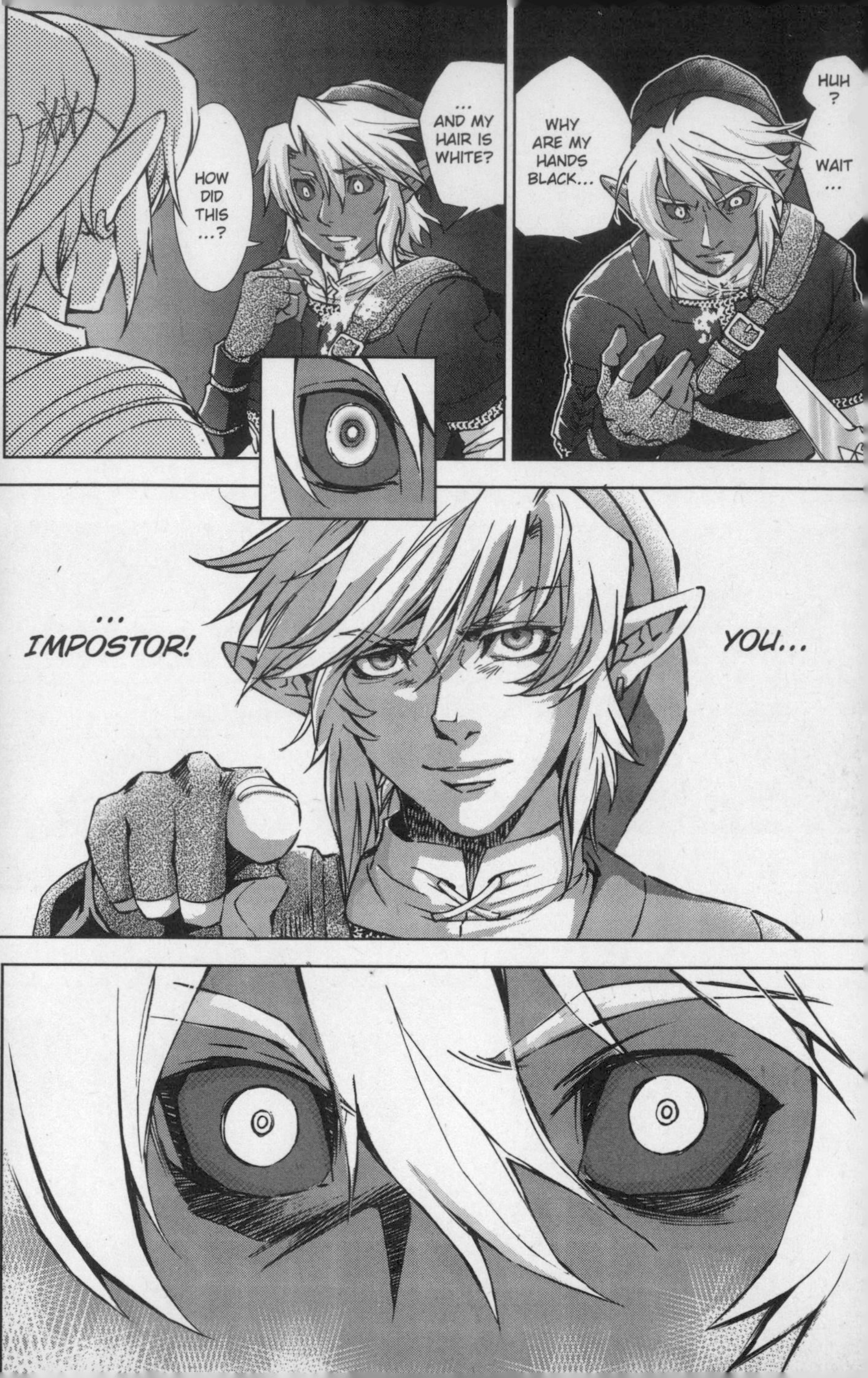
HUH?
WAIT...
WHY ARE MY HANDS BLACK...
... AND MY HAIR IS WHITE?
HOW DID THIS ...?
YOU...
... IMPOSTOR!

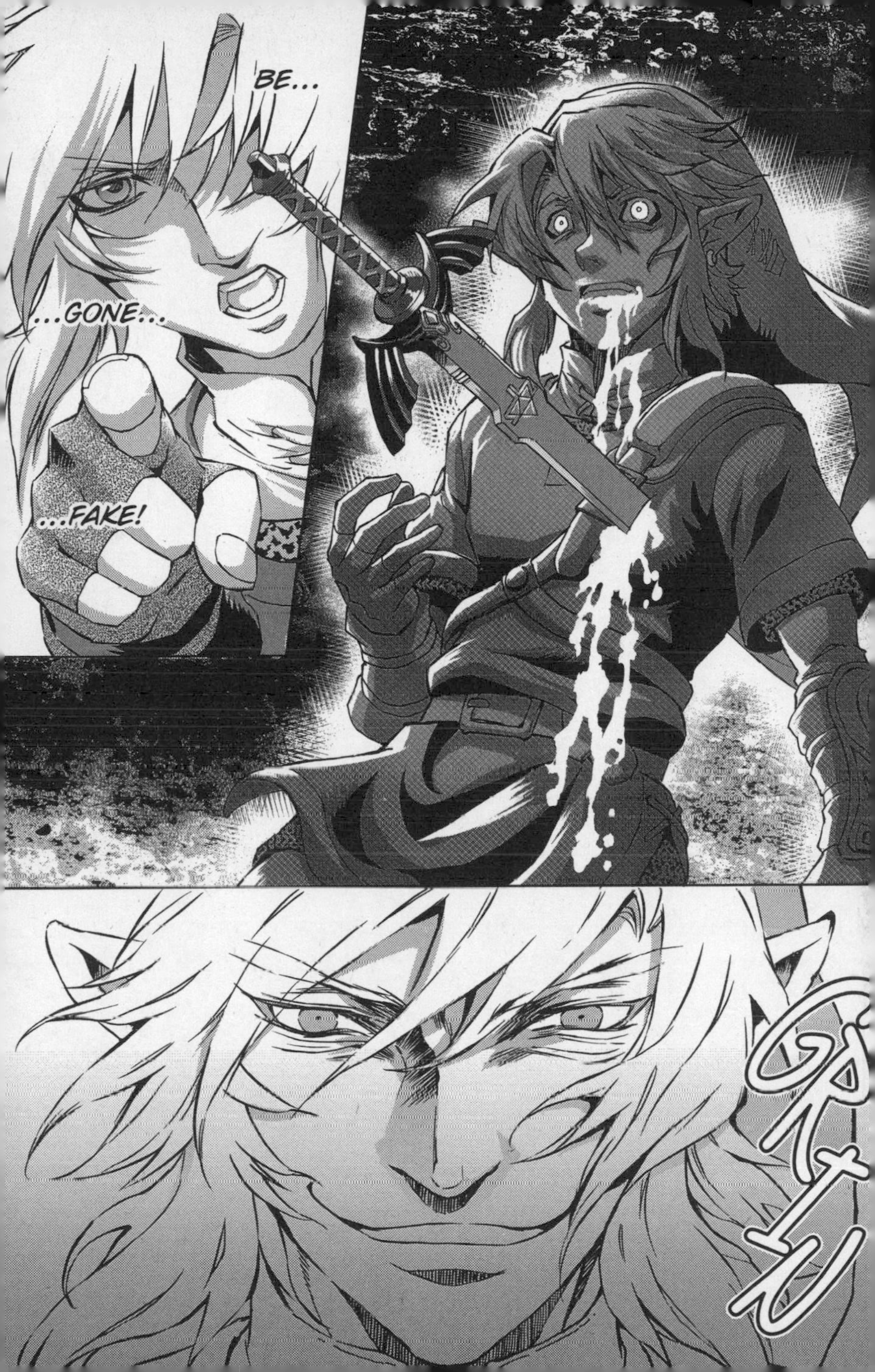
BE...
...GONE...
...FAKE!
GRIN

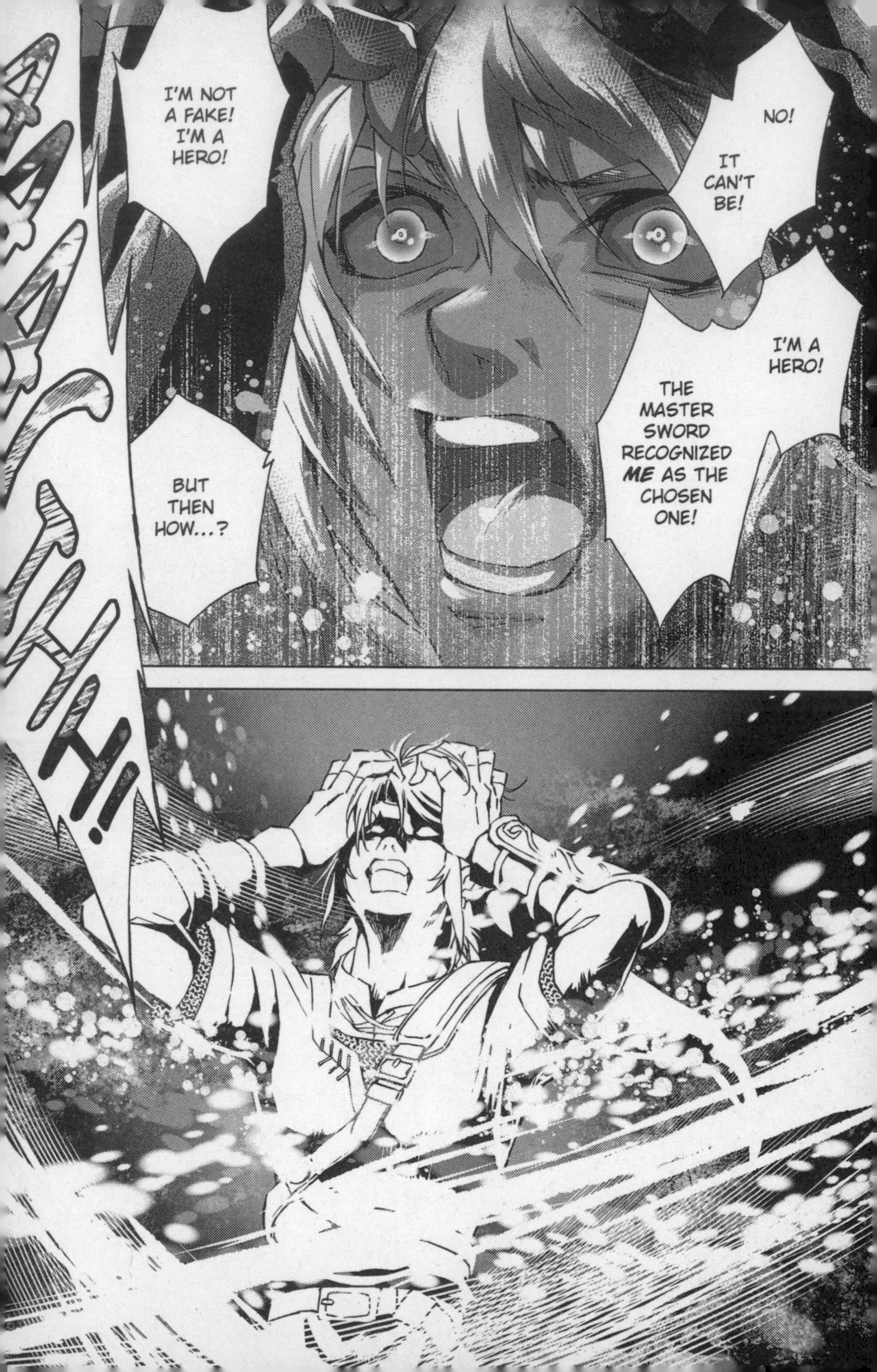
NO! IT CAN'T BE!
I'M A HERO!
THE MASTER SWORD RECOGNIZED ME AS THE CHOSEN ONE!
I'M NOT A FAKE! I'M A HERO!
BUT THEN HOW...?

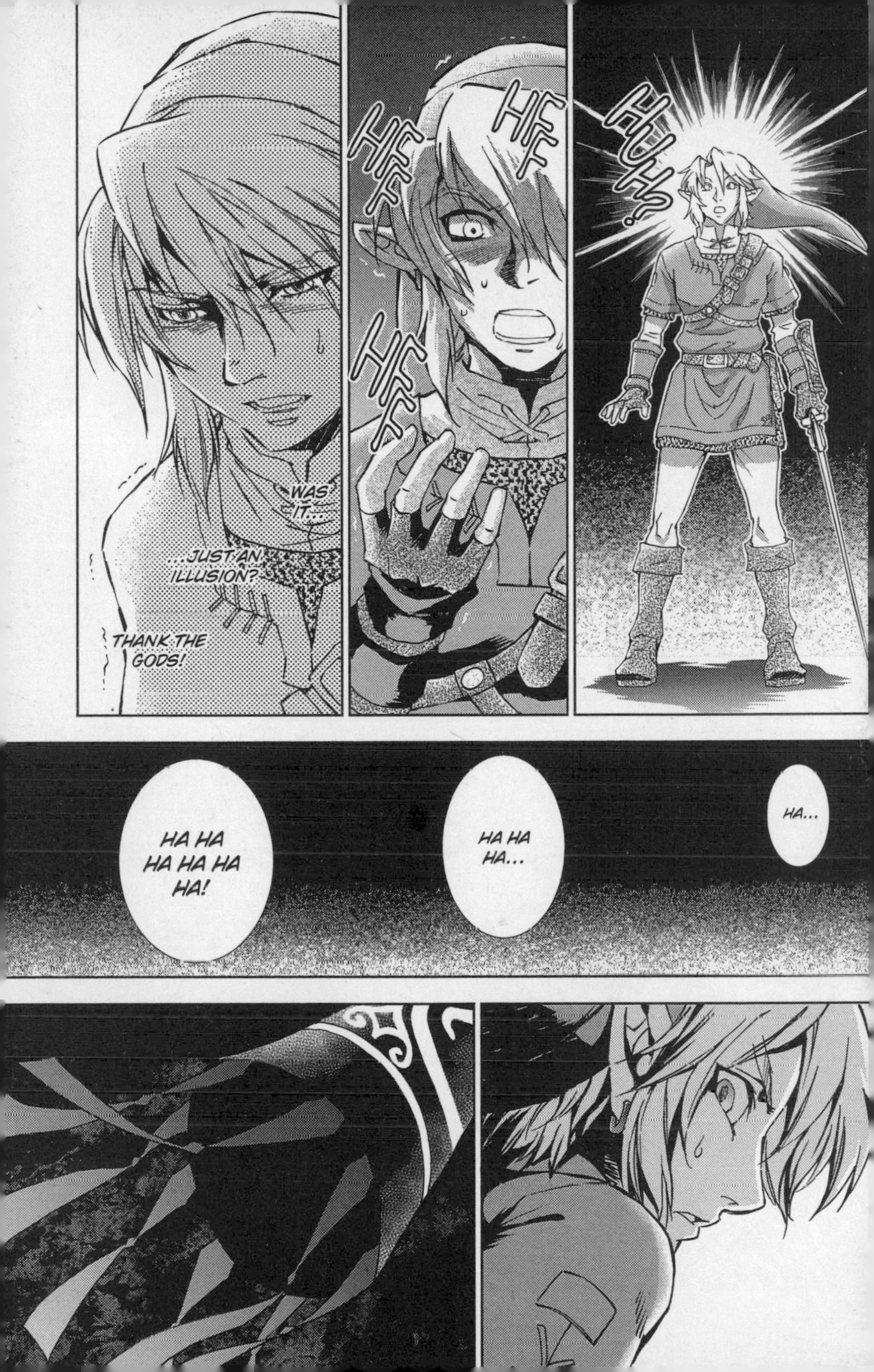
HUH?
HEF
HEF
HEF
WAS IT...
...JUST AN ILLUSION?
THANK THE GODS!
HA...
HA HA HA...
HA HA HA HA HA HA!

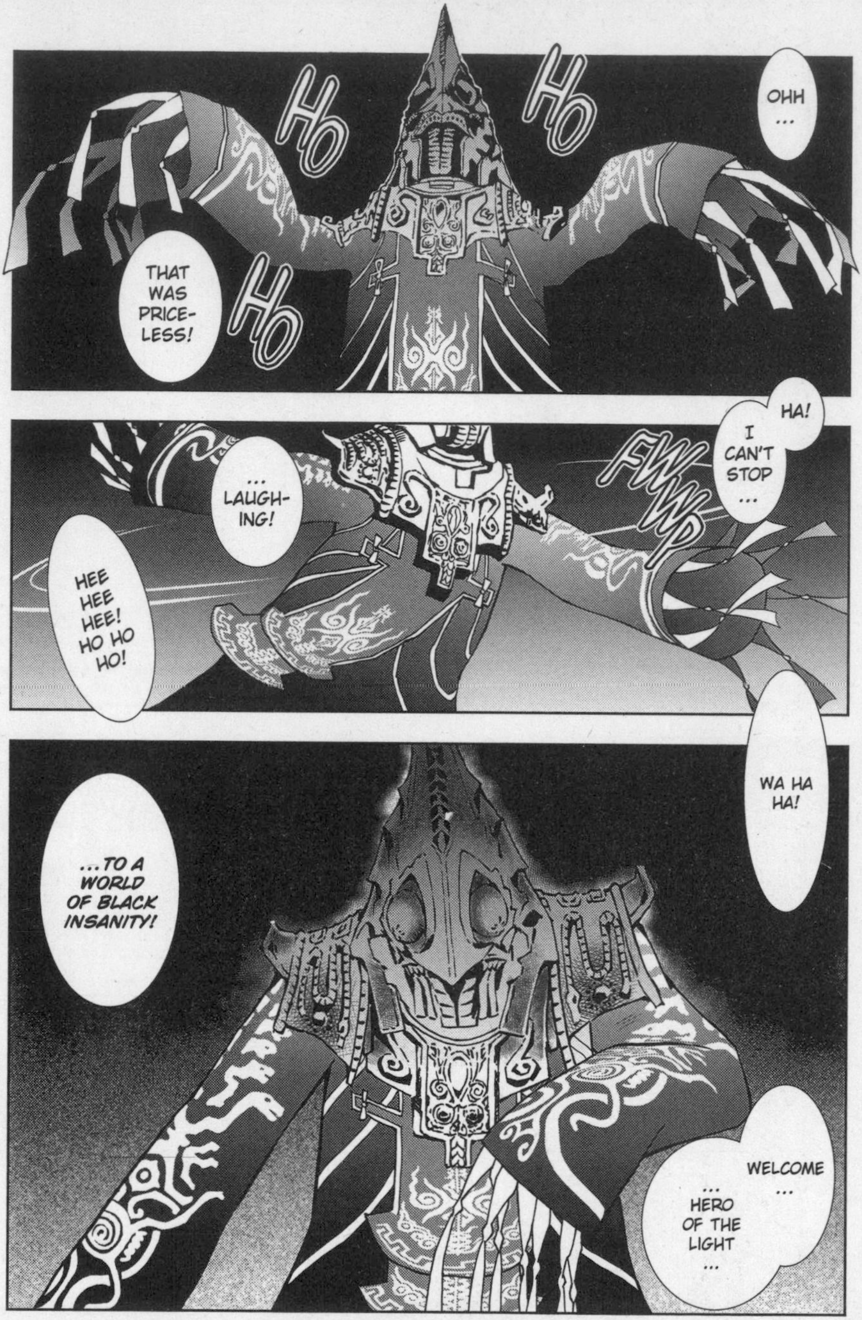
OHH ...
HO HO
HO
THAT WAS PRICE-LESS!
HA! I CAN'T STOP ...
FWWP
... LAUGH-ING!
HEE HEE HEE! HO HO HO!
WA HA HA!
WELCOME ... HERO OF THE LIGHT ...
...TO A WORLD OF BLACK INSANITY!

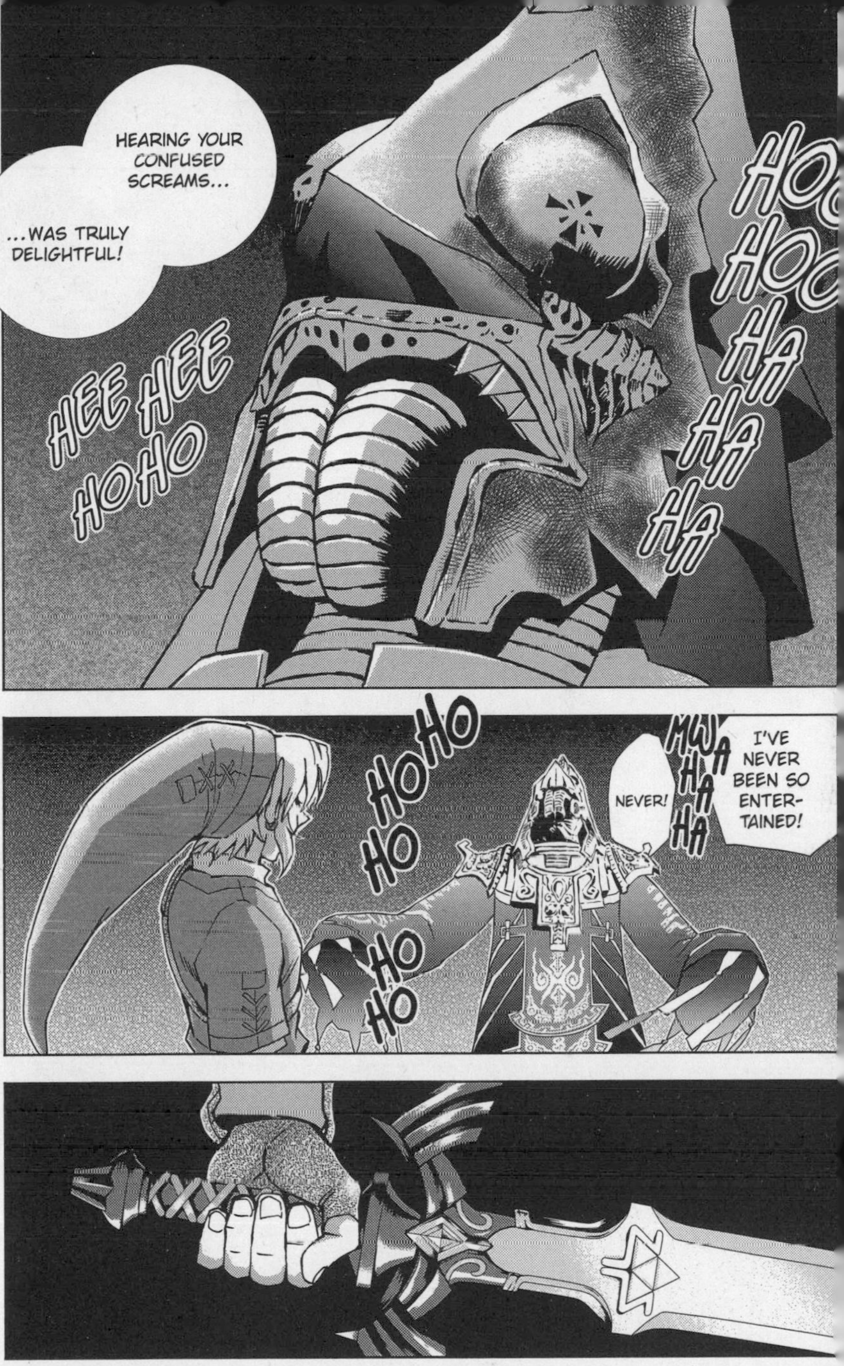
HOO HOO HA HA HA HA
HEARING YOUR CONFUSED SCREAMS...
...WAS TRULY DELIGHTFUL!
HEE HEE HO HO
I'VE NEVER BEEN SO ENTER-TAINED!
MWA HA HA HA
NEVER!
HO HO HO HO
HO HO HO HO

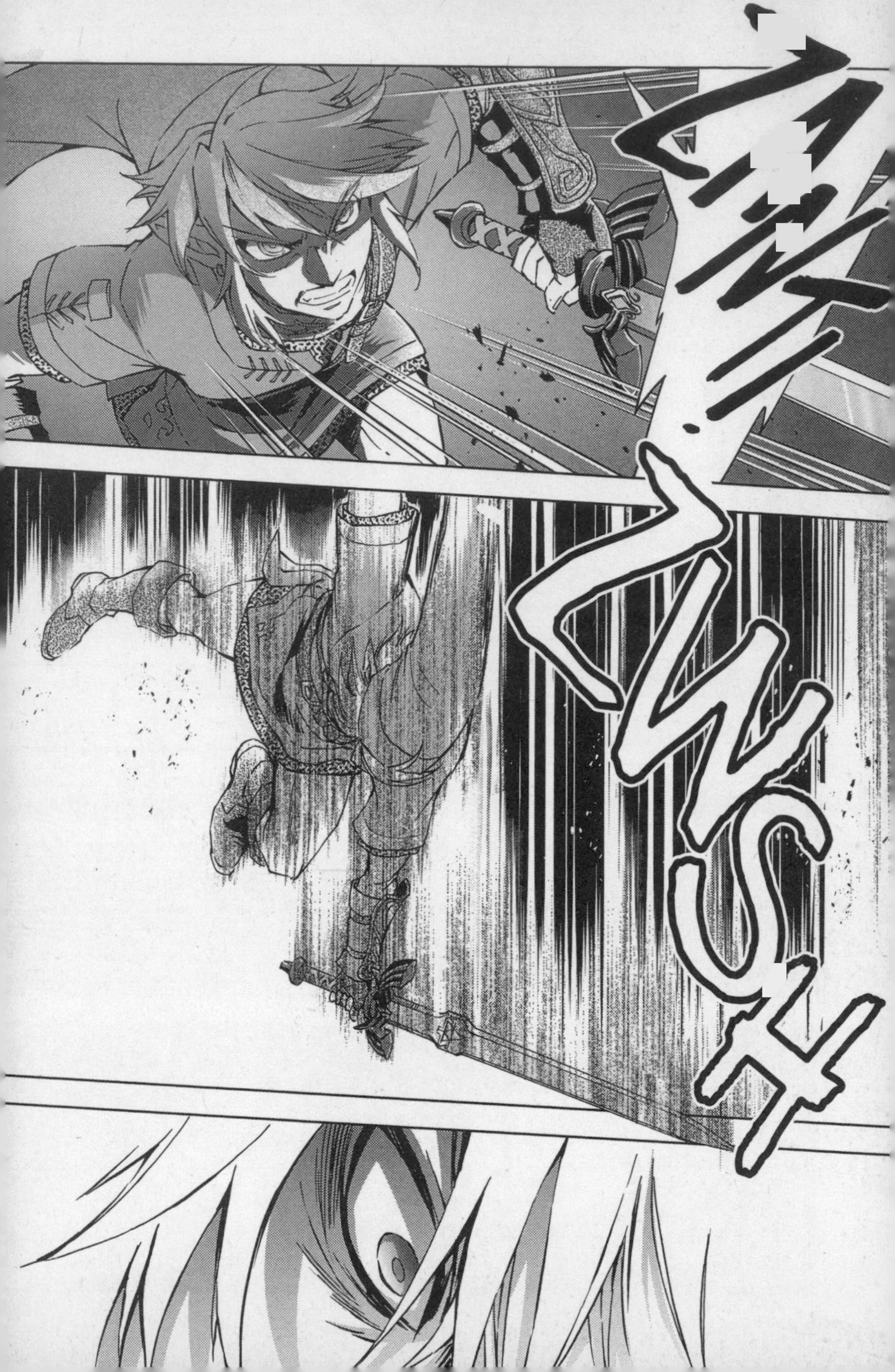

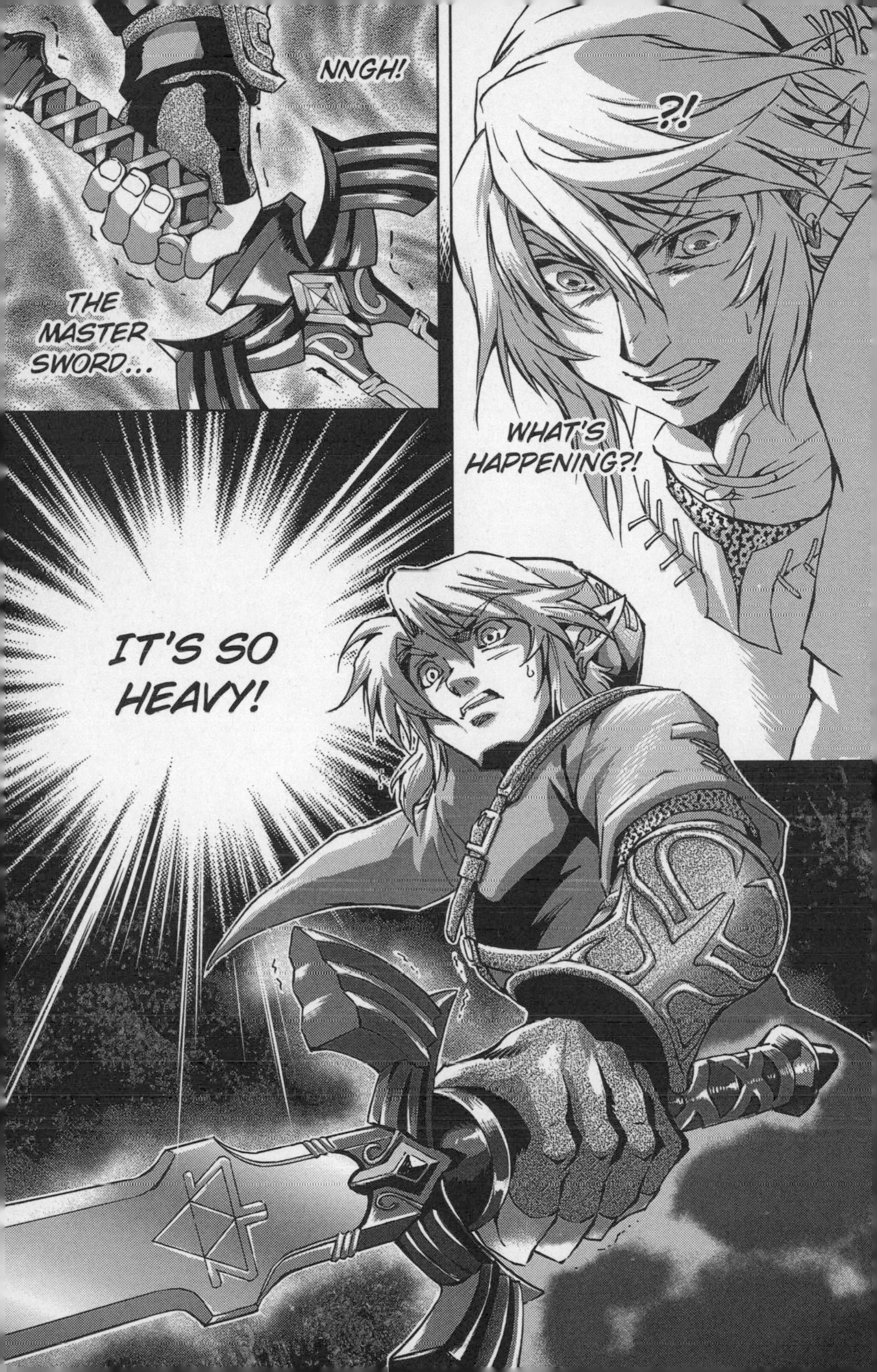
?!
WHAT'S HAPPENING?!
NNGH!
THE MASTER SWORD...
IT'S SO HEAVY!

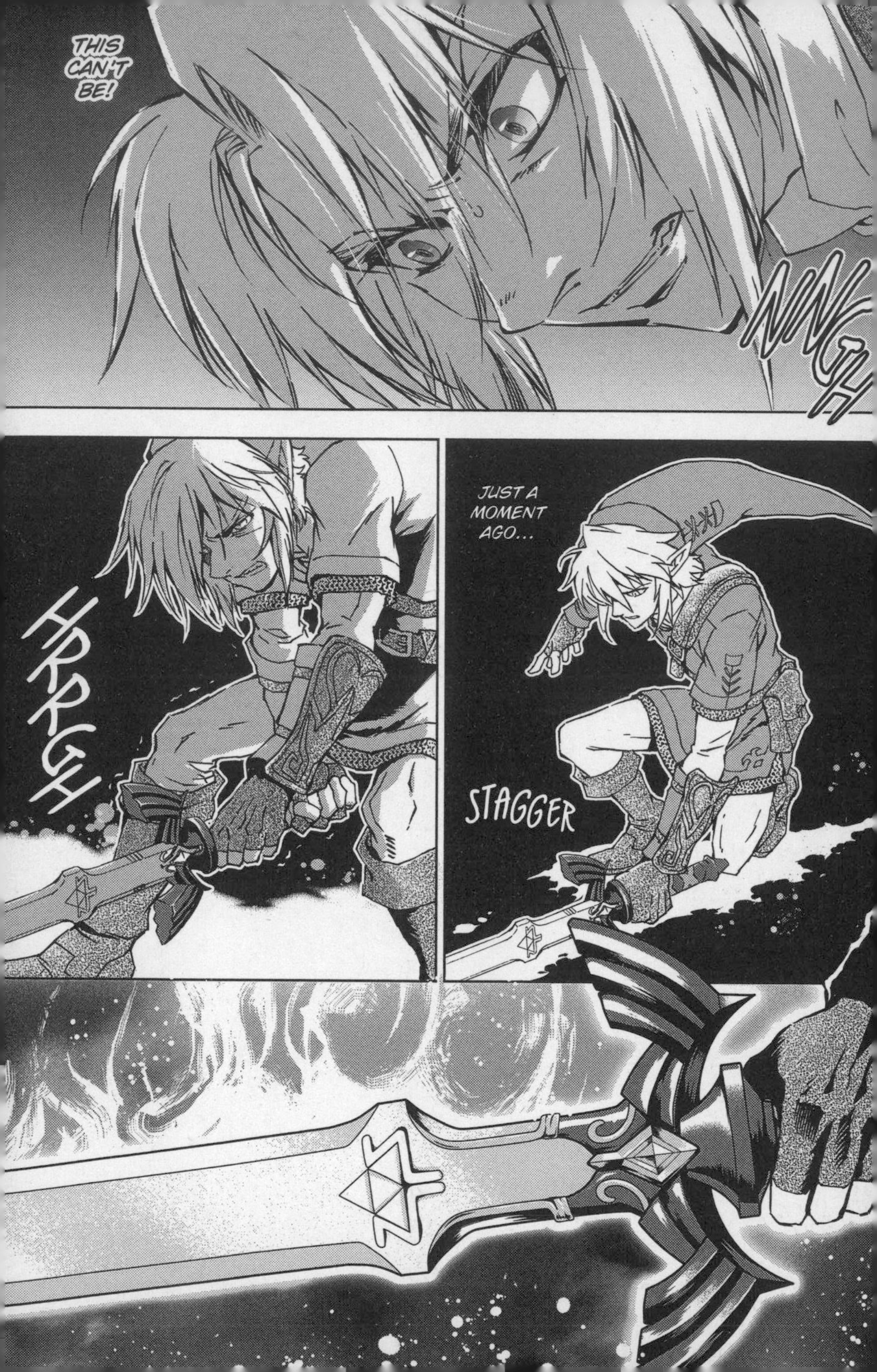
THIS CAN'T BE!
NNGH
JUST A MOMENT AGO...
STAGGER
HRRGH

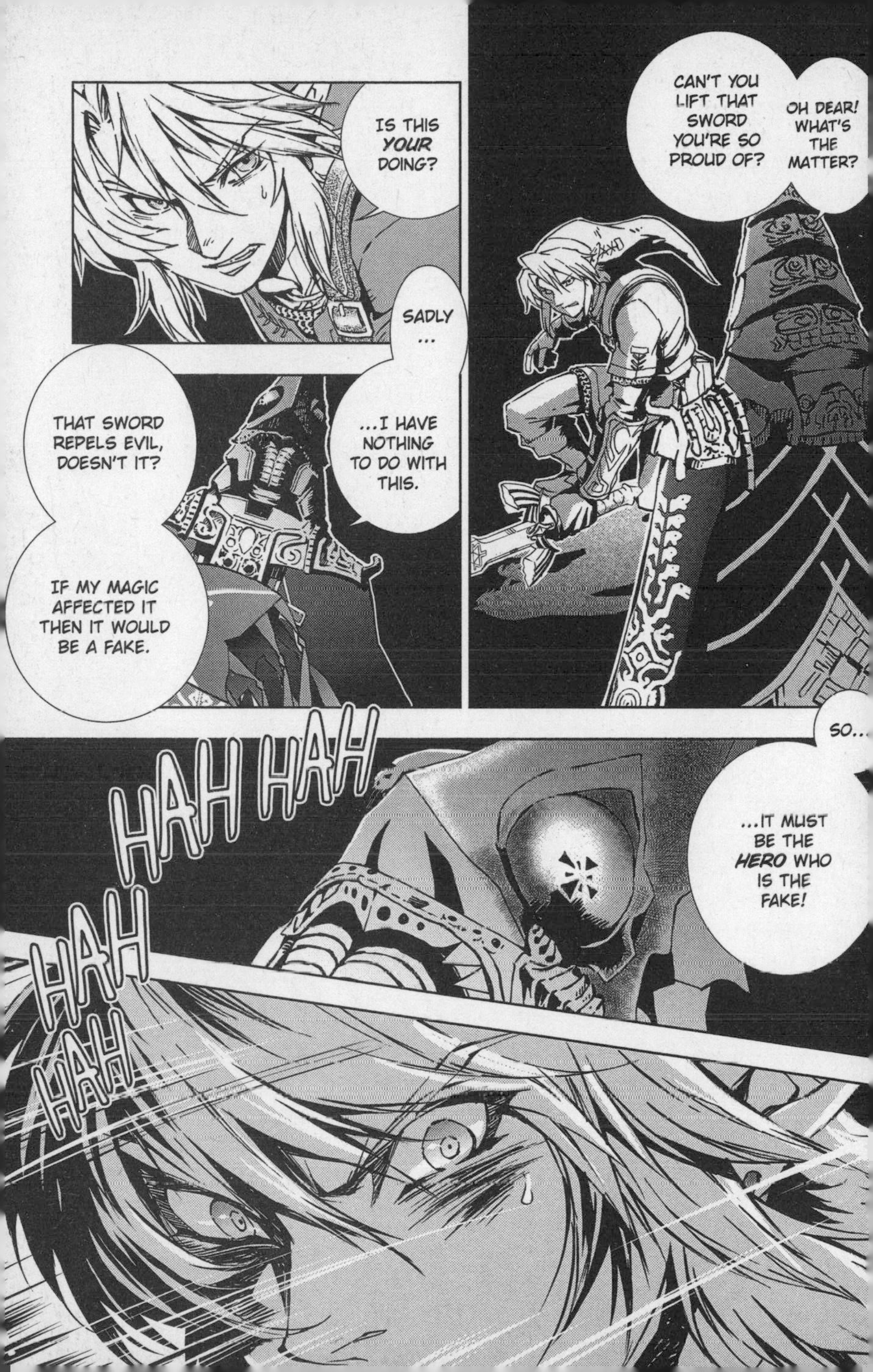
OH DEAR! WHAT'S THE MATTER?
CAN'T YOU LIFT THAT SWORD YOU'RE SO PROUD OF?
IS THIS *YOUR* DOING?
SADLY ...
...I HAVE NOTHING TO DO WITH THIS.
THAT SWORD REPELS EVIL, DOESN'T IT?
IF MY MAGIC AFFECTED IT THEN IT WOULD BE A FAKE.
SO...
...IT MUST BE THE *HERO* WHO IS THE FAKE!
HAH HAH
HAH HAH

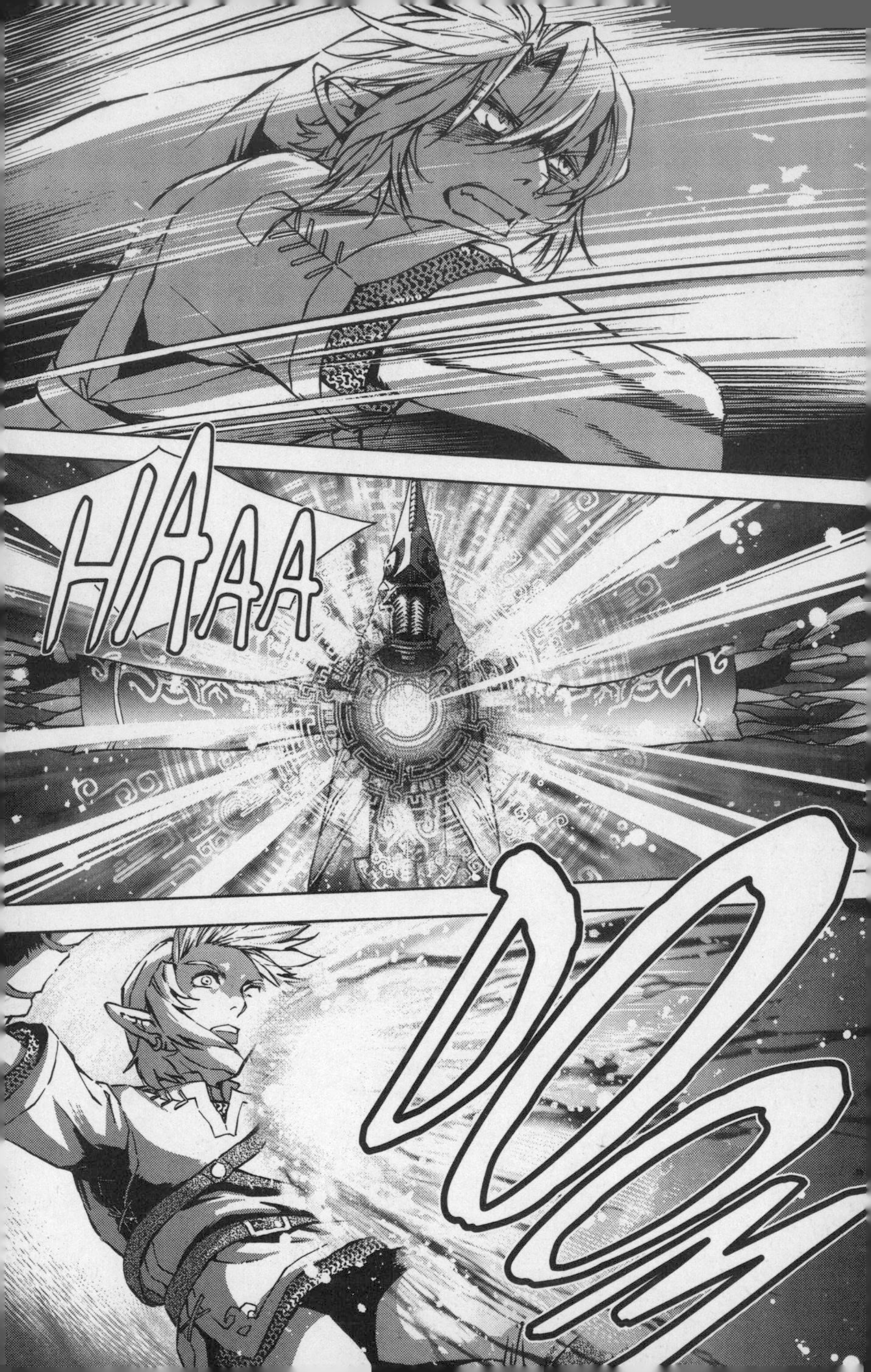
HAAA
DOOM

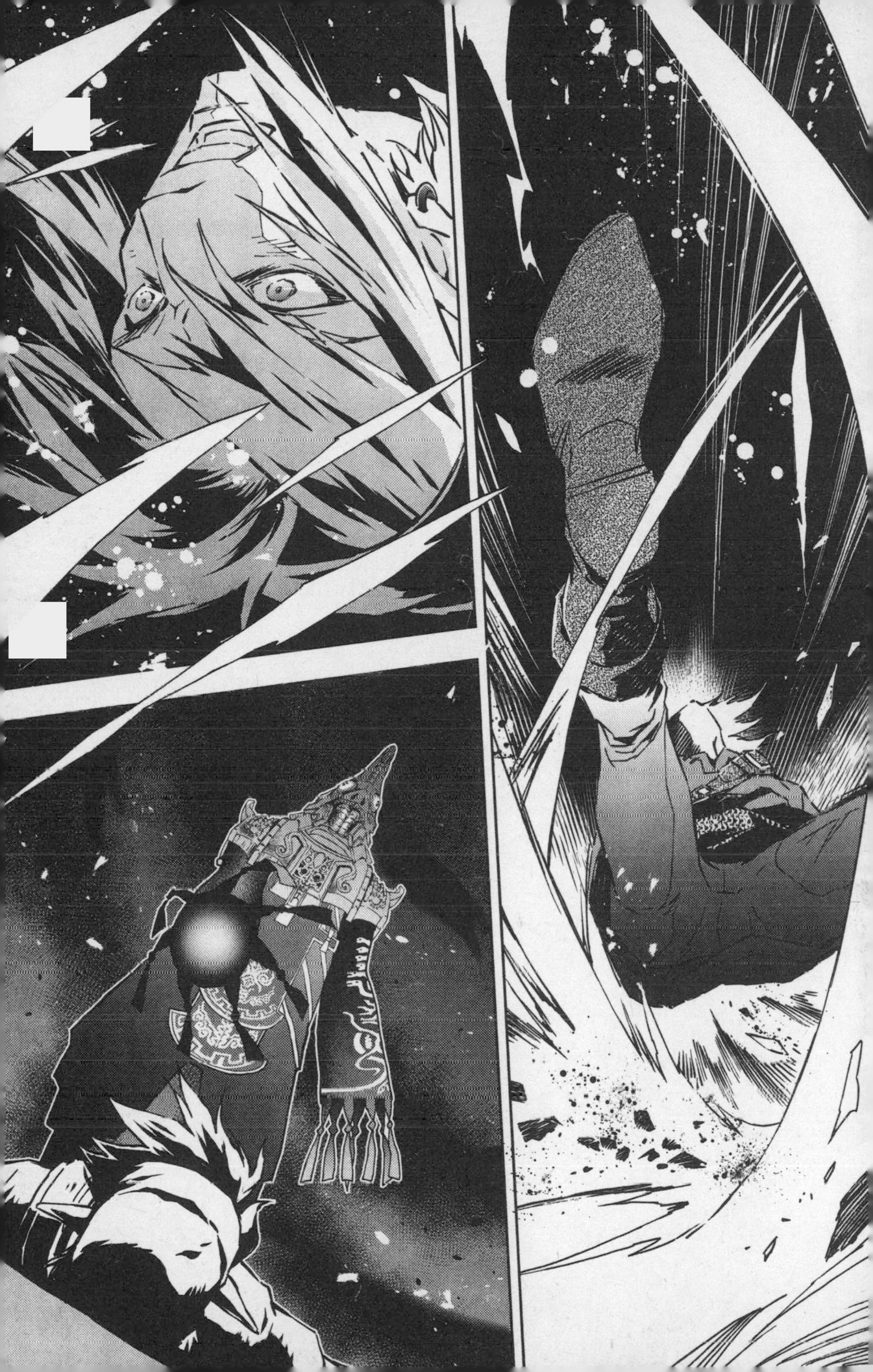

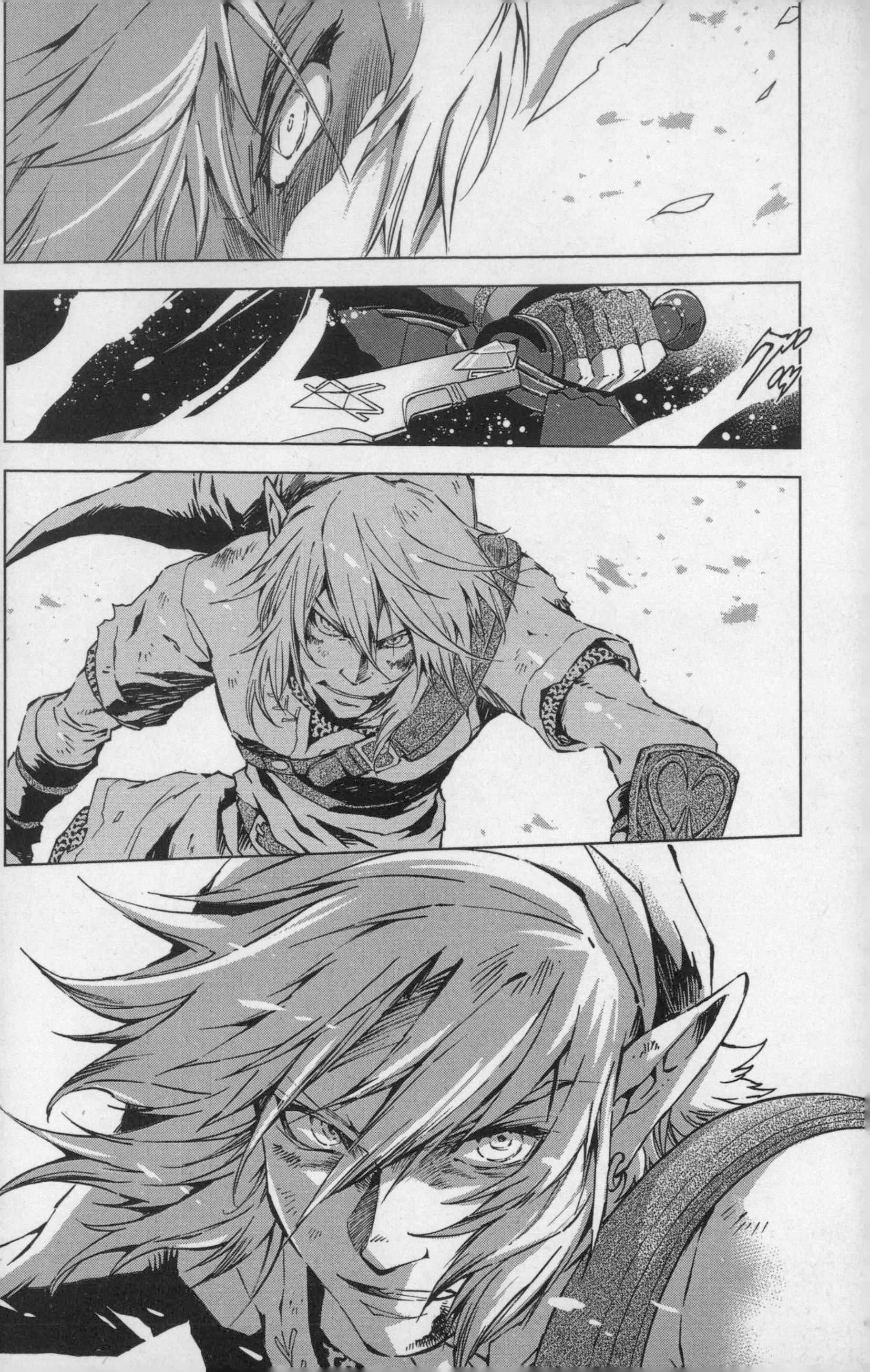

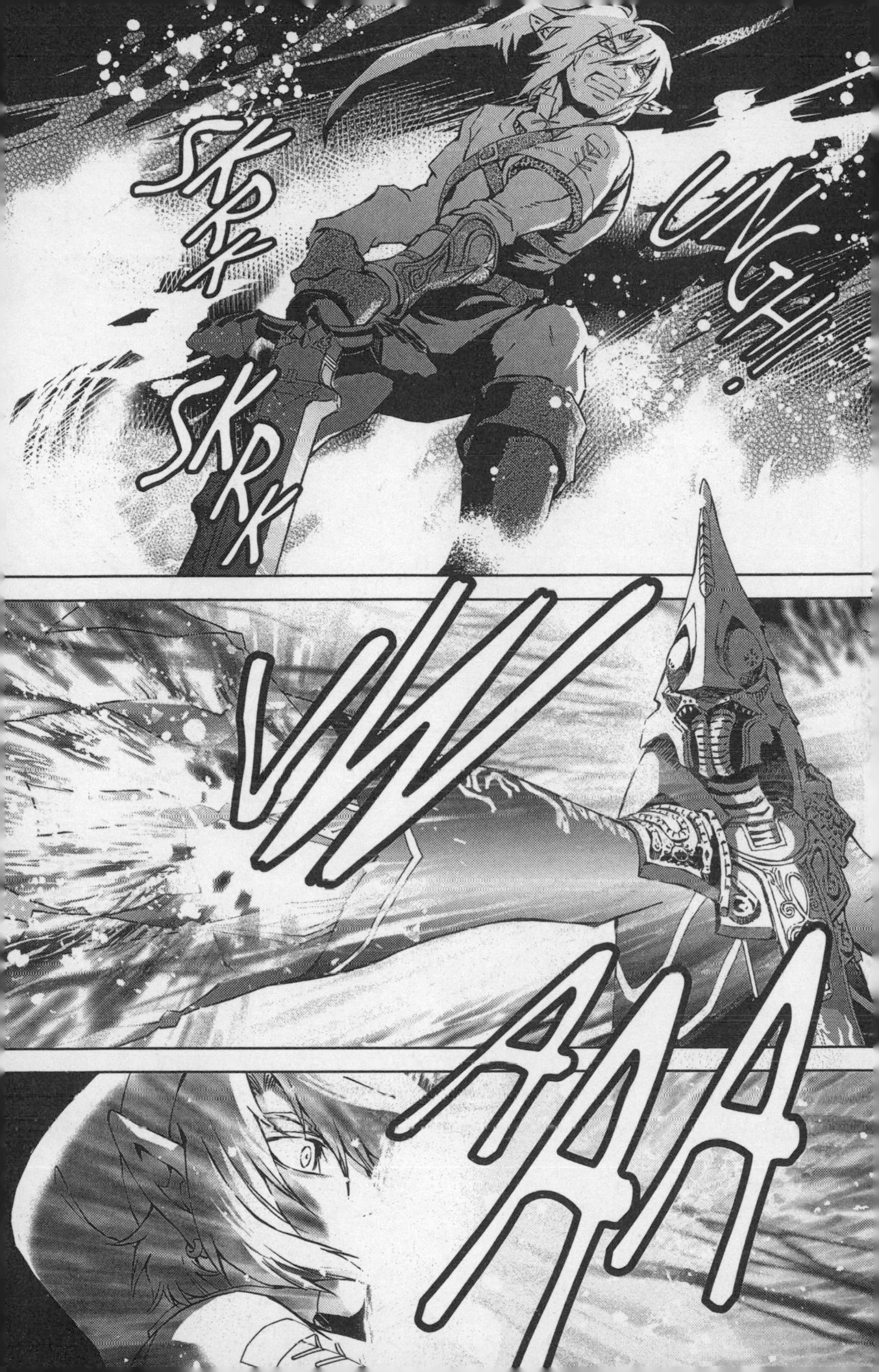
UNGH!
SKRK
SKRK
VWAAA

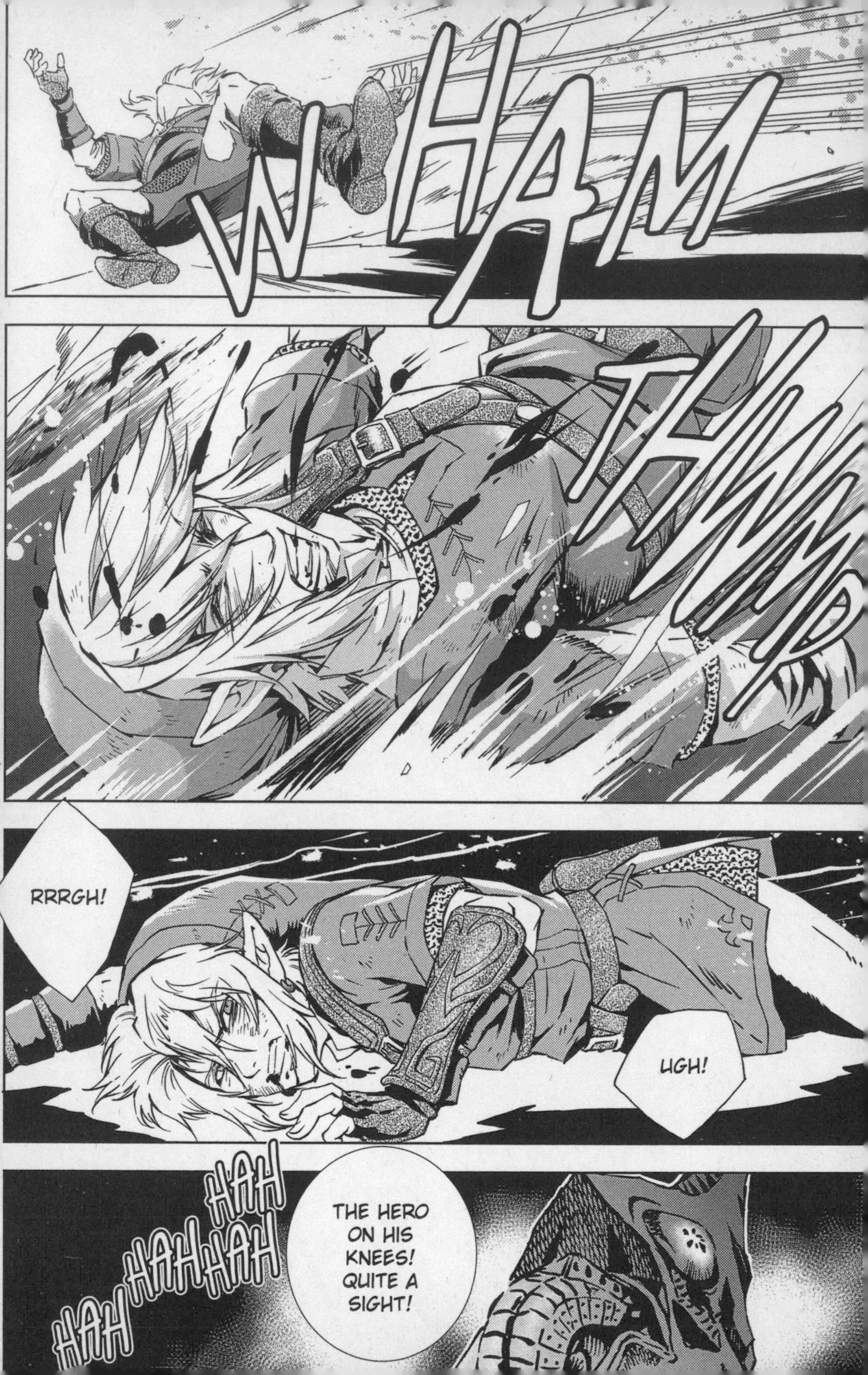
WHAM
THUMP
UGH!
RRRGH!
THE HERO ON HIS KNEES! QUITE A SIGHT!
HAH HAH HAH HAH HAH

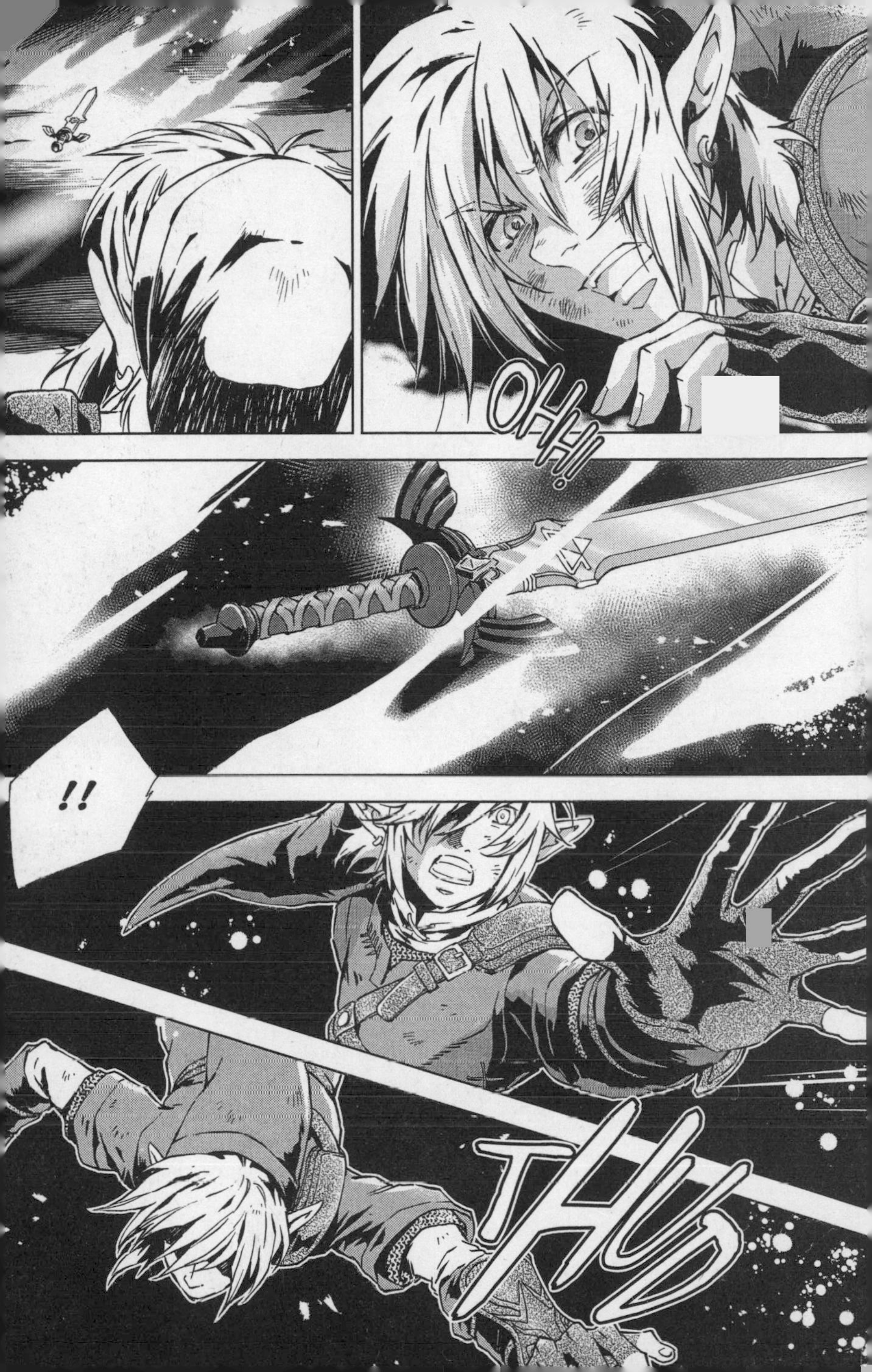
OHH!!
!!
THU

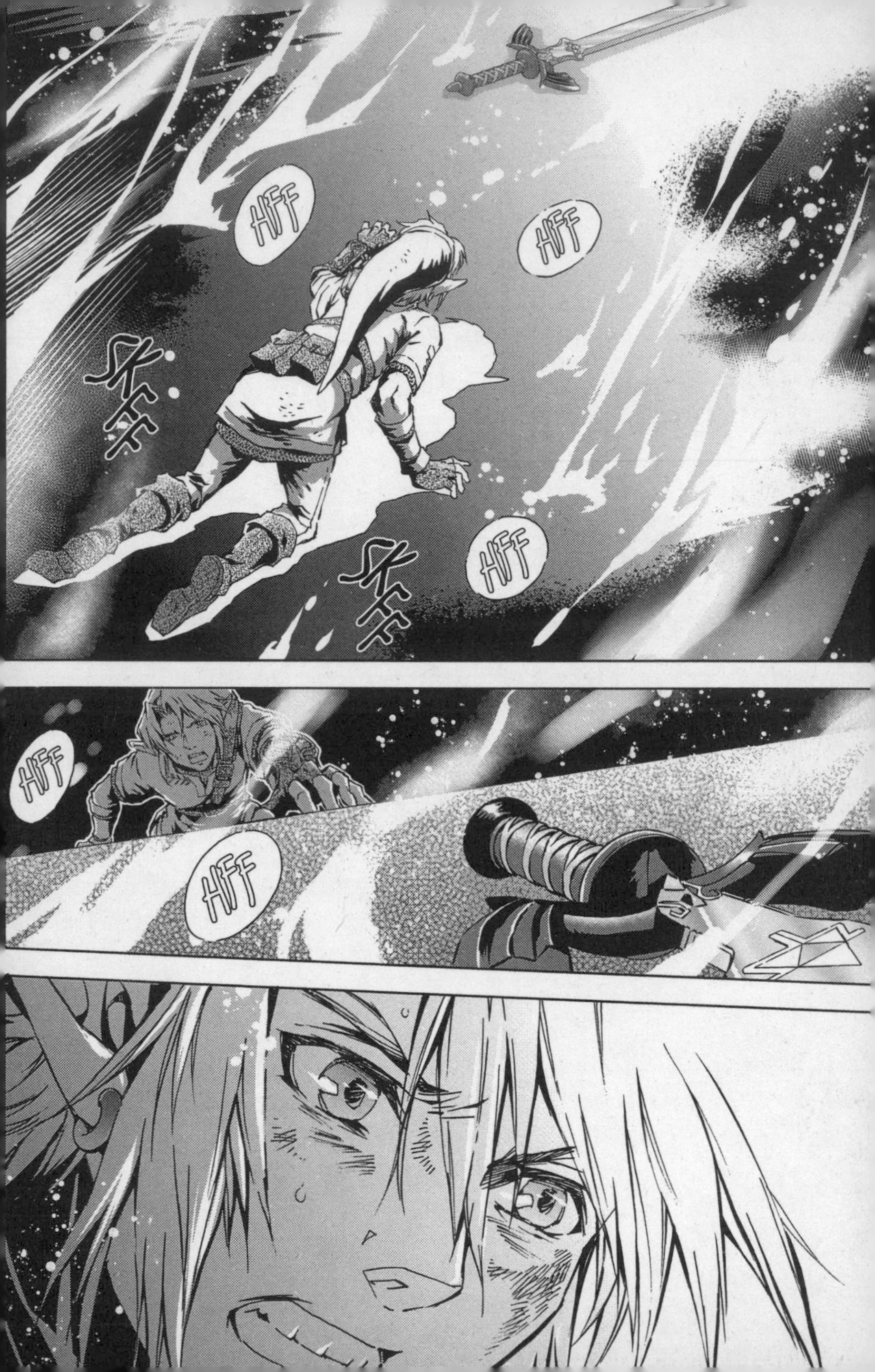
HFF
HFF
SKFF
HFF
SKFF
HFF
HFF

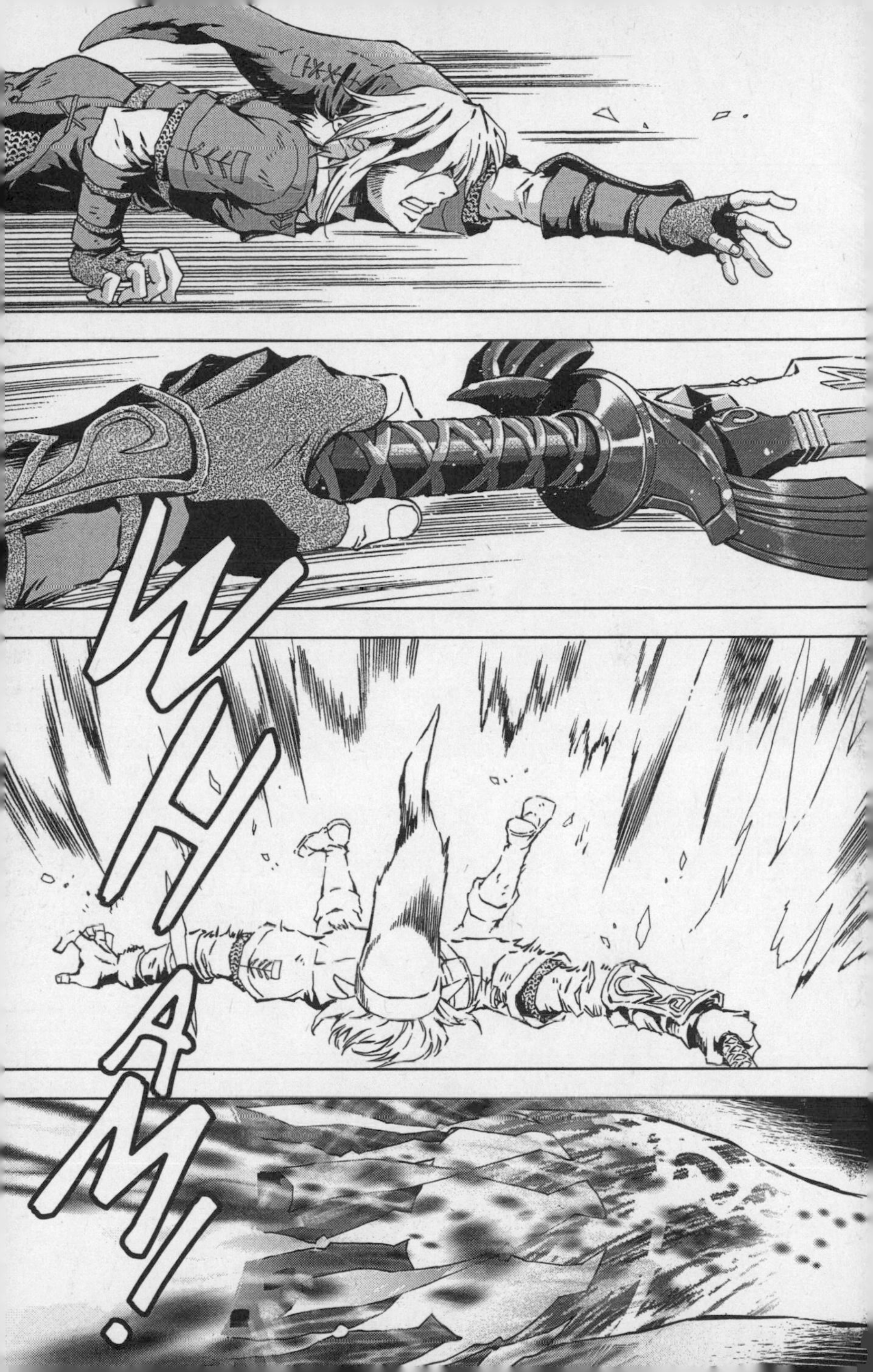
WHAM!

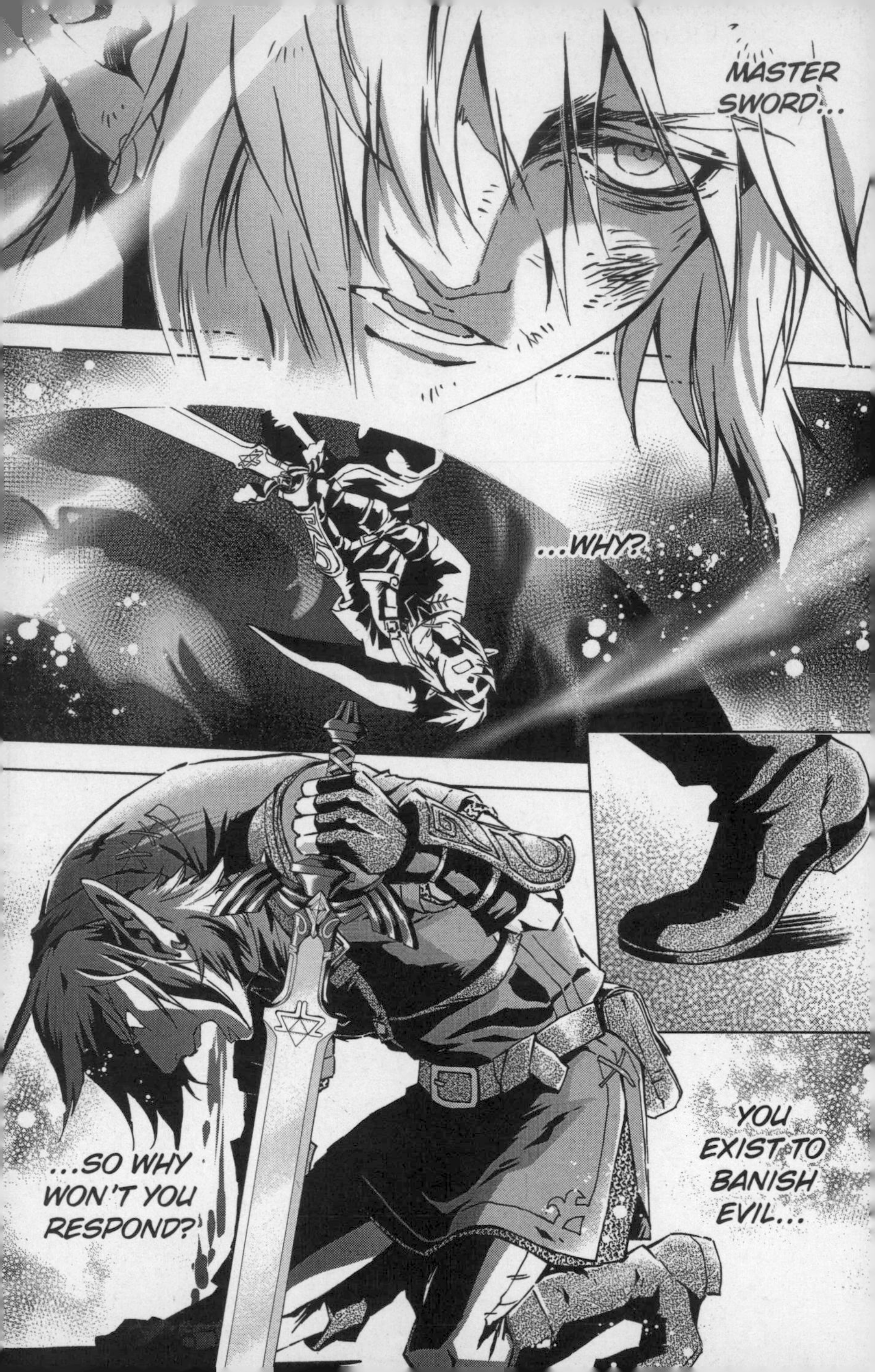
MASTER SWORD...
...WHY?
YOU EXIST TO BANISH EVIL...
...SO WHY WON'T YOU RESPOND?

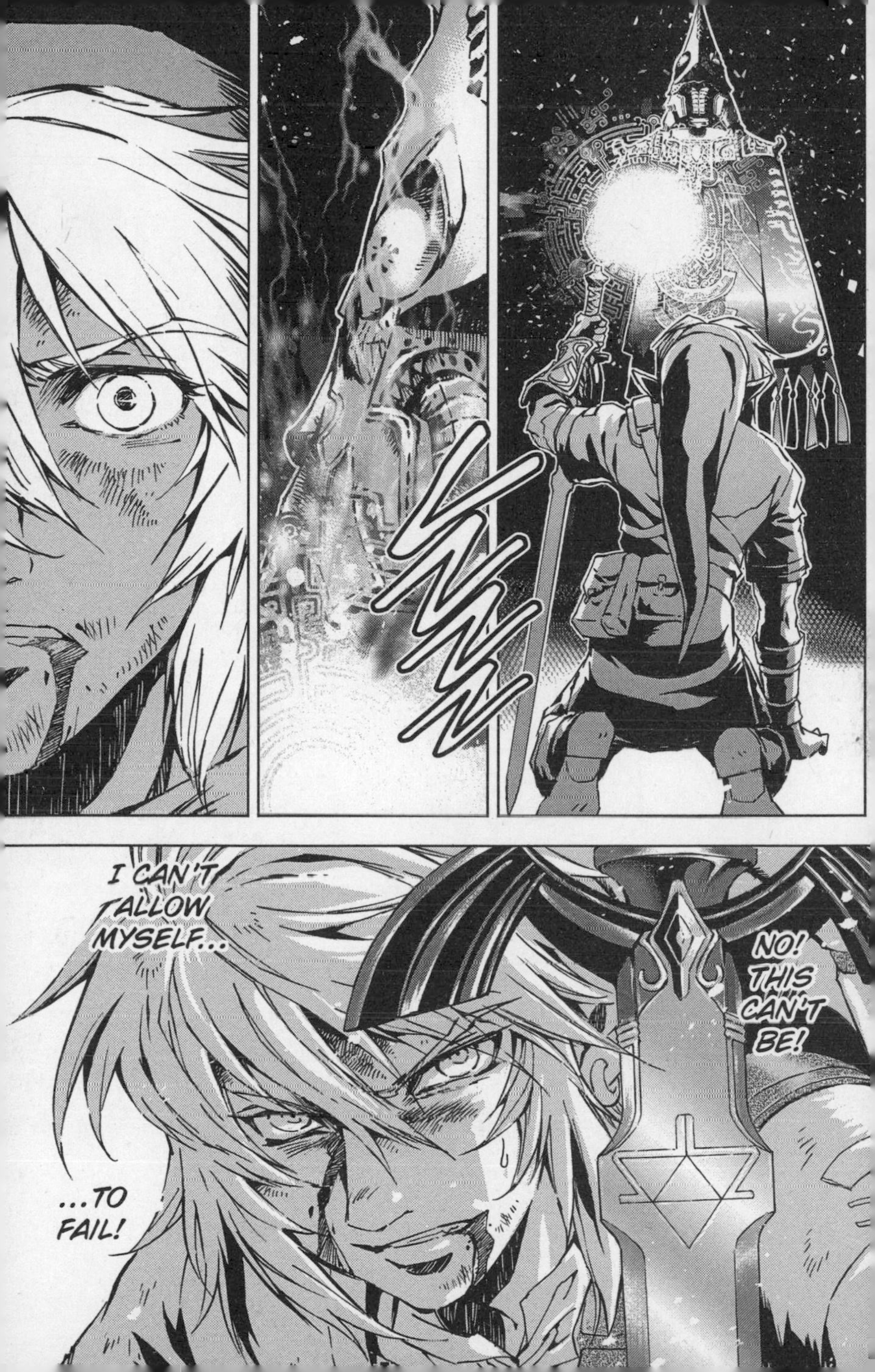
VNNNN
NO! THIS CAN'T BE!
I CAN'T ALLOW MYSELF...
...TO FAIL!

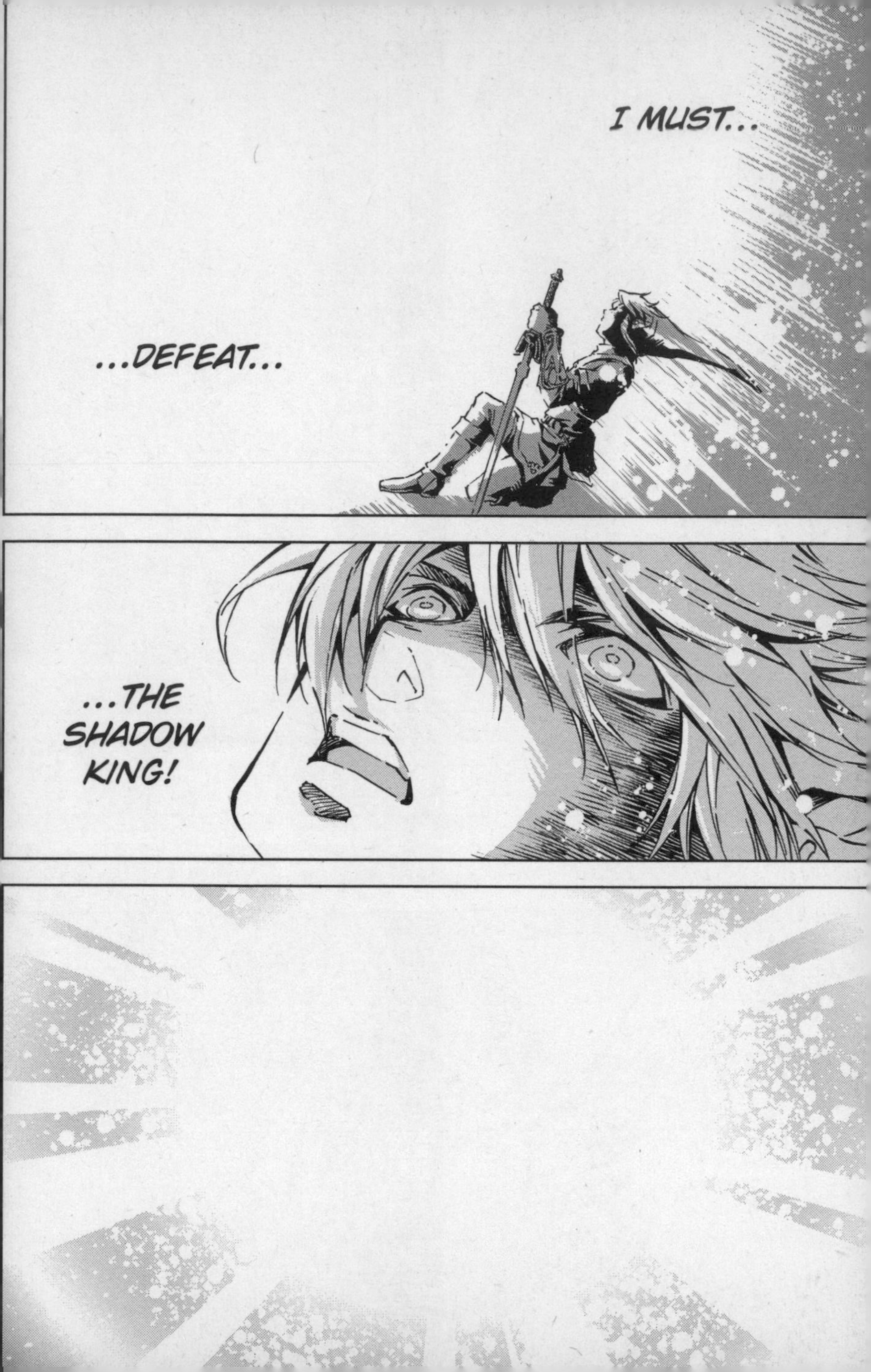
I MUST...
...DEFEAT...
...THE SHADOW KING!

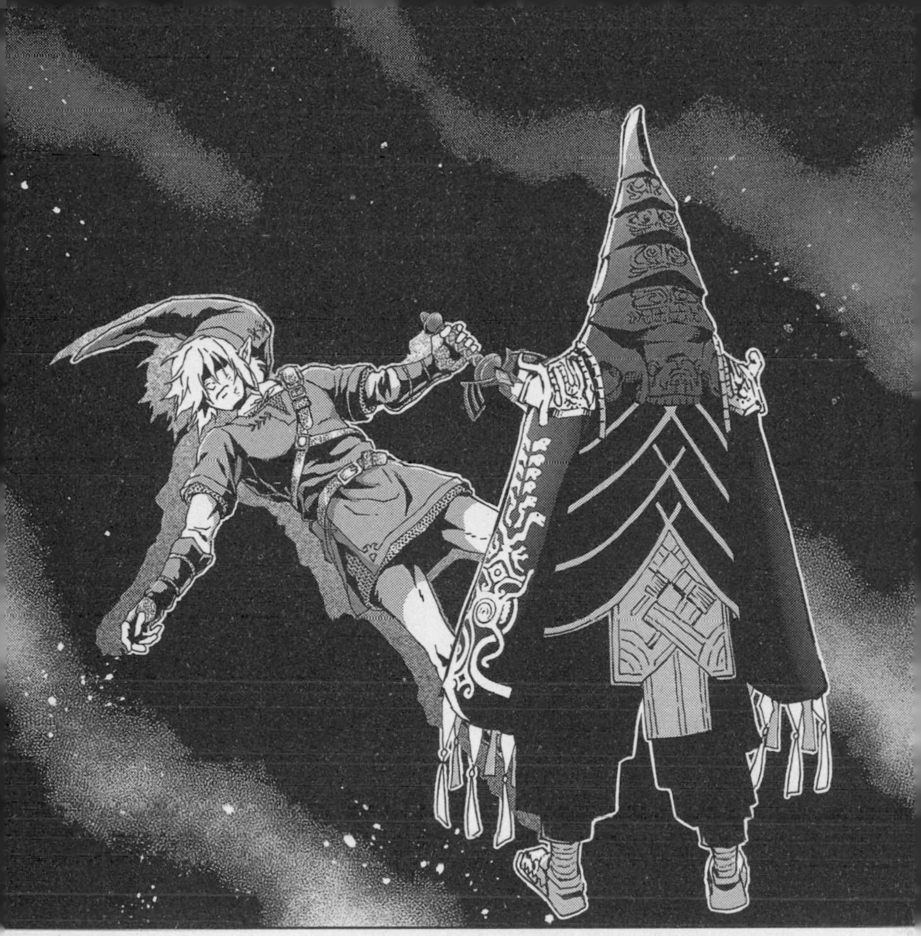

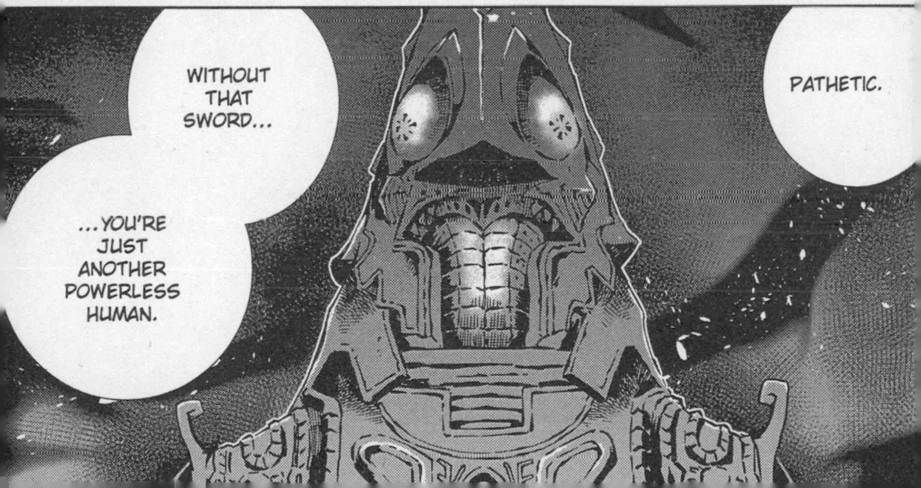
PATHETIC.
WITHOUT THAT SWORD...
...YOU'RE JUST ANOTHER POWERLESS HUMAN.

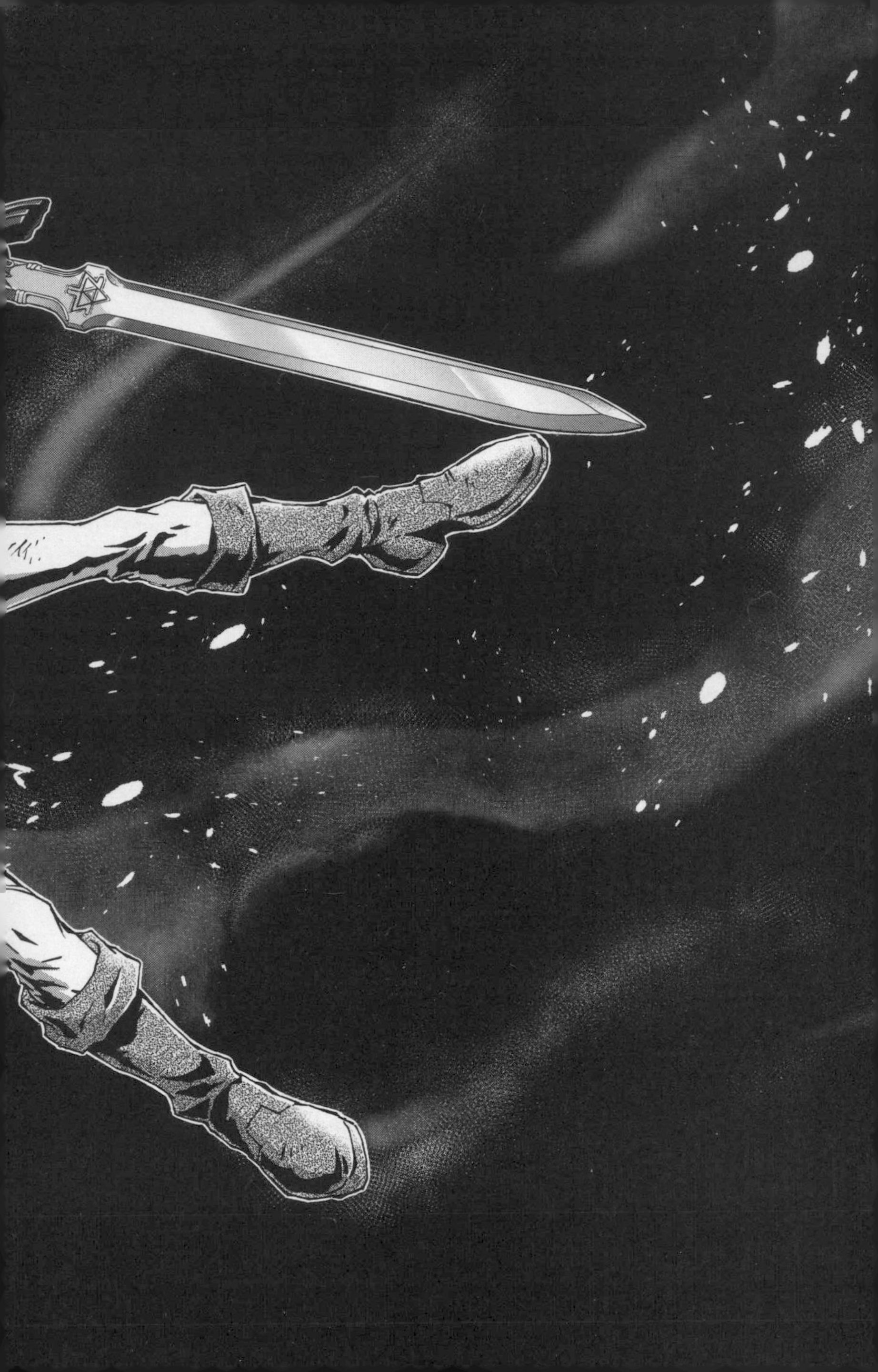

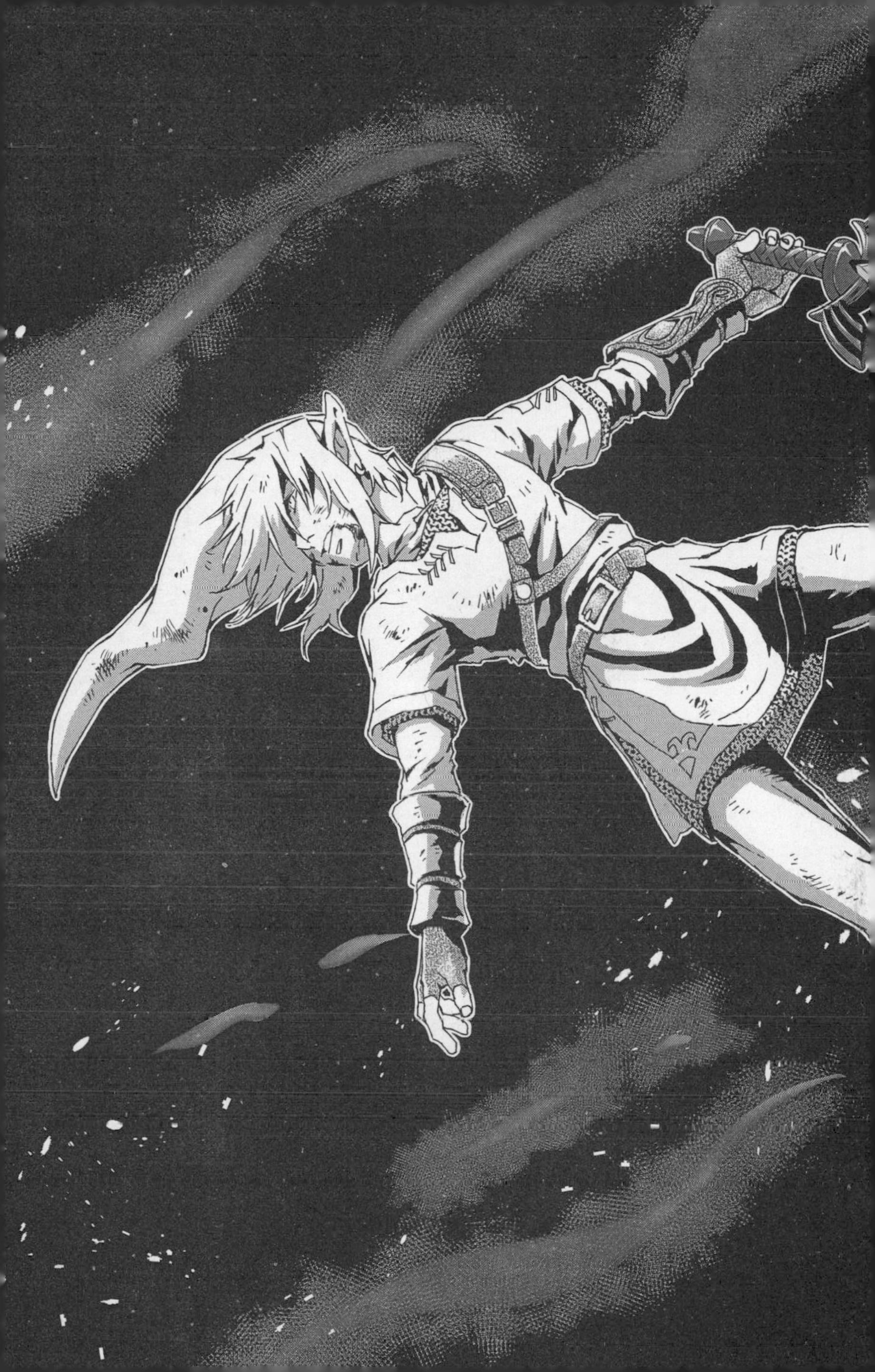

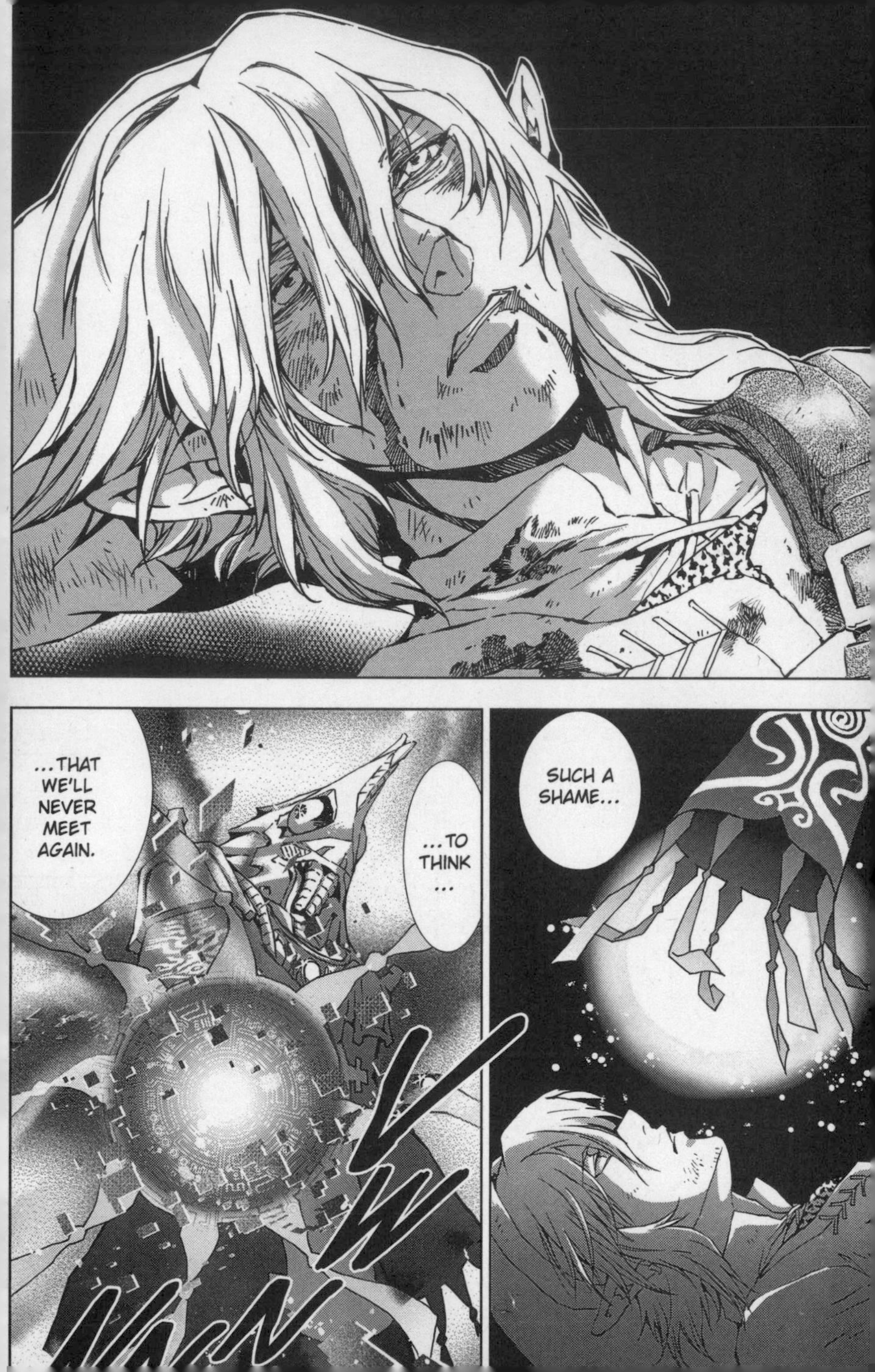
SUCH A SHAME...
...TO THINK...
...THAT WE'LL NEVER MEET AGAIN.

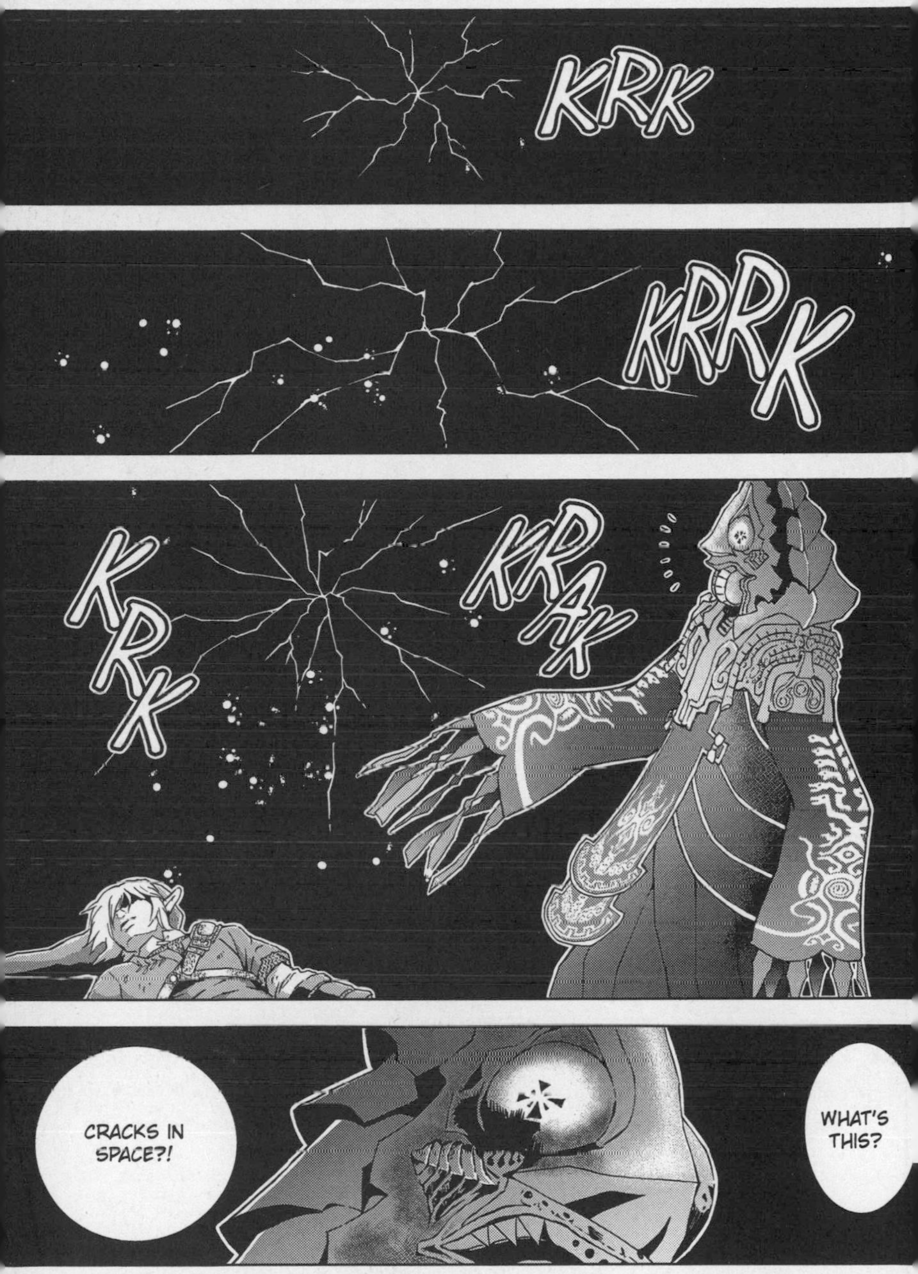
KRK
KRRK
KRAK
KRK
WHAT'S THIS?
CRACKS IN SPACE?!

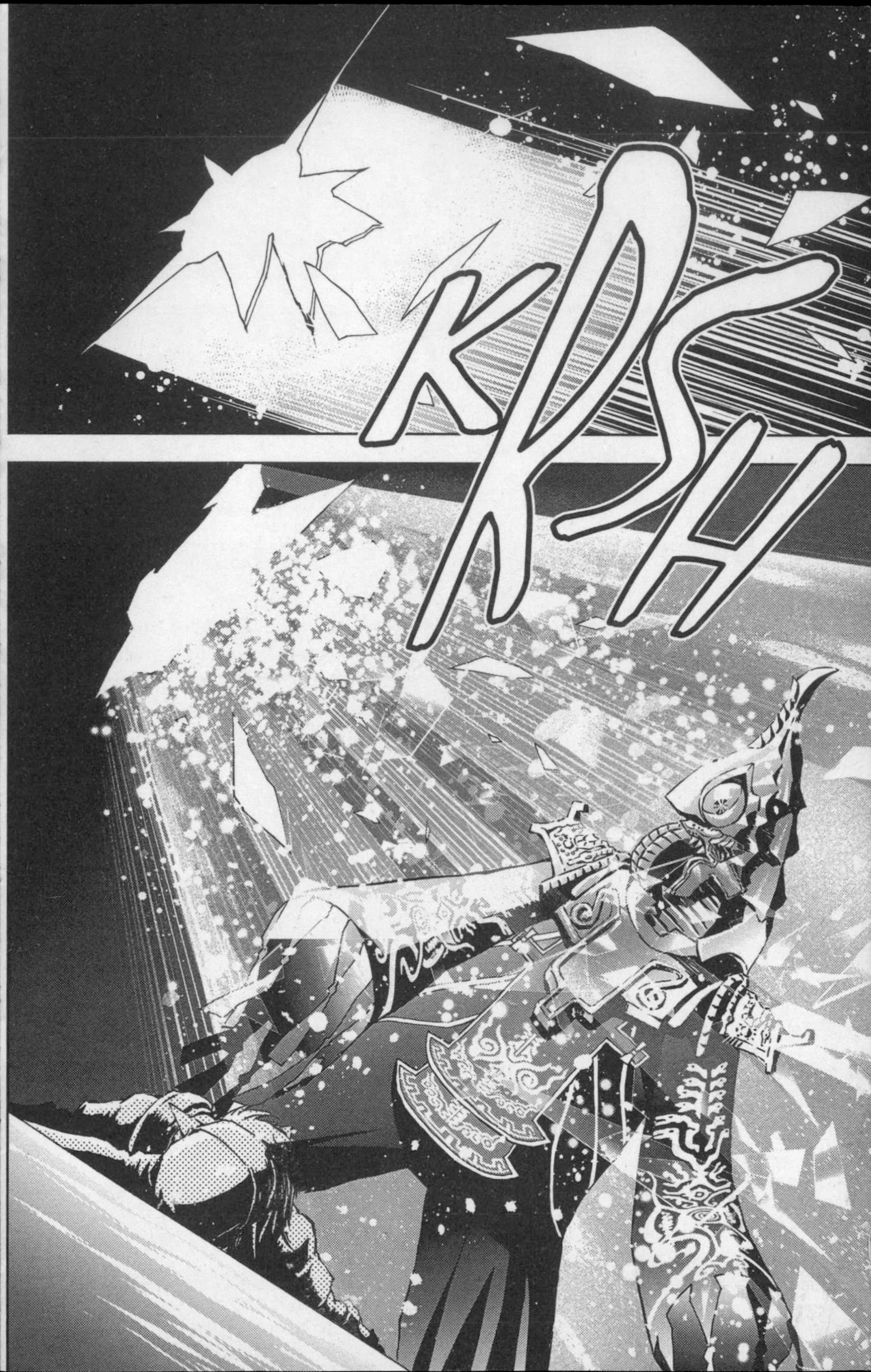
KRSSH

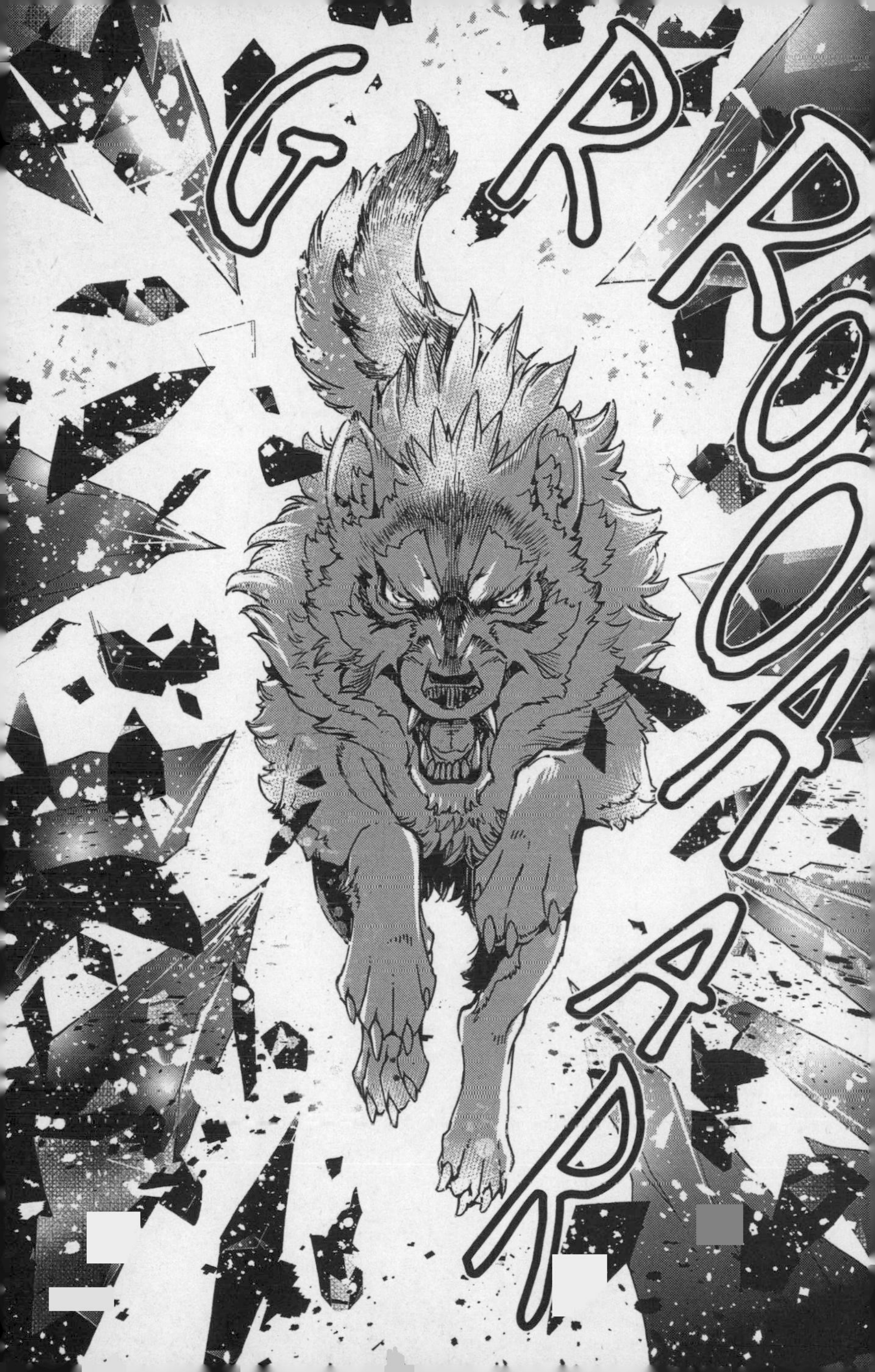
GRROOAAR

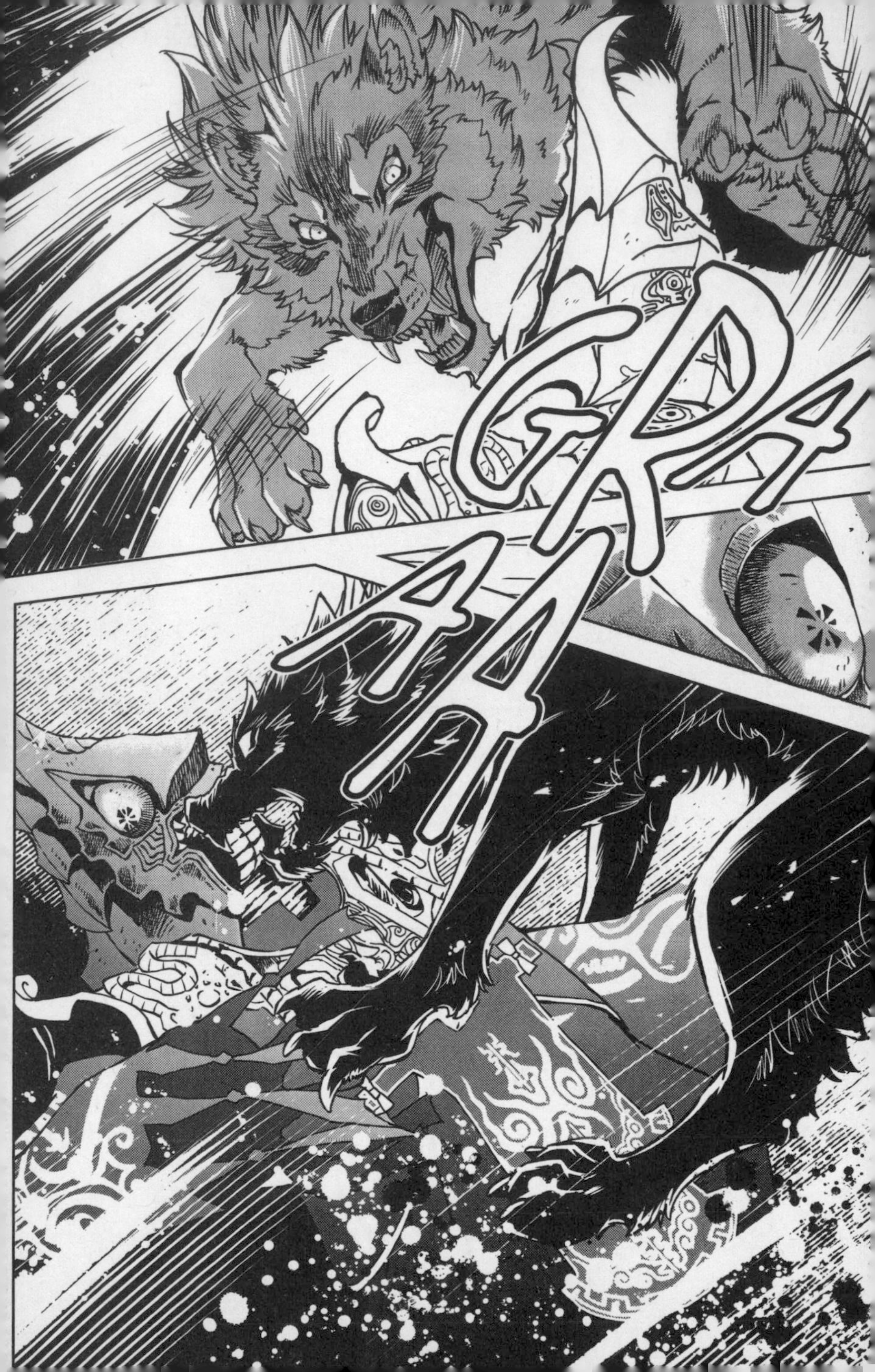
GRAAH

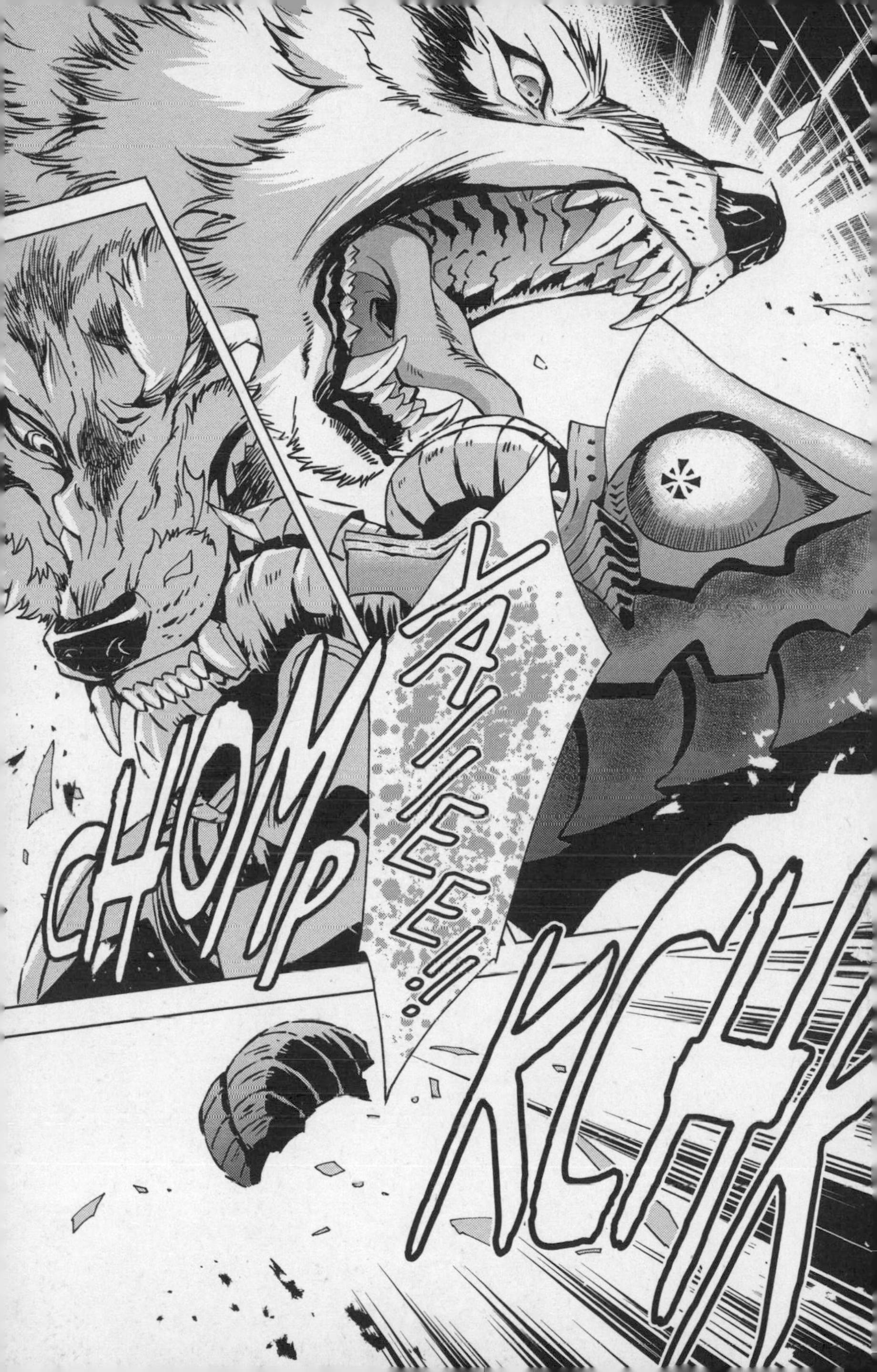
YAIIEEE!!...
CHOMP

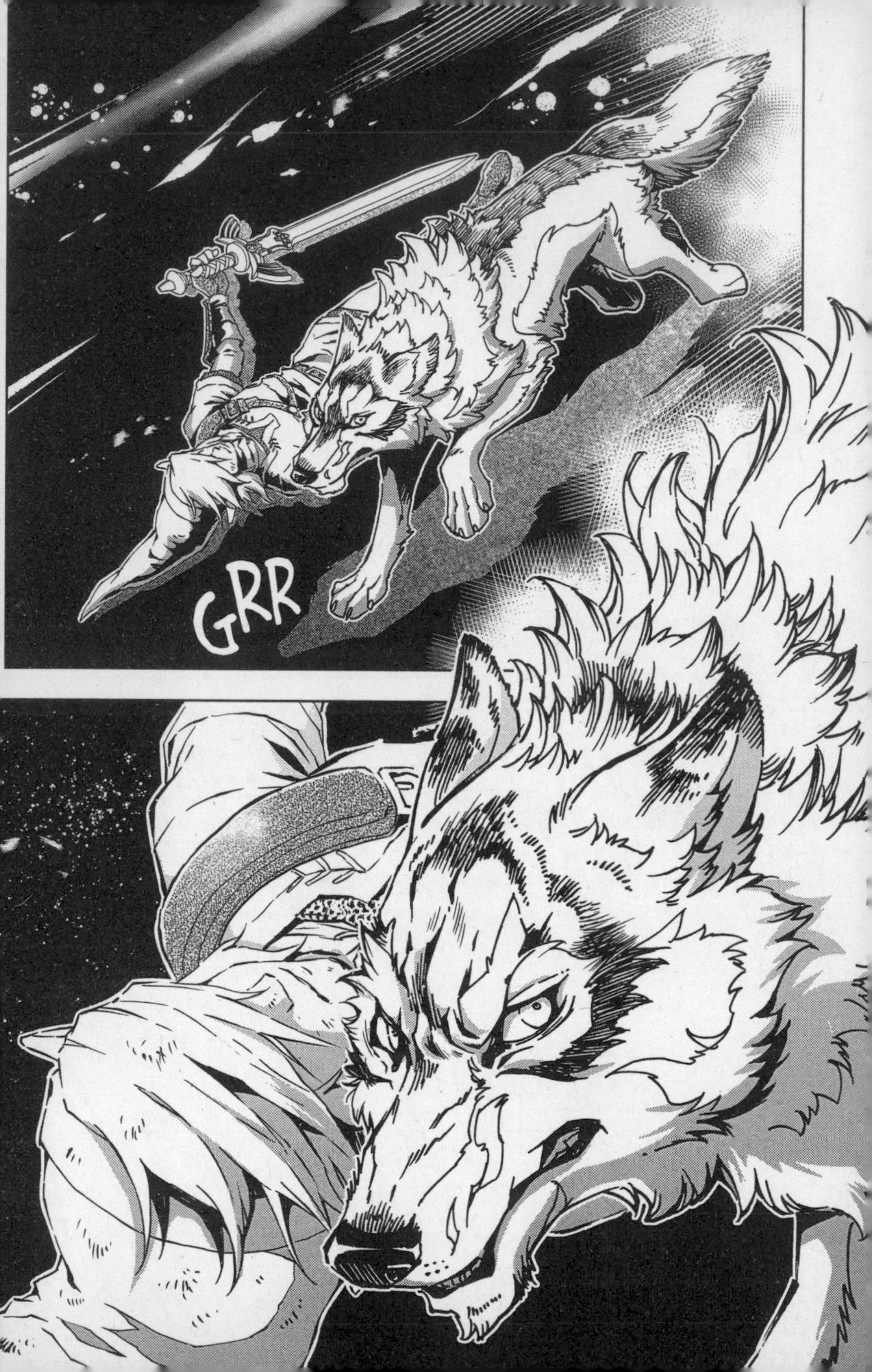
GRR

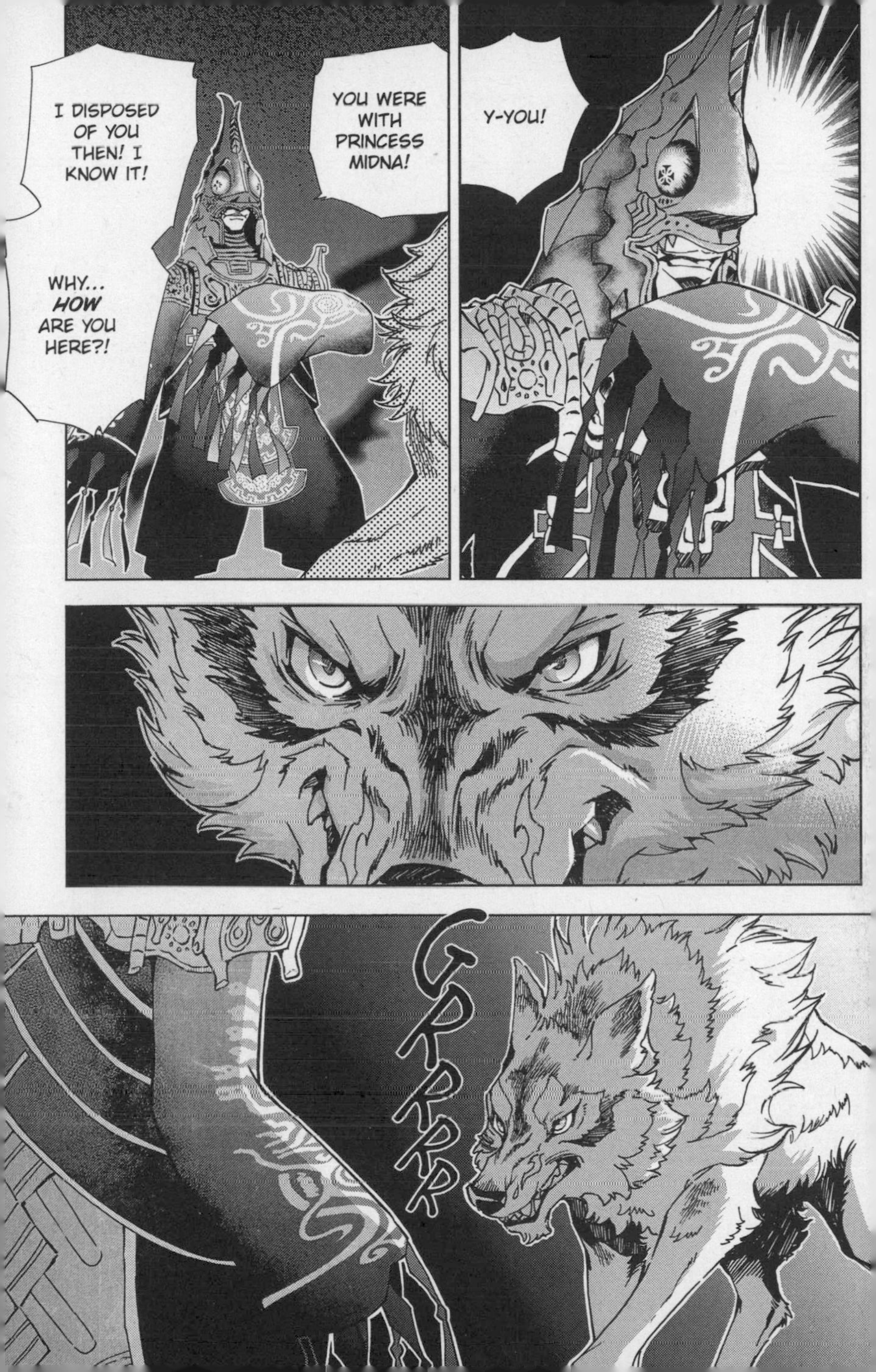
Y-YOU!
YOU WERE WITH PRINCESS MIDNA!
I DISPOSED OF YOU THEN! I KNOW IT!
WHY... *HOW* ARE YOU HERE?!
GRRRR

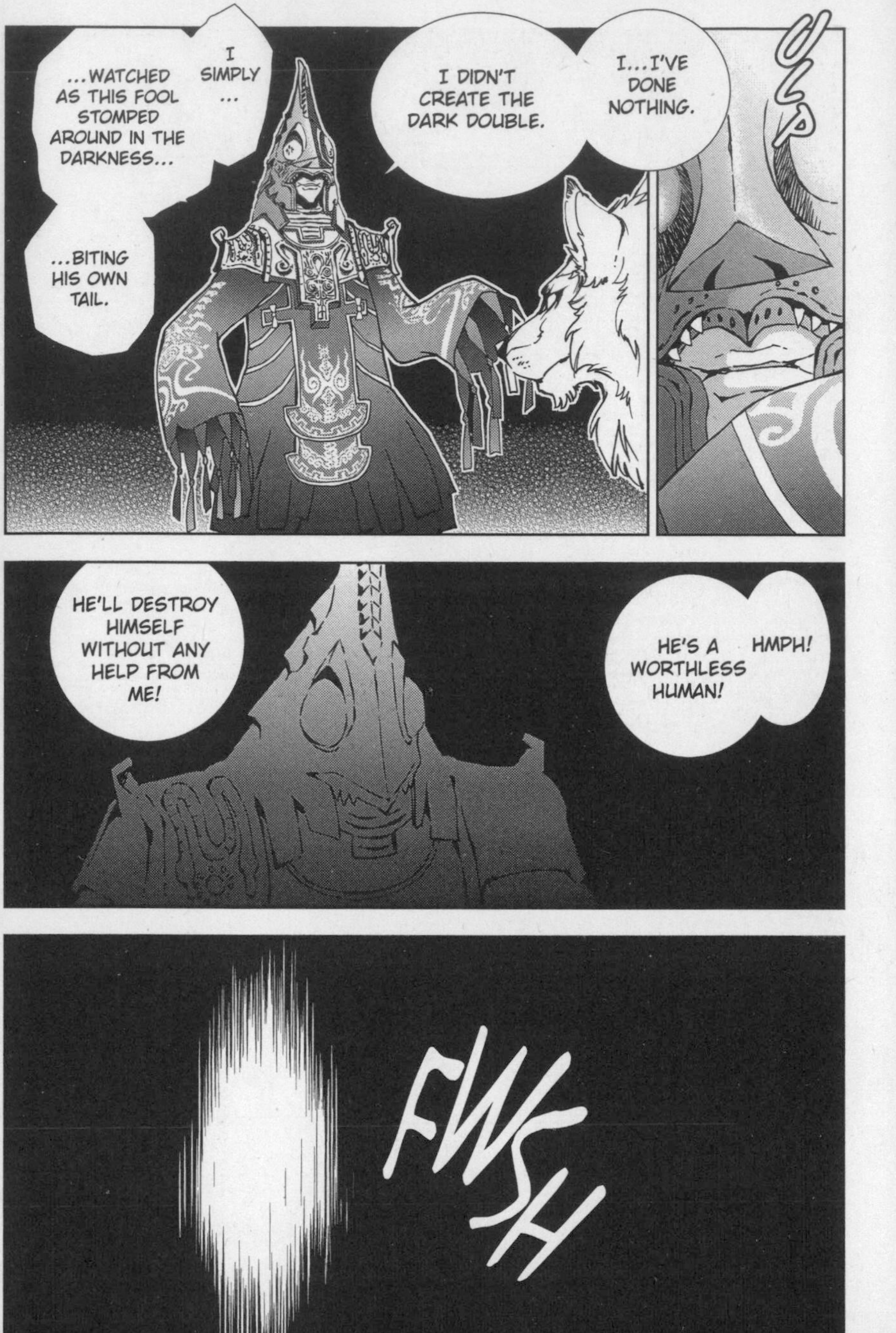
ULP
I...I'VE DONE NOTHING.
I DIDN'T CREATE THE DARK DOUBLE.
I SIMPLY ...
...WATCHED AS THIS FOOL STOMPED AROUND IN THE DARKNESS...
...BITING HIS OWN TAIL.
HMPH!
HE'S A WORTHLESS HUMAN!
HE'LL DESTROY HIMSELF WITHOUT ANY HELP FROM ME!
FWSH

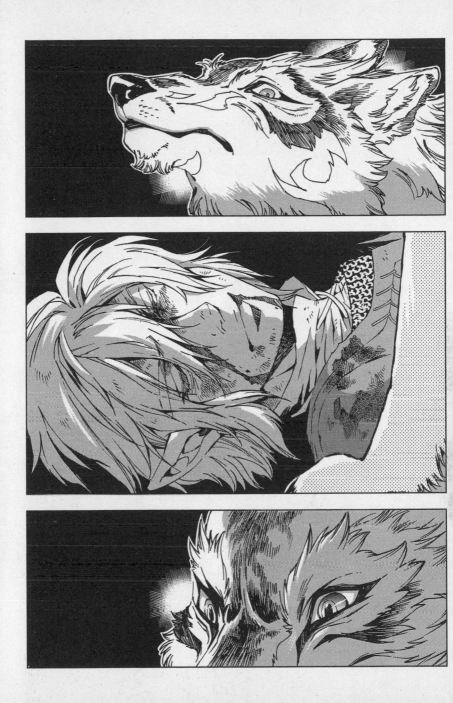

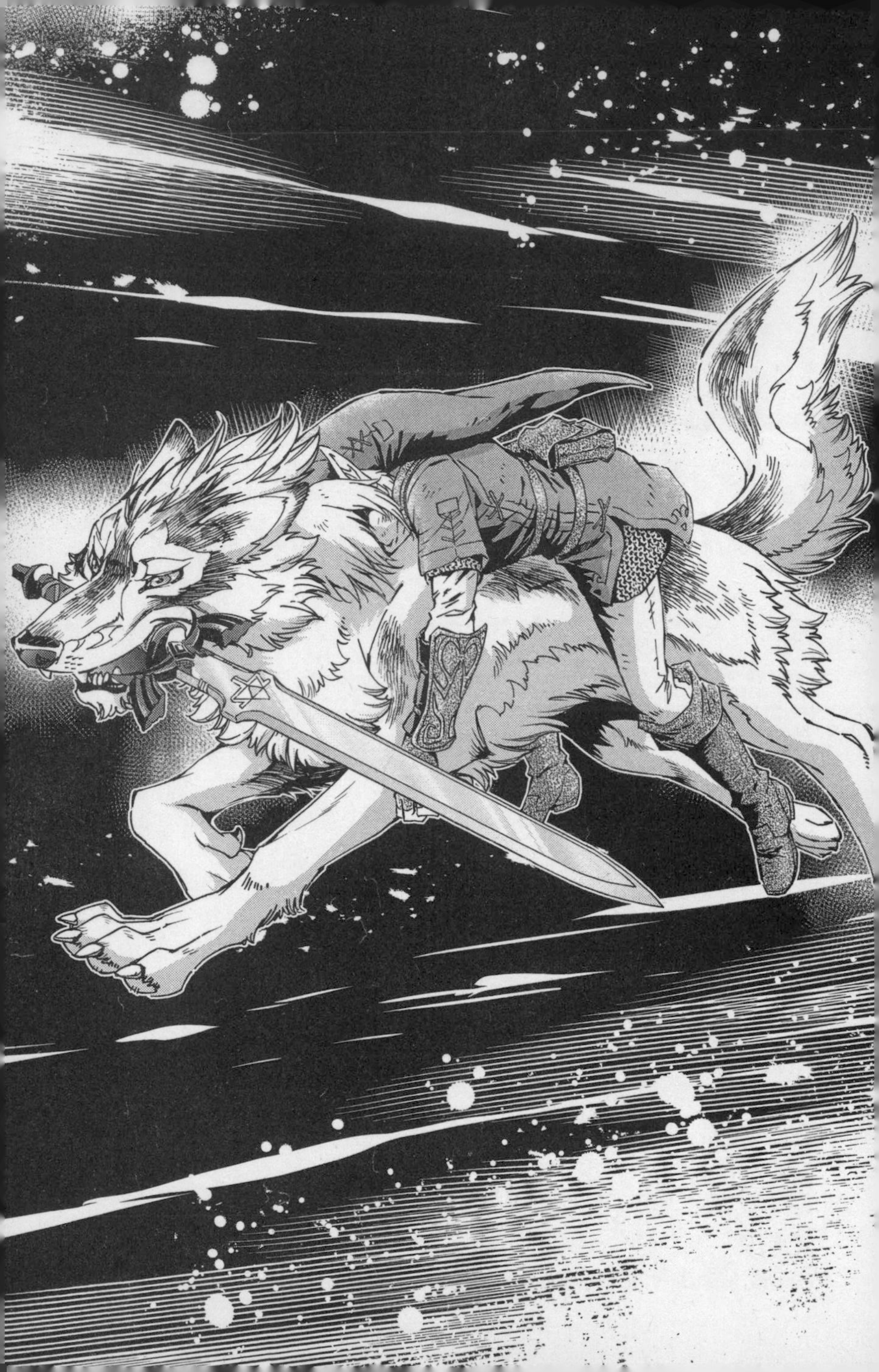

AUTHOR'S NOTE

It's been almost three years that we've known *TwiPri* Link and his story is reaching its climax! We haven't shown many developments such as Link falling to darkness, but it's happening now! The hero's trials continue!

Akira Himekawa is the collaboration of two women, A. Honda and S. Nagano. Together they have created ten manga adventures featuring Link and the popular video game world of *The Legend of Zelda*™. Their most recent work, *The Legend of Zelda*™: *Twilight Princess*, is serialized digitally on Shogakukan's MangaONE app in Japan.

THE LEGEND OF ZELDA

◆TWILIGHT PRINCESS◆

Volume 6—VIZ Media Edition

STORY AND ART BY

Akira Himekawa

DRAWING STAFF **mati.** / **Akiko Mori** / **Sakiho Tsutsui**

TRANSLATION **John Werry**

ENGLISH ADAPTATION **Stan!**

TOUCH-UP ART & LETTERING **Evan Waldinger**

DESIGNER **Shawn Carrico**

EDITOR **Mike Montesa**

THE LEGEND OF ZELDA: TWILIGHT PRINCESS
TM & © 2020 Nintendo. All Rights Reserved.

ZELDA NO DENSETSU TWILIGHT PRINCESS Vol. 6
by Akira HIMEKAWA
© 2016 Akira HIMEKAWA
All rights reserved.
Original Japanese edition published by SHOGAKUKAN.
English translation rights in the United States of America,
Canada, the United Kingdom, Ireland, Australia and
New Zealand arranged with SHOGAKUKAN.

Original design by Kazutada YOKOYAMA

The stories, characters and incidents mentioned
in this publication are entirely fictional.

Printed in the U.S.A.

Published by VIZ Media, LLC
P.O. Box 77010
San Francisco, CA 94107

10 9 8 7 6 5 4 3 2 1
First printing, January 2020

VIZ MEDIA
viz.com

THE LEGEND OF ZELDA

LEGENDARY EDITION

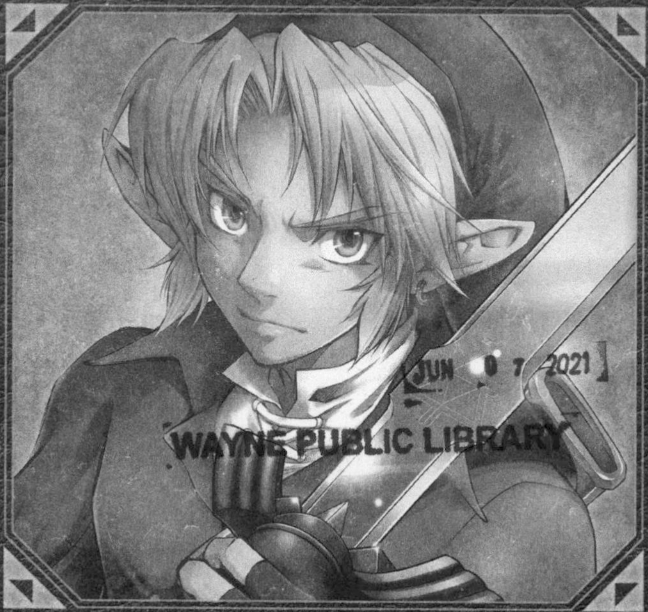

STORY AND ART BY

AKIRA HIMEKAWA

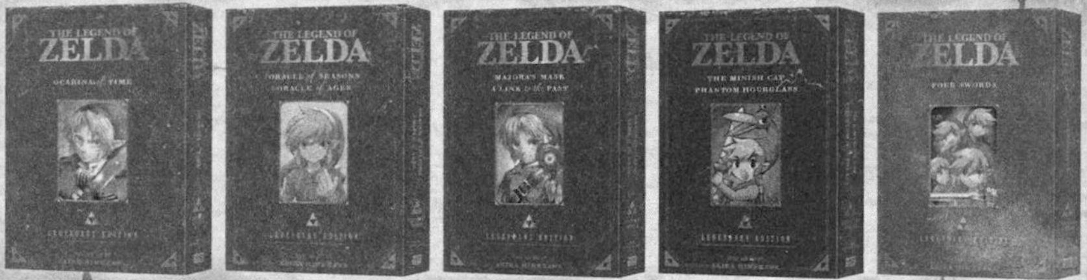
THE LEGEND OF ZELDA
OCARINA of TIME
THE LEGEND OF ZELDA
ORACLE of SEASONS
ORACLE of AGES
THE LEGEND OF ZELDA
MAJORA'S MASK
A LINK to the PAST
THE LEGEND OF ZELDA
THE MINISH CAP
PHANTOM HOURGLASS
THE LEGEND OF ZELDA
FOUR SWORDS

The Legendary Editions of *The Legend of Zelda*™ contain two volumes of the beloved manga series, presented in a deluxe format featuring new covers and color art pieces.

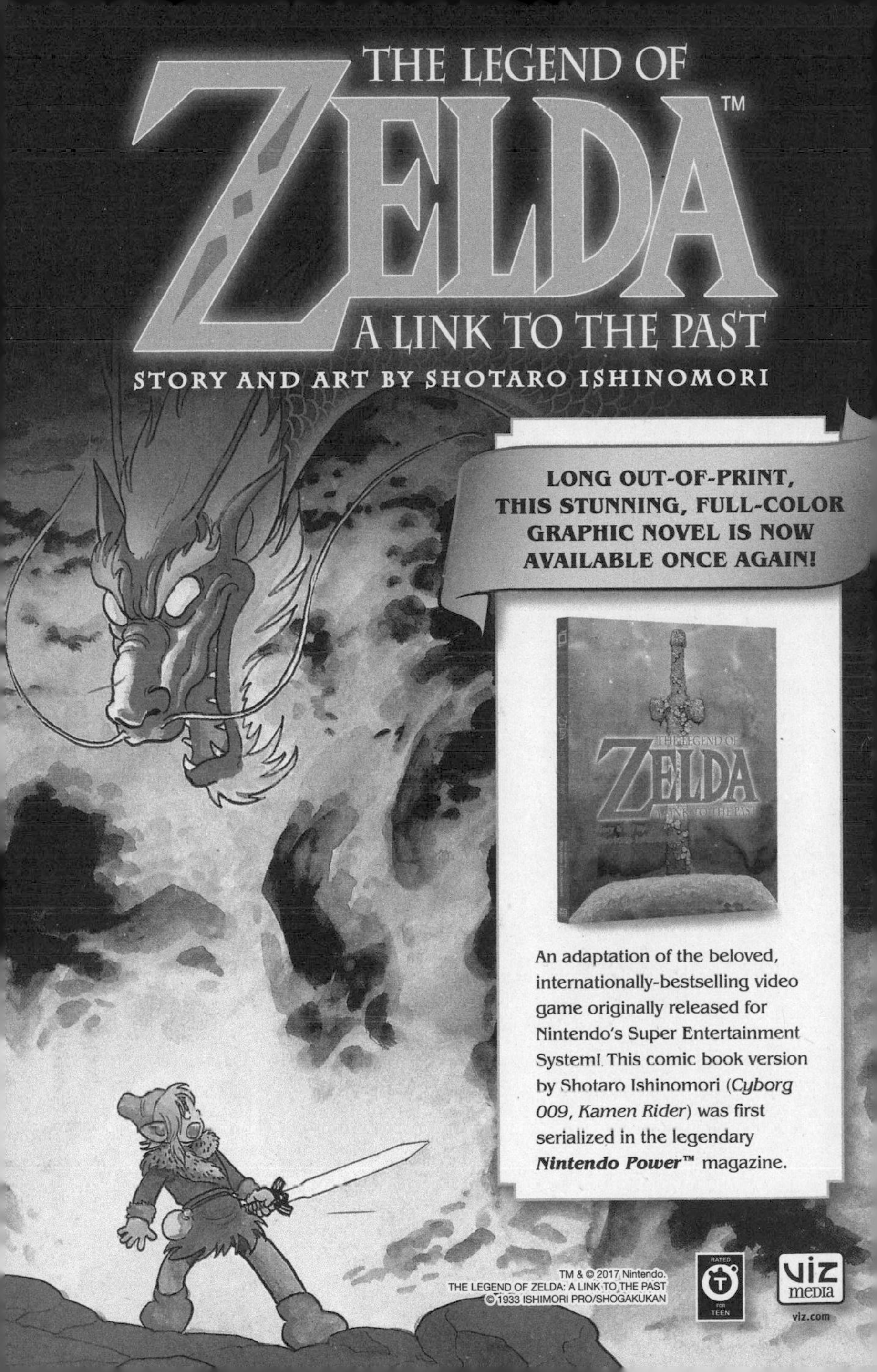
THE LEGEND OF
ZELDA™
A LINK TO THE PAST
STORY AND ART BY SHOTARO ISHINOMORI
LONG OUT-OF-PRINT, THIS STUNNING, FULL-COLOR GRAPHIC NOVEL IS NOW AVAILABLE ONCE AGAIN!
An adaptation of the beloved, internationally-bestselling video game originally released for Nintendo's Super Entertainment System! This comic book version by Shotaro Ishinomori (*Cyborg 009*, *Kamen Rider*) was first serialized in the legendary ***Nintendo Power*™** magazine.
TM & © 2017 Nintendo.
THE LEGEND OF ZELDA: A LINK TO THE PAST
© 1933 ISHIMORI PRO/SHOGAKUKAN
RATED T FOR TEEN
viz media
viz.com

Hey! You're Reading in the Wrong Direction!

This is the **end** of this graphic novel!

To properly enjoy this VIZ graphic novel, please turn it around and begin reading from **right to left.** Unlike English, Japanese is read right to left, so Japanese comics are read in reverse order from the way English comics are typically read.

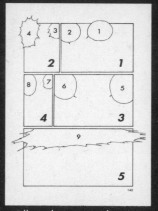

Follow the action this way

This book has been printed in the original Japanese format in order to preserve the orientation of the original artwork. Have fun with it!